UNIVERSITY OF NOTTINGHAM TELEPEN
6 00 212925 3
WITHDRAWN FROM THE LIBRARY

D1491957

DATE DUE FOR RETURN

UNIVERSITY LIBRARY

- 5 JUN 2002

SEM HALL 12

PLEASE PASS TO
CATALOGUING ON RETURN

NO DESCRIPTION

This book may be recalled before the above date

90014

THE IRELAND
OF
SIR JONAH BARRINGTON

Sir Jonah Barrington, K.C., engraved by J. Heath from a drawing
from life by Commerford. Photograph courtesy of the National
Library of Ireland

THE
IRELAND
OF
SIR JONAH
BARRINGTON

SELECTIONS FROM

HIS *Personal Sketches*

EDITED BY

HUGH B. STAPLES

PETER OWEN

London

Published in the British Commonwealth 1968

Copyright © 1967 by the University of Washington Press.
Library of Congress Catalog Card Number 67-21201. Manu-
factured by the Colonial Press Inc., Clinton, Massachusetts.
Designed by Diana Bower. Printed in the United States of
America.

Bound in Great Britain. Printed in the U.S.A.
Peter Owen
London

TO MY WIFE, MARY

PREFACE

MY AIM in editing the *Personal Sketches* has been to select from a large and heterogeneous collection of memoirs those accounts which appear to me to have the greatest interest for the present-day reader. In the original three-volume edition of 1827 and 1832, upon which the present text is wholly based, these sketches are presented according to no discernible principle of organization, chronological or otherwise. Furthermore, they vary greatly both in interest and in literary quality. My task was to cut the extant published material down to a length approximating one third of the original, and to rearrange it into some kind of logical order. Thus I have found it convenient to divide the book as a whole into four parts: "Life in the Country," in which Barrington describes conditions in the Irish countryside of his boyhood and retells stories he had heard handed down; "Life in Town," which embraces his young manhood and adult social career; "Some Irishmen of the Day"—a series of vignettes of famous personalities of the time; and "The National Scene," which focuses mainly on the abortive struggle for Irish independence in the last three years of the eighteenth century. This rearrangement is entirely arbitrary on my part, and bears no relation to the order of episodes in the original text. The titles of the four parts are mine; individual chapter headings are taken verbatim from Barrington's first edition of the *Personal Sketches*.

Even within individual chapters, Sir Jonah is frequently given to digressions that serve only to impede the flow of the narrative and to diminish the total effect. I have not, therefore, approached my editorial task with the same kind of reverential circumspection that one would accord, let us say, to *The Canterbury Tales,* or to an edition of Pope. On the contrary, I have done what a modern editor would do had Sir Jonah submitted the manuscript to him—excise the prolix and the platitudinous. This has meant that in almost every chapter I have omitted whole paragraphs. On the other hand, I have joined up, in some cases, brief sentences that typographically represent paragraphs in the original.

This may appear to some a rather high-handed procedure; yet, if the present text is compared to the original, I believe it will be found more readable, and readability has been a major concern. It seemed to me also that an elaborate record of every instance of editing would needlessly clutter up the text. I have of course not added anything to the text except for an occasional brief query, and all additions to the original text appear in square brackets [thus]. Neither have I rearranged any of the sentences or paragraphs within a given chapter, although the chapters themselves have been very considerably rearranged. In a very few cases where the references are to omitted material, and would therefore be unintelligible, or where the text becomes irrelevant and digressive, I have ventured to omit parts of sentences; these omissions are in each case indicated by ellipses [. . .].

I have been arbitrary also in respect to typography and orthography. I have in most cases preserved Sir Jonah's archaic spelling of such words as "cieling," "chesnut," and "decrepid" (especially if these spellings are to be found in the *O.E.D.*) because they seem to me to have a pleasing eighteenth-century flavor. On the other hand, in the interests of readability, I have ventured to bring titles such as "Speaker of the House" and "His Majesty" into accordance with modern usage by capitalizing them. For the most part, these changes are minor and have been done silently. Sir Jonah's often erratic use of italics has been preserved intact.

I have been sparing in the use of footnotes. Some of Barrington's own have been omitted, but wherever they appear, they are so labeled. My own have been added only in further explanation of matters that I felt might be unclear to the average educated reader. Even here, my motive has been to add to the interest of the text rather than to appear pedantic.

I should like to express my gratitude to the University of California at Davis for generous grants of faculty research funds, and to Mrs. Nancy Oliver Anderson, who typed much of the manuscript.

University of Cincinnati
January 1, 1967

CONTENTS

[xi]

III. SOME IRISHMEN OF THE DAY

IV. THE NATIONAL SCENE

ILLUSTRATIONS

INTRODUCTION

I stood well with all parties." So Sir Jonah Barrington speaks of his relationship to the other inhabitants of the Dublin boardinghouse where he lived as a fledgling barrister, and this declaration can be taken as a paradigm of his whole life, insofar as he reveals it in his *Personal Sketches*. This is the boast, justified by his own account and corroborated by his contemporaries, of a man hugely successful in the society of late eighteenth-century Dublin. It can be read also as an ironic epitaph on his political career. For the same ability to please everybody in private life, speeches in Parliament against the Union and friends in the Castle notwithstanding, meant to please nobody in the larger arena of Irish history. Thus Sir Jonah was neither hanged on Wexford Bridge like some of his friends in 1798, nor was he to remain a force in national affairs after 1800. Instead, he gradually faded away, an exile in Versailles, unwept for, unsung, and ultimately, with his removal from the Bench in 1830, dishonored.

He was born at Knapton, adjacent to Abbeyleix, in the Queen's County, apparently in 1760 (the relevant parish records for Abbeyleix go back only to 1780). Perhaps in the ancient Irish tradition of fosterage, he was brought up by his grandparents, first at the family demesne at nearby Cullenaghmore and, after his grandfather's death, at his grandmother's household in Dublin. In the capital, he attended Dr. Ball's school in Ship Street and, after further tutoring, entered Trinity College, probably at the age of fifteen or sixteen. After graduation he found himself at loose ends, living an idle life at his father's country seat, Blandsfort, the scene of

"Irish Dissipation in 1778." A couple of years later, the whole family moved into town, where his father took a mansion in Merrion Square. Probably in 1781, young Jonah fell in love with a "Miss D. W." who consented to become engaged if he would study for the legal profession in London. He accordingly left Ireland, presumably in 1781 or 1782, and during his absence his fiancee died "under very peculiar circumstances," but what they were he does not tell us.

He was called to the Bar in 1788 and entered the Irish Parliament as a member for Tuam in 1790, a seat he was to hold until 1798; during the final two stormy years of the Irish Parliament he represented Banagher. After the Act of Union was passed in 1800, he felt it necessary to resign, though he ran unsuccessfully for Parliament in 1803. In the meantime, his legal and financial fortunes were on the rise. Apparently as a reward for some parliamentary opposition to John Philpot Curran and Henry Grattan, Barrington received a lucrative sinecure in the Custom House and was advanced to the dignity of King's Counsel over the heads of a number of senior barristers in 1793. Sometime before 1798 he married, though the circumstances of his marriage, to say nothing of his wife's name, are never mentioned in the *Sketches*. He reached the apex of his career in 1798, when he was appointed Judge of the Admiralty Court. Although his opposition to the Act of Union effectively removed him from a direct role in the government, he was allowed to keep his tenure as judge, and even to act by proxy. Furthermore, he was knighted in 1807. But, partly to escape his creditors, he seems to have lived more or less permanently in France from about 1815 on —certainly he was in Paris during the Hundred Days. His enemies allege that he tried to blackmail the English government with his detailed knowledge of Castlereagh's bribery of his former colleagues and, failing in this, be-

gan to publish his *Historic Memoirs*. It is apparently
not possible to ascertain the whole truth of this matter,
but it is a fact that the first half of these "exposés" was
published in five parts between 1809 and 1815.

In 1825 or 1826 the writing of the *Personal Sketches*
must have begun, as the first two volumes appeared in
1827. Barrington, who had always had expensive tastes,
was by now running out of money, as two independent
sources reveal. In the first place, the parliamentary inves-
tigation showed that he had misappropriated sums of
money paid into the Admiralty Court on three separate
occasions. Moreover, John Prendergast in his account
of the life of the famous Dublin antiquarian, Charles
Haliday, has this to say:

> Amongst Daniel Haliday's [Charles Haliday's brother]
> acquaintances at Paris was Sir Jonah Barrington, then en-
> gaged in completing his celebrated "History of the Union,
> with authentic details of the bribery used to effect that great
> political measure." Sir Jonah's anti-Union sentiments har-
> monized with those of Daniel Haliday, and they formed
> such an intimacy that Daniel Haliday gave him a share of
> his apartments and even supplied him with money, as appears
> by unpaid promissory notes found amongst Daniel Haliday's
> papers after his death. In fact, Sir Jonah's "Historic Mem-
> oirs of Ireland" [i.e., Volume II of the 1835 edition]
> were completed and his "Personal Sketches" written in Dan-
> iel Haliday's rooms at Paris.*

It should be added that Sir Jonah acknowledges this
debt to Haliday in the Preface to the 1833 edition of the
Historic Memoirs (which appeared in Paris under the
title of *Rise and Fall of the Irish Nation*) in these words:

> I cannot terminate these observations, without expressing
> how much the arrangement and the correctness of this vol-
> ume, owe to the research, and revision, of my zealous and
> talented friend, Doctor Halliday [sic] of Paris. That con-

* Charles Haliday, *The Scandinavian Kingdom of Dublin*,
edited with Some Notice of the Author's Life, by John P.
Prendergast (Dublin, 1881), p. lxxxviii.

geniality of sentiment which generated out of mutual friendship, excited that exertion, and gives me the pleasing opportunity, of saying, how much my esteem has been encreased,
by a more intimate knowledge of his mind and of his principles.

PARIS, 1st May, 1833

Perhaps feeling, as an Irish exile in Paris now approaching seventy, that he no longer owed anything to
England, he finished the second volume of the *Historic
Memoirs* and with unflagging energy completed the third
volume of the *Personal Sketches,* which appeared in
1832. And then, two years later, he died.

Considering these circumstances of his life, it is no
wonder that Barrington, even more than most writers of
memoirs, is a confirmed *laudator temporis acti;* like John
Stanislaus Joyce, who seems in some respects to have
modeled his own life on Sir Jonah's, he is a "praiser of
his own past." Indeed, the two men share a good many
qualities in common: family pride, conviviality, ready
and mordant wit, improvidence, a heightened sense of the
forms of social intercourse, popularity, and, above all,
a feeling for the original phrase. There is, however, an
important difference: whereas John Stanislaus Joyce is
remembered chiefly as an irresponsible progenitor, Sir
Jonah was an important member of the Protestant Ascendancy. As such, he had the advantages enjoyed by the
tiny minority of landholders who had ruled Ireland on
the local level for nearly two hundred years. As a matter
of course, his education at Trinity College was finished
by reading law in England. His legal and forensic
achievements were a function of his breeding. His duels
were fought with ball and pistol; his utterances against
the Act of Union are a matter of public record. Above
all, his two literary works, both written in his sixties,
comprise a significant contribution to the record of Irish
life and letters.

Thus, although the time span of some of these sketches extends back to earlier times, they are mainly a chronicle of what appeared to Sir Jonah as the Golden Age of Dublin—the years between 1782 and 1800. It was an age of great architectural triumphs, one that produced the Four Courts, the Custom House, and many of the most impressive private mansions of Dublin. It was an age of great oratory, both at the Bar and in the Irish House of Commons, which had become the focus of national pride flourishing in an unprecedented atmosphere of independence. It was a prosperous and expansive age, that of Henry Flood and Henry Grattan, Thomas Ivory and James Gandon, Curran, Lord Edward Fitzgerald, and Wolfe Tone. And, in his own and lesser way, the age of Sir Jonah Barrington.

Of course there was another side to Irish life, and one that made this kind of magnificence possible: the nearly feudal, wholly agrarian condition of the illiterate Catholic peasantry. An American reader familiar with documents of the period is reminded constantly of parallels between Georgian Ireland and the ante-bellum South. The Irish serf, like the Negro slave, did all the hard work and had little more than bare subsistence to show for it. His religion, his language, his customs, and his ignorance set him apart from his masters, who, like the Southern aristocrats, made sure of keeping such distinctions as permanently obvious as possible both by the passage of the Penal Laws and by illegal coercion. To such hereditary members of the ruling class as Sir Jonah, "Paddy" provided a fascinating, though ultimately inscrutable, figure of fun, to whom was attributed all the comical absurdities of Uncle Remus or Amos and Andy, and all the ineradicable superstitiousness of Miss Watson's Jim. But, ruled by a wise, benign (if absent-minded) master like Sir Jonah's grandfather, he was assured of his minimal wants and was even treated with something like affection. The obvious abuses and inequities of this system are not very much explored by Barrington; for him, the revenges of the "Whiteboys" on rack-renting agents are attributed to absentee landlords; the skulls broken against the windmill on Vinegar Hill reflect the dangerous contagion of democracy; indeed, the Fall of the Irish Nation in 1800 seems to be due, in Barrington's opinion, to the defection of the "half-mounted gentlemen" (read "Snopeses"), English imperialists (read "carpetbaggers"), and misguided Irish idealists (read "Abolitionists").

Sir Jonah's values, and those of much of the world he lived in and described, are plainly aristocratic. The characters who stream past our eyes in the *Personal Sketches* are judged by the symmetry and nobility of their bodies and features, by the correctness or eccentricity of their dress, by the felicity or awkwardness of their bearing, manners, and speech. Their political opinions are less important to Barrington than the manner in which they are expressed or put into operation. Wealth, power, even ostentation is admired, though only on the part of gentlemen. Above all, one must adhere to the Code, which takes its most obviously symbolic form in the rules of dueling, which was for Barrington what bull-fighting was for Hemingway. Barrington condones private immorality, as in the case of the Earl of Kingston (who was a gentleman), but not public chicanery, as in the case of Castlereagh (who was *not*). To be a man for all seasons, to sit a good horse, to drink one's share (and—if a "hard-goer"—more than one's share), to excel in witty repartee, to speak cogently on one's feet for three or four or five hours at a stretch at the Bar or in Parliament, to "stand well with all parties"—these are the principal criteria of Barrington's world, and there may still, perhaps, be something to be said for them.

There is something to be said also for Sir Jonah's respect for the written word, which extends beyond the legal to the literary. So active a way of life as he led would seem to afford little leisure for literature. Or so it would seem to a modern, who has forgotten that there was a world in which something like total leisure was possible. The fact is that Barrington, for a man of his class, was well read, and he did not consider that a gentleman demeaned himself by wielding a pen with as much flourish as he would a smallsword. Accordingly, when his age and his fortunes precluded more active pleasures, he began, as he tells us in his introduction to the *Personal Sketches:*

> . . . to consider what species of employment might lightly wear away the long and tedious winter-evenings of a demi-invalid; and recollecting that I could neither live for ever nor was *sure* of being the "last man," I conceived the idea of looking over and burning a horse-load or two of letters, papers, and fragments of all descriptions, which I had been carrying about in old trunks (not choosing to leave them at any body's mercy), and to which I had been perpetually adding.

He had earlier been working on his *Historic Memoirs,* an account of the Irish Parliament in the heyday of its independence, and the events leading up to the Act of Union of 1800. This is a long work, amounting to over eight hundred quarto pages in the definitive 1835 edition, and it is a serious contribution to Irish history, written in the style of a lesser Gibbon. It is evidently with a feeling of relief that Barrington the lawyer and judge turned away from this task to indulge another part of his personality—that of the *bon vivant* and wit, the lynx-eyed and silver-tongued observer of Dublin society.

So, in his sixties, in a borrowed room and with borrowed money, Sir Jonah Barrington sat down to assess the events of a not altogether misspent life, to recall for posterity that which had been amusing, and to paint a broad canvas of a way of life that had already passed away. The most important episode of his life—the fight against the Union—he had already chronicled in sober, deliberate prose. This left him free for subsidiary concerns and pointed the way for a less inhibited kind of writing. His legal training had prepared him for the major task and, as a historian, he writes like a lawyer. But a great part of the *Personal Sketches* deals with what we should now call sociology, and, happily, in this endeavor he writes like a novelist.

What kinds of things struck him as exciting, memorable, and informative? What areas of contemporary sensibility did he aim at exploiting? He was right in believing that then, as now, most people are immersed in a life of physical sensation, and it is his tremendous appetite for the sensational that gives his *Sketches* the air of pungent immediacy that still appeals to a very different kind of audience. Hence the frequent and minute descriptions of food and drink, which make reading this book inadvisable for anyone on a diet, alcoholic or otherwise. On the other hand, like Dickens, Barrington never exploits the other great area of physical human enjoyment. One would almost infer that his people are so busy eating, drinking, arguing, dueling, conniving, and generally raising a ruction as to leave neither time nor energy for sex.

For a man who obviously took a keen relish in the life of the senses, Barrington's prudery seems almost abnormal, and the strictures against the dangers of exposing young ladies to dramatic presentations strike a false note, as Bacchus diminishes into Mrs. Grundy. The reasons for this are probably partly autobiographical: he seems to have the feeling that sex was not a subject for gentlemen to write about. Similarly, we note an equal reticence to speak about his own domestic career. We gain no very clear impression of "Lady B.," as he always calls her—somehow the abbreviation seems significant. Over and above a sense of personal decorum, it must be remembered that Barrington was, perhaps rather desperately, hoping to reach the ever increasing numbers of contemporary middle-class readers, whose taste hampered the expression of almost every writer up to the days of Hardy, and even after.

But if sex is taboo, death remains in these pages a never ending source of satisfaction and fascination. There is no subject on which Sir Jonah loves to dwell like the manner and circumstances of a man's losing his life or, more especially, his head. Sometimes the context of the decapitation theme is historical, as in the case of Charles I; sometimes political, as in the case of Bagenal Harvey and his fellow victims; sometimes apocryphal, as in the case of the Irish peasant who cut off his own head while engaged in spearing a salmon. Without urging that this preoccupation with violence has symbolic overtones, one can at least assert that the author's interest in sudden death is to modern tastes macabre (a dominant quality of Irish comedy, as Vivian Mercier has shown), but hardly morbid.

Or not very morbid. These were, after all, precarious times, in which political mistakes had consequences rather more catastrophic than in our own. Aside from the political arena, the ordinary conditions of life approached something like those of the American frontier. And in this respect, it is no wonder that we are reminded often in these pages of Faulkner and Mark Twain, both of whom treat events essentially tragic with an air of *sang froid* that Barrington would certainly have admired.

One of the great resources of frontier life is humor, and perhaps its most typical aspect takes the form of the Tall Tale. This is a mode that, with few exceptions, has never really taken hold in English literature. It is something typically American, but we ought not to forget that it is also (and has been for many more centuries) typically

Irish. An English don wrote the greatest fantasy in the language, but the greatest of all Tall Tales was certainly written by an Irish dean. At any rate, Barrington has a pronounced gift for this kind of narrative, and often, like freshmen contemplating *A Modest Proposal,* we are hard put to decide at just what point our author takes leave of sober fact. Not that it matters. The story of Elizabeth Fitzgerald of Moret Castle is as true a reflection of the anarchic conditions in seventeenth-century Ireland as the Grangerford-Shepherdson episode of *Huckleberry Finn* is of nineteenth-century Arkansas. The sallies of Curran and Sir Boyle Roche may seem to us a bit heightened, but that they are a true record of contemporary wit is borne out by many other historians. The stories of "Achmet Borumborad," "Skinning a Black Child," and "The Enniscorthy Boar" are clearly Tall Tales, but good ones. All three are funny; all three aim at human gullibility and false pretension, and all are, however exaggerated, illuminating footnotes to the Never-Never Land of late eighteenth-century Ireland.

Sir Jonah Barrington may have been derelict in his duties on the Admiralty Bench, but he was a judge of character, and a good judge, too. The *Personal Sketches* owe part of their interest and importance to the series of vignettes of contemporary Irishmen. It was possible in the small world of ruling-class Georgian Ireland to know almost everyone personally, and, by his own account, Sir Jonah did. He is, to be sure, one of the great name-droppers in history, but the fact is that the names were there to drop. So he was able to rescue the characteristic leaders of Irish society from the oblivion of duller memoirists, and sometimes even from the formality of their own recorded speeches and letters. In this area Barrington's novelistic flair shines forth. The dress, the stance, the idiosyncrasies; above all, the impression of living speech he captures as skillfully as Boswell. The latter,

more single-minded, more perspicuous, luckier in his subject, has achieved more, but Sir Jonah deserves a place
beside Aubrey in the ranks of the great English minia-
turists.

His weakness is to be too easily amused, too quickly diverted. He has the necessary gifts of the novelist and the
biographer save the crucial one—the capacity to think in
terms of the larger perspective. These *Sketches* were composed on a kind of *ad hoc* basis, with the consequence that
for every portrait of Archibald Rowan Hamilton, we
have a platitudinous disquisition on the operation of the
memory; for every account of undergraduate pranks at
Trinity College in the 1780's, we have a sententious dia-
tribe against the "inferior" theater of the day. The first,
three-volume octavo edition (1827–32), upon which the
present text is based, runs to almost fourteen hundred
pages—a fact that gives at once an indication of Sir
Jonah's abundance and a rationale for editing him.

He has not been so much neglected as he has been
forgotten. Indeed, it must be confessed that the present
editor came across these sketches only because both Joyce
and Yeats borrowed from them, and it seemed worth-
while to read what writers gifted with so fine an ear had
admired. Both, perhaps, were attracted by the macabre
and the grotesque in Barrington, and by his inveterate
Irishness. Yeats's ancestors were neighbors of Sir Jonah's
maternal grandparents in Galway; Joyce must have seen
something of his own father in this book, and so, one
ventures to assert, did his father, since it was one of the
very few volumes he possessed. Both men drew heavily
on the Irish past in their own work; indeed, it is impossible to understand either Joyce or Yeats without a more
comprehensive knowledge of Irish political and social history than is gained in the ordinary way outside of Ireland itself. It is my hope that this edition of selections
from the *Sketches* may lead other readers to a re-exam-

ination of other accounts of the period and to such modern syntheses as those of Maurice Craig and Constantia Maxwell.

But even for the nonspecialist there is God's plenty in these pages. Sir Jonah Barrington, as both his portrait and his prose testify, was a man with a sense of style. Though there may be a few tedious passages in his *Sketches,* there is no sloppy writing. The author has put as much care into his literary productions as he would have done, say, into the preparations for a duel or a dinner. His style is flexible, even Protean, and one that readily adapts itself to the ever changing demands of mood and subject. When the topic is serious, he reverts to the highly Latinate periods characteristic of the educated man of his century. Thus he writes of the trial of the Earl of Kingston:

> The grave and awful solemnity of that trial made a very deep impression on my memory: and, coupled with the recollection that it proclaimed indisputably the sovereignty of the Irish nation, its effect on a contemplative mind was of a penetrating nature ["Singular Customs in the Irish Parliament"].

On the other hand, Barrington has a perfect command of the racy vernacular, which serves him in good stead on such appropriate occasions as the reaction of his father's huntsman when requested to pay a toll-keeper:

> "Is it me pay the pike?" said Matthew ". . . me? The devil a cross of wages I got from the master this many a day, and if I did, do you think, Master Jonah, the liquor would not be after having it out of me by this time?" and he then attempted to drive on *without* paying, as he used to do at Cullenaghmore ["A Wedding in Olden Days"].

Most often, however, his prose is a nice blending of the ornate and the plain, so that the mixture characteristically has a sardonic, mock heroic quality, as in the following passage describing his first duel:

[xxvi]

My friend Crosby, without any sort of salutation or prologue, immediately cried out "Ground, gentlemen! ground,
ground! damn measurement!" and placing me on his selected
spot, whispered into my ear *"Medio tutissimus ibis:* never
look at the head or heels: *hip* the maccaroni! the hip for
ever, my boy! hip, hip!"—when my antagonist's second, advancing and accosting mine, said, Mr. Daly could not
think of going any further with the business; that he found
it was totally a mistake on his part, originating through
misrepresentation, and that he begged to say he was extremely sorry for having given Mr. Barrington and his
friend the trouble of coming out, hoping they would excuse
it and shake hands with him. To this arrangement, I certainly had no sort of objection; but Crosby, without hesitation, said, "We cannot do that *yet,* sir: I'll *show* you we
can't: (taking a little manuscript book out of his breeches
pocket,) there's the *rules!*—look at that, sir," continued he,
"see No. 7;—no apology can be received *after* the parties
meet, *without a fire.* You see, there's the rule," pursued
Crosby, with infinite self-satisfaction; "and a young man on
his *first blood* cannot break rule, particularly with a gentleman so used to the sport as Mr. Daly. Come, gentlemen,
proceed! proceed!" ["The Fire-Eaters"].

Add to Sir Jonah's command of two essentially different
dialects, his eye for significant, telling detail (as in the
description of Parsons Hoye); his penchant for the
original phrase (as in the case of Mr. Dennis, who "had
outdone his usual outdoings," and thereby lost his ears),
and his novelist's trick of shifting from the past tense to
the present to reinforce an air of immediacy, and you
have a prose style at once adaptable and richly textured.
Whether the writings of so worthy a fellow deserve to be
revived, the reader is now invited to judge for himself.

I

LIFE IN THE COUNTRY

MY FAMILY CONNEXIONS

I WAS born at Knapton, near Abbeyleix, in the Queen's County, at that time the seat of my father, but now of Sir George Pigott. I am the third son and fourth child of John Barrington, who had himself neither brother nor sister; and at the period of my birth, my immediate connexions were thus circumstanced.

My family, by ancient patents, by marriages, and by inheritance from their ancestors, possessed very extensive landed estates in Queen's County, and had almost unlimited influence over its population, returning two members to the Irish Parliament for Ballynakill, then a close borough.

Cullenaghmore, the mansion where my ancestors had resided from the reign of James the First, was then occupied by my grandfather, Colonel Jonah Barrington. He had adopted me as soon as I was born, brought me to Cullenaghmore, and with him I resided until his death.

That old mansion (the Great House as it was called) exhibited altogether an uncouth mass, warring with every rule of symmetry in architecture. The original castle had been demolished, and its materials converted to a much worse purpose: the front of the edifice which succeeded it was particularly ungraceful; a Saracen's head (our crest) in coloured brick-work being its only ornament, whilst some of the rooms inside were wainscoted with brown oak, others with red deal, and some not at all. The walls of the large hall were decked (as is customary) with fishing-rods, fire-arms, stags' horns, foxes' brushes, powder-flasks, shot-pouches, nets, and dog-collars; here and there relieved by the extended skin of a kite or a king-fisher, nailed up in the vanity of their destroyers: that of a monstrous eagle, which impressed itself indelibly on my mind, surmounted the chimney-piece, accompanied by a card announcing the name of its slaughterer—"Alexander Barrington;"—who, not being a *rich* relation, was subsequently entertained in the Great House two years, as a compliment for his present. A large parlour on each side of the hall, the only embellishments of which were some old portraits, and a multiplicity of hunting, shooting, and racing prints, with red tape nailed round them by way of frames, completed the reception-rooms; and as I was the only child in the house, and a most inquisitive brat, every different article was explained to me.

I remained here till I was nine years old; I had no play-fellows to take off my attention from whatever I observed or was taught; and so strongly do those early impressions remain engraven on my memory, naturally most retentive, that even at this long distance of time I fancy I can see the entire place as it stood then, with its old inhabitants moving before me:—their faces I most clearly recollect.

The library was a gloomy closet, and rather scantily furnished with everything but dust and cobwebs: there were neither chairs nor tables; but I cannot avoid recollecting many of the principal books, because I read such of them as I could comprehend, or as were amusing; and looked over all the prints in them a hundred times. While trying to copy these prints, they made an indelible impression upon me; and hence I feel confident of the utility of embellishments in any book intended for the instruction of children. I possessed many of the books long after my grandfather's death, and have some of them still. I had an insatiable passion for reading from my earliest days, and it has occupied the greater proportion of my later life. *Gulliver's Travels, Robinson Crusoe, Fairy*

Tales, and *The History of the Bible,* all with numerous plates, were my favourite authors and constant amusement: I believed every word of them except the fairies, and was not entirely sceptical as to those good people neither.

I fancy there was then but little variety in the libraries of most country gentlemen; and I mention as a curiosity, the following volumes, several of which, as already stated, I retained many years after my grandfather and grandmother died:—*The Journals of the House of Commons; Clarendon's History; The Spectator* and *Guardian; Killing No Murder; The Patriot King;* Bailey's *Dictionary;* some of Swift's Works, George Falkner's Newspapers; Quintus Curtius in English; Bishop Burnet; *A Treatise on Tar-water,* by some bishop;* *Robinson Crusoe; Hudibras; History of the Bible,* in folio; Nelson's *Fasts and Feasts; Fairy Tales; The History of Peter Wilkins; Glums and Gouries;* somebody's *Justice of Peace;* and a multiplicity of Farriery, Sporting, and Gardening Books, &c. which I lost piecemeal, when making room for law-books—probably not half so good, but at least much more experimental.†

Very few mirrors in those days adorned the houses of the country gentlemen:—a couple or three shaving-glasses for the gentlemen, and a couple of pretty large dressing-glasses, in black frames, for the ladies' use, composed, I believe, nearly the entire stock of reflectors at my grandfather's, except tubs of spring water, which answered for the maid-servants.

A very large and productive, but not neatly dressed-up garden, adjoined the house. The white-washed stone images; the broad flights of steps up and down; the terraces, with the round fish-pond,—rivetted my attention, and gave an impressive variety to this garden, which

* George Berkeley.
† For notes on this library, see Appendix.

[5]

I shall ever remember, as well as many curious incidents which I witnessed therein.

At the Great House all disputes amongst the tenants were then settled,—quarrels reconciled,—old debts arbitrated: a kind Irish landlord reigned despotic in the ardent affections of the tenantry, their pride and pleasure being to obey and to support him.

But there existed a happy reciprocity of interests. The landlord of that period protected the tenant by his influence—any wanton injury to a tenant being considered as an insult to the lord; and if either of the landlord's sons were grown up, no time was lost by him in demanding satisfaction from any gentleman for mal-treating even his father's blacksmith. No gentleman of this degree ever distrained a tenant for rent: indeed the parties appeared to be quite united and knit together. The greatest abhorrence, however, prevailed as to tithe proctors, coupled with no great predilection for the clergy who employed them. These latter certainly were, in principle and practice, the real country tyrants of that day, and first caused the assembling of the White Boys.*

I have heard it often said that, at the time I speak of, every estated gentleman in the Queen's County was *honoured* by the gout. I have since considered that its extraordinary prevalence was not difficult to be accounted for, by the disproportionate quantity of acid contained in their seductive beverage, called rum-shrub—which was then universally drunk in quantities nearly incredible, generally from supper-time till morning, by all country gentlemen, as they said, to keep down their claret.

My grandfather could not refrain, and therefore he suffered well:—he piqued himself on procuring, through

* Clandestine groups of peasants organized in the latter part of the eighteenth century to oppose by terrorizing tactics the collection of rents. They were called "White Boys" because of their method of disguising themselves with white cloth—à la Ku Klux Klan.

the interest of Batty Lodge, (a follower of the family who had married a Dublin grocer's widow,) the very first importation of oranges and lemons to the Irish capital every season. Horse-loads of these, packed in boxes, were immediately sent to the Great House of Cullenagh-more; and no sooner did they arrive, than the good news of *fresh fruit* was communicated to the Colonel's neigh-bouring friends, accompanied by the usual invitation. Night after night the revel afforded uninterrupted pleas-ure to the joyous gentry: the festivity being subsequently renewed at some other mansion, till the Gout thought proper to put the whole party *hors de combat;* having the satisfaction of making cripples for a few months such as he did not kill.

Whilst the convivials bellowed with only toe or finger agonies, it was a mere bagatelle; but when Mr. Gout marched up the country, and invaded the head or the stomach, it was then called *no joke;* and Drogheda usquebaugh, the hottest-distilled drinkable liquor ever invented, was applied to for aid, and generally drove the tormentor in a few minutes to his former quarters. It was, indeed, counted a specific; and I allude to it the more par-ticularly, as my poor grandfather was finished thereby.

It was his custom to sit under a very large branching bay-tree in his arm-chair, placed in a fine sunny aspect at the entrance of the garden. I particularly remember his cloak, for I kept it twelve years after his death: it was called a *cartouche* cloak, from a famous French robber who, it was said, invented it for his gang for the purposes of evasion. It was made of very fine broad-cloth; of a bright blue colour on one side, and a bright scarlet on the other: so that on being turned, it might deceive even a vigilant pursuer.

There my grandfather used to sit of a hot sunny day, receive any rents he could collect, and settle any accounts which his indifference on that head permitted him to think

[7]

of. He was rather a short man, with a large red nose—strong made; and wore an immense white wig, such as the portraits give to Dr. Johnson. He died at eighty-six years of age, of shrub-gout and usquebaugh, beloved and respected. I cried heartily for him; and then became the favourite of my grandmother, the best woman in the world, who went to reside in Dublin, and prepare me for college.

Colonel John Barrington, my great-grandfather, for some time before his death, and after I was born, resided at Ballyroan. My grandfather having married Margaret, the daughter of Sir John Byrne, Bart., had taken to the estates and mansion, and gave an annuity to my great-grandfather, who died, one hundred and four years old, of a fever, having never shown any of the usual decrepitudes or defects of age—he was the most respectable man by tradition of my family, and for more than seventy years a Parliament man.

Sir John Byrne, Bart. my maternal great-grandfather, lived at his old castle, Timogee, almost adjoining my grandfather Barrington: his domains, close to Stradbally, were nearly the most beautiful in the Queen's County. On his decease, his widow, Lady Dorothea Byrne, an Englishwoman, whose name had been Warren, I believe a grand-aunt to the late Lady Bulkley, resided there till her death; having previously seen her son give one of the first and most deeply to be regretted instances of what is called forming English connexions. Sir John Byrne, my grand-uncle, gone to England, married the heiress of the Leycester family:—the very name of Ireland was then odious to the English gentry; and previous terms were made with him, that his children should take the cognomen of Leycester, and drop that of Byrne; that he should quit Ireland, sell all his paternal estates there, and become an Englishman. He assented; and the last Lord Shelburne purchased, for less than half their value, all his fine estates, of which the Marquis of Lansdown is now the proprietor.

After the father's death, the son became, of course, Sir Peter Leycester, the predecessor of the present Sir John Fleming Leycester: thus the family of Byrne, descended from a long line of Irish princes and chieftains, condescended to become little amongst the rank of English commoners; and so ended the connexion between the Byrnes and Barringtons.

My mother was the daughter of Patrick French, of Peterswell, county of Galway, wherein he had large estates: my grandmother (his wife) was one of the last remaining to the first house of the ancient O'Briens. Her brother, my great-uncle, Donatus, also emigrated to England, and died fifteen or sixteen years since, at his mansion, Blatherwick, in Cheshire, in a species of voluntary obscurity, inconsistent with his birth and large fortune. He left great hereditary estates in both countries to the enjoyment of his *mistress,* excluding the legitimate branches of his family from all claims upon the manors or demesnes of their ancestors. The law enabled him to do what a due sense of justice and pride would have interdicted.

The anomaly of political principles among the Irish country gentlemen at that period was very extraordinary. They professed what they called *"unshaken loyalty;"* and yet they were unqualified partizans of Cromwell and William, two decided *usurpers*—one of them having dethroned his father-in-law, and the other decapitated his king.

The fifth of November was celebrated in Dublin for the preservation of a Scottish king from gunpowder in London: then the thirtieth of January was much approved of by a great number of Irish, as the anniversary of making his son, Charles the First, shorter by the head; and then the very same Irish celebrated the restoration of

[9]

Charles the Second, who was twice as bad as his father; and whilst they rejoiced in putting a crown upon the head of the son of the king who could not quietly keep his own head on, they never failed to drink bumpers to the memory of *Old Noll,* who had cut that king's head off. To conclude, in order to commemorate the whole story, and make their children remember it, they dressed up a fat calf's head on every anniversary of King Charles's throat being cut, and with a smoked ham placed by the side of it, all parties partook thereof most happily, washing down the emblem and its accompaniment with as much claret as they could hold.

Having thus proved their loyalty to James the First, and their attachment to his son's murderer, and then their loyalty to one of his grandsons, to another of whom they were disloyal, they next proceeded to celebrate the birthday of William of Orange, a Dutchman, who turned their king, his father-in-law, out of the country, and who, in all probability, would have given the Irish another calf's head for their celebration, if his said father-in-law had not got out of the way with the utmost expedition, and gone to live upon charity in France, with the natural enemies of the British nation.

One part of the Irish people then invented a toast, called "The glorious, pious, and immortal memory of William, the Dutchman;" whilst another raised a counter-toast, called "The memory of the chesnut-horse," that broke the neck of the same King William. But in my mind (if I am to judge of past times by the corporation of Dublin) it was only to coin an excuse for getting loyally drunk as often as possible, that they were so enthusiastically fond of *making sentiments,* as they called them. (Could His Majesty, King William, learn in the other world that he has been the cause of more broken heads and drunken men, since his departure, than all his predecessors, he must be the proudest ghost and most conceited skeleton that ever entered the gardens of Elysium.)

As to the politics of my family, we had, no doubt, some very substantial reasons for being both Cromwellians and Williamites; the one confirmed our grants, and the other preserved them for us: my family, indeed, had certainly not only those, but other very especial reasons to be pleased with King William; and though he gave them nothing, they kept what they had, which might have been lost but for his usurpation. During the short reign of James the Second in Ireland, those who were not for him were considered to be against him, and of course were subjected to the severities and confiscations usual in all civil wars. Amongst the rest, my great-grandfather, Colonel John Barrington, being a Protestant, and having no predilection for King James, was ousted from his mansion and estates at Cullenaghmore by one O'Fagan, a Jacobite wig-maker and violent partizan, from Ballynakill. He was, notwithstanding, rather respectfully treated, and was allowed forty pounds a year so long as he behaved himself.

However, he only behaved well for a couple of months; at the end of which time, with a party of his faithful tenants, he surprised the wig-maker, turned him out of possession in his turn, and repossessed himself of his mansion and estates. The wig-maker, having escaped to Dublin, laid his complaint before the authorities; and a party of soldiers were ordered to make short work of it, if the colonel did not submit on the first summons.

The party demanded entrance, but were refused; and a little firing from the windows of the mansion took place. Not being, however, tenable, it was successfully stormed: the old gamekeeper, John Neville, killed, and my great-grandfather taken prisoner, conveyed to the drum-head at Raheenduff, tried as a rebel by a certain

Cornet M'Mahon, and in due form ordered to be hanged in an hour.

At the appointed time, execution was punctually proceeded on; and so far as tying up the colonel to the crossbar of his own gate, the sentence was actually put in force. But at the moment the first haul was given to elevate him, Ned Doran, a tenant of the estate, who was a trooper in King James's army, rode up to the gate—himself and horse in a state of complete exhaustion. He saw with horror his landlord strung up, and exclaimed,—

"Holloa! holloa! blood and ouns, boys! cut down the colonel! cut down the colonel! or ye'll be all hanged yeerselves, ye villains of the world, ye! I am straight from the Boyne Water,* through thick and thin: ough, by the hokys! we're all cut up and kilt to the devil and back agin—Jemmy's scampered, bad luck to him, without a 'good bye to yees!'—or, 'kiss my r——p!'—or the least civility in life!"

My grandfather's hangmen lost no time in getting off, leaving the colonel slung fast by the neck to the gateposts. But Doran soon cut him down, and fell on his knees to beg pardon of his landlord, the holy Virgin, and King William from the Boyne Water.

This occurrence of my great-grandfather fixed the political creed of my family. On the 1st of July, the orange lily was sure to garnish every window in the mansion: the hereditary petereroes† scarcely ceased cracking all the evening, to glorify the victory of the Boyne Water, till one of them burst, and killed the gardener's wife, who was tying an orange ribbon round the mouth of it, which she had *stopped* for fear of *accidents*.

The tenantry, though to a man Papists, and at that

* The Battle of the Boyne was fought on July 1, 1690. The victory of William III's forces spelled an end to the attempts of James II to regain the throne of England.

† A peterero is an antique kind of gun that could fire stones, pieces of iron, and the like.

time nearly in a state of slavery, joined heart and hand in these rejoicings, and forgot the victory of their enemy while commemorating the rescue of their landlord. A hundred times have I heard the story repeated by the "Cotchers," * as they sat crouching on their hams, like Indians, around the big turf fire. Their only lament was for the death of old John Nevill, the game-keeper. His name I should well remember; for it was his grandson's wife, Debby Clarke, who nursed me.

This class of stories and incidents was well calculated to make indelible impressions on the mind of a child, and has never left mine.—The old people of Ireland (like the Asiatics) took the greatest delight in repeating their legendary tales to the children, by which constant repetition their old stories became in fact hereditary, and I dare say neither gained nor lost a single sentence in the recital for a couple of hundred years. The massacres of Queen Elizabeth were quite familiar to them; and by an ancient custom of every body throwing a stone on the spot where any celebrated murder had been committed, upon a certain day every year, it is wonderful what mounds were raised in numerous places, which no person, but such as were familiar with the customs of the poor creatures, would ever be able to account for.

* I.e., "cottagers."

ELIZABETH FITZGERALD

A GREAT-AUNT of mine, Elizabeth Fitzgerald, whose husband, Stephen, possessed the castle of Moret,* near Bally-Brittis and not very far from Cullenagh, did not fare quite so well as my great-grandfather, before mentioned.

She and her husband held their castle firmly during the troubles. They had forty good warders; their local enemies had no cannon, and but few guns. The warders, protected by the battlements, pelted their adversaries with large stones, when they ventured to approach the walls; and in front of each of that description of castles, there was a hole, perpendicularly over the entrance, wherefrom any person, himself unseen, could drop down every species of defensive material upon assailants.

About the year 1690, when Ireland was in a state of great disorder, and no laws were really regarded, numerous factious bodies were formed in every part of the country to claim old rights, and take possession of estates under legal pretences.

My uncle and aunt, or rather my aunt and uncle (for she was said to be far the most effective of the two), at one time suffered the enemy (who were of the faction of the O'Cahils, and who claimed my uncle's property, which they said Queen Elizabeth had turned them out of,) to approach the gate in the night-time. There were neither outworks nor wet fosse; the assailants therefore, counting upon victory, brought fire to consume the gate, and so gain admittance. My aunt, aware of their designs, drew all her warders to one spot, large heaps of great

* I.e., Morretta Castle, near Ballybrittas, County Leix.

[14]

stones being ready to their hands at the top of the castle.

When the O'Cahils had got close to the gate, and were directly under the loop-hole, on a sudden streams of boiling water, heated in the castle coppers, came showering down upon the heads of the crowd below: this extinguished their fire, and cruelly scalded many of the besiegers.

The scene may be conceived which was presented by a multitude of scalded wretches, on a dark night, under the power and within the reach of all offensive missiles. They attempted to fly; but whilst one part of the warders hurled volleys of weighty stones *beyond* them, to deter them from *retreating,* another party dropped stones more ponderous still on the heads of those who, for protection, crouched close under the castle-walls: the lady of the castle herself, meantime, and all her maids, assisting the chief body of the warders in pelting the Jacobites with every kind of destructive missile, till all seemed pretty still; and wherever a groan was heard, a volley quickly ended the troubles of the sufferer.

The old traditionists of the country often told me, that at daybreak there were lying above one hundred of the assailants under the castle-walls—some scalded, some battered to pieces, and many lamed so as to have no power of moving off: but my good aunt kindly ordered them all to be put out of their misery, as fast as ropes and a long gallows, erected for their sakes, could perform that piece of humanity.

After the victory, the warders had a feast on the castle-top, whereat each of them recounted his own feats. Squire Fitzgerald, who was a quiet easy man, and hated fighting, and who had told my aunt, at the beginning, that they would surely kill him, having seated himself all night peaceably under one of the parapets, was quite delighted when the fray was over. He had walked out into his garden outside the walls to take some tranquil air, when an ambuscade of the hostile survivors surrounded and carried him off. In vain his warders sallied—the squire was gone past all redemption!

It was supposed he had paid his debts to Nature—if any he owed—when, next day, a large body of the O'Cahil faction appeared near the castle. Their force was too great to be attacked by the warders, who durst not sally; and the former assault had been too calamitous to the O'Cahils to warrant them in attempting another. Both were therefore standing at bay, when, to the great joy of the garrison, Squire Fitzgerald was produced, and one of the assailants, with a white cloth on a pike, advanced to parley.

The lady attended his proposals, which were very laconic. "I'm a truce, lady!—Look here, (showing the terrified squire,) we have your husband in hault—yee's have yeer castle *sure* enough. Now we'll change, if you please: we'll render the squire and you'll render the keep; and if yees won't do that same, the squire will be throttled before your two eyes in half an hour."

"Flag of truce!" said the heroine, with due dignity and without hesitation; "mark the words of Elizabeth Fitzgerald, of Moret Castle: they may serve for your own wife upon some future occasion. Flag of truce! I *won't* render my keep, and I'll tell you why—Elizabeth Fitzgerald may get another husband, but Elizabeth Fitzgerald may never get another castle; so I'll keep what I have, and if you can't get off faster than your legs can readily carry you, my warders will try which is hardest, your skull or a stone bullet."

The O'Cahils kept their word, and old Squire Stephen Fitzgerald, in a short time, was seen dangling and performing various evolutions in the air, to the great amusement of the Jacobites, the mortification of the warders, and chagrin (which however was not without a mixture of consolation) of my great-aunt, Elizabeth.

[16]

This magnanimous lady, after Squire Stephen had been duly cut down, waked, and deposited in a neighbouring garden, conceived that she might enjoy her castle with tranquillity: but, to guard against every chance, she replenished her stony magazine; had a wide trench dug before the gate of the castle; and pit-falls, covered with green sods, having sharp stakes driven within, scattered round it on every side—the passage through these being only known to the faithful warders. She contrived, besides, a species of defence that I have not seen mentioned in the *Peccata Hibernia,** or any of the murderous annals of Ireland: it consisted of a heavy beam of wood, well loaded with iron at the bottom, and suspended by a pulley and cord at the top of the castle, and which, on any future assault, she could let down through the projecting hole over the entrance;—alternately, with the aid of a few strong warders above, raising and letting it drop smash among the enemy who attempted to gain admittance below,—thereby pounding them as if with a pestle and mortar, without the power of resistance on their part.

The castle-vaults were well victualled, and at all events could safely defy any attacks of hunger; and as the enemy had none of those despotic engines called cannon, my aunt's garrison were in all points in tolerable security. Indeed, fortunately for Elizabeth, there was not a single piece of ordnance in the country, except those few which were mounted in the Fort of Dunnally,† or travelled with the king's army: and, to speak truth, fire-arms then would have been of little use, since there was not sufficient gunpowder among the people to hold an hour's hard fighting.

With these and some interior defences, Elizabeth

* Barrington is punning on the title of Sir James Stafford's *Pacata Hibernia* (1633)—a very biased account (favorable to the English) of warfare between England and Ireland in the reign of Elizabeth.

† I.e., Dún Aillinne, a large royal fort at Kilcullen, County Kildare.

imagined herself well armed against all marauders, and quietly awaited a change of times and a period of general security.

Close to the castle there was, and I believe still remains, a dribbling stream of water, in which there is a large stone with a deep indenture on the top. It was always full of limpid water, and called St. Bridget's Well,—that holy woman having been accustomed daily to kneel in prayer on one knee, till she wore a hole in the top of the granite by the cap of her pious joint.

To this well, old Jug Ogie, the oldest piece of furniture in Moret Castle, (she was an hereditary cook,) daily went for the purpose of drawing the most sacred crystal she could, wherewith to boil her mistress's dinner; and also, as the well was naturally consecrated, it saved the priest a quantity of trouble in preparing holy water for the use of the warders.

On one of these sallies of old Jug, some fellows (who, as it afterwards appeared, had with a very deep design lain in ambush) seized and were carrying her off, when they were perceived by one of the watchmen from the tower, who instantly gave an alarm, and some warders sallied after them. Jug was rescued, and the enemy fled through the swamps; but not before one of them had his head divided into two equal parts by the hatchet of Keeran Karry,* who was always at the head of the warders, and the life and soul of the whole garrison.

The dead man turned out to be a son of Andrew M'Mahon, a faction-man of Reuben;† but nobody could then guess the motive for endeavouring to carry off old Jug. However, that matter soon became developed.

* Rather suspiciously, a servant of this name turns up as a member of the Barrington retinue at Major Barrington's wedding.

† This refers to Reban Castle, near Athy, County Kildare, on the river Barrow.

Elizabeth was accounted to be very rich,—the cleverest woman of her day,—and she had a large demesne into the bargain: and finding the sweets of independence, she refused matrimonial offers from many quarters; but as her castle was, for those days, a durably safe residence, such as the auctioneers of the present time would denominate *a genuine undeniable mansion,* the country squires determined she *should* marry one of them, since marry willingly she would not—but they nearly fell to loggerheads who should *run away* with her. Almost every one of them had previously put the question to her by *flag of truce,* as they all stood in too much awe of the lady to do it personally: and at length, teased by their importunities, she gave notice of her intention to hang the next flag of truce who brought any such impudent proposals.

Upon this information, they finally agreed to decide by lot who should be the hero to surprise and carry off Elizabeth, which was considered a matter of danger on account of the warders, who would receive no other commandant.

Elizabeth got wind of their design and place of meeting, which was to be in the old castle of Reuben, near Athy. Eleven or twelve of the squires privately attended at the appointed hour, and it was determined that whoever should be the lucky winner, was to receive the aid and assistance of the others in bearing away the prize, and gaining her hand. To this effect, a league offensive and defensive was entered into between them—one part of which went to destroy Elizabeth's warders root and branch; and to forward their object, it was desirable, if possible, to procure some inmate of the castle, who, by fair or foul means, would inform them of the best mode of entry: this caused the attempt to carry off old Jug Ogie.

However, they were not long in want of a spy: for Elizabeth, hearing of their plan from the gassoon* of Reuben (a nephew of Jug's), determined to take advantage of it. "My lady," said Jug Ogie, "pretend to turn me adrift in a dark night, and give out that my gassoon here was found robbing you—they'll soon get wind of it, and I'll be the very person the squires want—and then you'll hear all."

The matter was agreed on, and old Jug Ogie and the gassoon were turned out, as thieves, to the great surprise of the warders and the country. But Jug was found and hired, as she expected; and soon comfortably seated in the kitchen at Castle Reuben, with the gassoon, whom she took in as kitchen-boy. She gave her tongue its full fling,—told a hundred stories about her "devil of a mistress,"—and undertook to inform the squires of the best way to get to her apartment.

Elizabeth was now sure to learn every thing so soon as determined on. The faction had arranged all matters for the capture:—the night of its execution approached:—the old cook prepared a good supper for the quality—the squires arrived, and the gassoon had to run only three miles to give the lady the intelligence. Twelve cavaliers attended, each accompanied by one of the ablest of his faction, for they were all afraid of each other, whenever the wine should rise upwards.

The lots, being formed of straws of different lengths, were held by the host, who was disinterested, and the person of Elizabeth, her fortune, and Moret castle, fell to the lot of Cromarty O'Moore, one of the Cremorgan squires, and, according to tradition, as able-bodied, stout a man as any in the whole county. The rest all swore to assist him till death; and one in the morning was the time appointed for the surprise of Elizabeth and her castle—

* A youth, young servant, from French *garçon*.

while in the mean time they began to enjoy the good supper of old Jug Ogie.

Castle Reuben had been one of the strongest places in
the county, situated in the midst of a swamp, which
rendered it nearly inaccessible. It had belonged to a natural son of one of the Geraldines, who had his throat
cut by a game-keeper of his own; and nobody choosing
to interfere with the sportsman, he remained peaceably
in possession of the castle, and now accommodated the
squires with it during their plot against Elizabeth.

That heroic dame, on her part, was not inactive; she
informed her warders of the scheme to force a new master
on her and them; and many a round oath she swore (with
corresponding gesticulations, the description of which
would not be over agreeable to modern readers,) that she
never would grant her favours to man, but preserve her
castle and her chastity to the last extremity.

The warders took fire at the attempt of the squires.
They always detested the defensive system; and probably
to that hatred may be attributed a few of the robberies,
burglaries, and burnings, which in those times were little
more than occasional pastimes.

"Arrah! lady," said Keeran Karry, "how many rogues
'ill there be at Reuben, as you larn, to-night?—arrah!"
"I hear only four-and-twenty," said Elizabeth, "besides
the M'Mahons."

"Right, a'nuff," said Keeran, "the fish in the Barrow
must want food this hard weather; and I can't see why
the rump of a rapparee* may not make as nice a tit-bit
for them as any thing else."

All then began to speak together, and join most heartily
in the meditated attack.

"Arrah! run for the priest," says Ned Regan, "may
be you'd like a touch of his reverence's office first, for
fear there might be any sin in it."

* An outlaw, plunderer, from Gaelic *rapaire,* rapier.

"I thought you'd like him with your brandy, warders," said Elizabeth with dignity, "I have him below: he's praying a little, and will be up directly. The whole plan is ready for you, and Jug Ogie has the signal. Here, Keeran," giving him a green ribbon with a daub of old Squire Fitzgerald, who was hanged, dangling to the ribbon, "if you and the warders do not bring me their captain's ear, you have neither the courage of a weazel, nor—nor" (striking her breast hard with her able hand) "even the revenge of a woman in you."

"Arrah, be asy, my lady!" said Keeran, "be asy! by my sowl, we'll bring you four-and-twenty pair, if your ladyship have any longing for the ears of such villains."

"Now, warders," said Elizabeth, who was too cautious to leave her castle totally unguarded, "as we are going to be just, let us be also generous; there's only twenty-four of them, besides the M'Mahons, will be there. Now it would be an eternal disgrace to Moret, if we went to over-power them by numbers: twenty-four chosen warders, Father Murphy and the corporal, the gassoon and the piper, are all that shall leave the castle to-night; and if Castle Reuben is let to stand till day-break to-morrow, I hope none of you will come back to me again."

The priest now made his appearance, he certainly seemed rather as if he had not been idle below during the colloquy on the leads; and the deep impressions upon the bottle which he held in his hand, gave grounds to suppose that he had been very busy and earnest in his devotions.

"My flock!" said Father Murphy, rather lispingly.

"Arrah!" said Keeran Karry, "we're not sheep to-night: never mind your flocks just now, Father! give us a couple of glasses a piece!—time enough for mutton-making."

"You are right, my chickens!" bellowed forth Father Murphy, throwing his old black surtout over his shoulder, leaving the empty sleeves dangling at full liberty, and putting a knife and fork in his pocket for ulterior operations:—"I forgive every mother's babe of you every thing you choose to do till sun-rise: but if you commit any sin after that time, as big even as the blacks of my nele, I can't take charge of yeer sowls, without a chance of disappointing you."

All was now in a bustle:—the brandy circulated merrily, and each warder had in his own mind made mincemeat of three or four of the Reuben faction, whose ears they fancied already in their pockets. The priest marked down the *"De profundis"* in the leaves of his double manual, to have it ready for the burials:—every man took his skeen* in his belt—had a thick club, with a strong spike at the end of it, slung with a stout leather thong to his wrist; and under his coat, a sharp broad hatchet with a black blade and a crooked handle. And thus, in silence, the twenty-five Moret warders set out with their priest, the piper, and the gassoon with a copper pot slung over his shoulders, and a piece of a poker in his hand, on their expedition to the castle of Reuben.

Before twelve o'clock, the warders, the priest, Keeran Karry, and the castle piper, had arrived in the utmost silence and secrecy. In that sort of large inhabited castle, the principal entrance was through the farm-yard, which was, indeed, generally the only assailable quarter. In the present instance, the gate was half open, and the house lights appeared to have been collected in the rear, as was judged from their reflection in the water of the Barrow, which ran close under the windows. A noise was heard, but not of drunkenness;—it was a sound as of preparation for battle. Now and then a clash of steel, as if persons were practising at the sword or skeen for the offensive, was going forward in the back hall; and a loud laugh was occasionally heard. The warders foresaw it

* A dagger, from Irish *sgian.*

[23]

would not be so easy a business as they had contemplated, and almost regretted that they had not brought a less chivalrous numerical force.

It was concerted that ten men should creep upon their hands and feet to the front entrance, and await there untill, by some accident, it might be sufficiently open for the ferocious rush which was to surprise their opponents.

But Keeran, always discreet, had some forethought that more than usual caution would be requisite. He had counted on dangers which the others had never dreamt of, and his prudence, in all probability, saved the lives of many of the warders. He preceded his men, crawling nearly on his breast; he had suspected that a dog overheard them, and a bark soon confirmed the truth of that suspicion, and announced the possibility of discovery. Keeran, however, was prepared for this circumstance; he had filled his pockets with pieces of bacon impregnated with a concentrated preparation of nux vomica, then, and at a much later period, well known to the clergy and spirituals, I cannot tell for what purpose, nor shall I here inquire. Its effect on dogs was instantaneous; and the savoury bacon having rendered them quite greedy to devour it, it had now an immediate effect on two great mastiffs and a wolfdog who roamed about the yard at nights. On taking each a portion, they quickly resigned their share of the contest without further noise.

Keeran advanced crawling to the door; he found it fast, but having listened, he soon had reason to conjecture that the inmates were too well armed and numerous to make the result of the battle at all certain.—He crept back to the hedge—and having informed the warders of the situation in which they were placed, they one and all swore that they would enter or die. The priest had lain himself down under a hay-stack in the outer hay-yard, and the piper had retired nobody knew where, nor in fact did any body care much about him, as he was but a very indifferent chanter.

Keeran now desired the warders to handle their hatchets, and be prepared for an attack so soon as they should see the front door open and hear three strokes on the copper kettle.—The gassoon had left that machine on a spot which he had described near the gate, and Keeran requested that, in case of any fire, they should not mind it till the kettle sounded. He then crawled away, and they saw no more of him.

The moments were precious, and seemed to advance too fast. At one o'clock a body armed possibly better than themselves, and probably more numerous, would surely issue from the castle on their road to Moret, well prepared for combat. The result in such a case might be very precarious. The warders by no means felt pleased with their situation; and the absence of their leader, priest, and piper gave no additional ideas of conquest or security. In this state of things near half an hour had elapsed, when of a sudden they perceived, on the side of the hay-yard towards their own position, a small blaze of fire issue from a corn-stack—in a moment another, and another! The conflagration was most impetuous; it appeared to be devouring every thing, but as yet was not perceived by the inmates at the rear of the house. At length volumes of flame illuminated by reflection the waters of the river under the back windows. The warders now expecting the sally, rubbed their hands well with bees' wax, and grasped tightly their hatchets, yet moved not:—breathless, with a ferocious anxiety, they awaited the event in almost maddening suspense. A loud noise now issued from the interior of the house; the fire was perceived by the garrison—still it might be accidental— the front door was thrown open, and near thirty of the inmates poured out, some fully, others not fully armed.

They rushed into the hay-yard—some cried out it was "treachery!" whilst others vociferated "accident! accident!"—All was confusion, and many a stout head afterwards paid for its incredulity.

At that moment the copper kettle was beaten rapidly and with force:—a responsive sound issued from the house—the garrison hesitated, but hesitation was quickly banished; for on the first blow of the kettle, the warders, in a compact body, with hideous yells, rushed on the astonished garrison, who had no conception who their enemies could be. Every hatchet found its victim;—limbs, features, hands, were chopped off without mercy—death or dismemberment followed nearly every blow of that brutal weapon, whilst the broad sharp skeens soon seached the bodies of the wounded, and almost half the garrison were annihilated before they were aware of the foe by whom they had been surprised. The survivors, however, soon learned the cause (perhaps merited) of their comrades' slaughter. The war cry of "A Gerald!—a Gerald! —a Gerald!"—which now accompanied every crash of the murderous hatchet, or every plunge of the broad-bladed skeen, informed them who they were fighting with:—fifteen or sixteen still remained unwounded of the garrison—their case was desperate. Keeran Karry now headed his warders. The gassoon rapidly and fiercely struck the copper, in unison with the sound of the fatal weapons, whilst the old and decrepid Jug Ogie, within the castle, repeated the same sound, thereby leading the garrison to believe that to retreat inside the walls would only be to encounter a fresh enemy.

The affair, however, was far from being finished;— the survivors rapidly retired, and got in a body to the position first occupied by Keeran's warders. They were desperate—they knew they must die, and determined not to go alone to the other regions. The flames still raged with irresistible fury in the hay-yard. It was Keeran who had set fire to the corn and hay, which materials produced an almost supernatural height of blaze and impetuosity of conflagration. The survivors of the garrison were at once fortified, and concealed from view, by a high holly hedge, and awaited their turn to become assailants:—it soon arrived. From the midst of the burning ricks in the hay-yard a shrill and piercing cry was heard to issue, of "Ough, murther—murther!—the devil—the devil! ough Holy Virgin, save me! if there is any marcy, save me!" The voice was at once recognised by the warriors of Moret as that of their priest Ned Murphy, who had fallen asleep under a hay-stack, and never awakened till the flames had seized upon his cloak. Bewildered, he knew not how to escape, being met, wherever he ran, by crackling masses. He roared and cursed to the full extent of his voice: and gave himself up for lost, though fortunately, as the materials of his habit did not associate with flame, he was not dangerously burned, although he suffered somewhat in his legs. No sooner did they perceive his situation, than the warders, each man forgetting himself, rushed to save their "clergy," on whom they conceived their own salvation entirely to depend. They now imagined that the fight was ended, and prepared to enjoy themselves by the plunder of Castle Reuben.

This was the moment for the defeated garrison:—with a loud yell of "a Moore, a Moore! a Moore!" they fell in their turn upon the entangled warders in the hay-yard, five of whom had been wounded and one killed in the first fray, whilst many had subsequently thrown down their hatchets to receive their pastor, and had only their spikes and skeens wherewith to defend themselves. The battle now became more serious, because more doubtful, than at its commencement. Several of the warders were wounded, and four more lay dead at the entrance to the hay-yard; their spirit was dashed, and their adversaries laid on with the fury of desperation. Keeran Karry had

[27]

received two sword-thrusts through his shoulder and could fight no more; but he could do better—he could command. He called to the warders to retreat and take possession of the castle, which was now untenanted: this step saved them; they retired thither with all possible rapidity, pursued by the former garrison of the place, who however were not able to enter with them, but killed another man before the doors were fast closed. Keeran directed the thick planks and flag stones to be torn up, thereby leaving the hall open to the cellar beneath, as had been done at Moret. The enemy were at bay at the door, and could not advance, but, on the other hand, many of the warders having, as we before stated, flung away their hatchets, were ill armed. The moment was critical: Keeran, however, was never at a loss for some expedient; he counted his men; five had been killed in the hay-yard, and one just outside the walls; several others were wounded, amongst whom was the piper, who had been asleep. Keeran told the warders that he feared the sun might rise on their destruction, if something were not immediately done. "Are there," said he, "five among ye, who are willing to swap your lives for the victory?" Every man cried out for himself—and I!—I!—I!—echoed through the hall. "Well!" said Keeran, who without delay directed five men, and the gassoon with the copper kettle, to steal out at the back of the castle, creep through the hedges, and get round directly into the rear of the foe before they attacked; having succeeded in which, they were immediately to advance beating the vessel strongly.—"They will suppose," said the warlike Keeran, "that it is a reinforcement, and we shall then return the sound from within. If they believe it to be a reinforcement, they will submit to mercy: if not, we'll attack them front and rear—and as our numbers are pretty equal, very few of us on either side will tell the story to our childer! but we'll have as good chance as them villains."

This scheme was carried into immediate execution, and completely succeeded. The enemy, who were now grouped outside the door, hearing the kettle in the rear, supposed that they should be at once attacked by sally and from behind. Thinking that they had now only to choose between death and submission, the mercy, which was offered, they accepted;—and peep-o'day being arrived, the vanquished agreed to throw their arms into the well,—to swear before the priest that they never would disturb, or aid in disturbing, Lady Elizabeth or the castle of Moret,—that no man on either side should be called upon by law for his fighting that night; and finally, that the person who had succeeded in drawing the lot for Elizabeth, should deliver up the lock of his hair that grew next his ear to testify his submission: this latter clause, however, was stipulated needlessly, as Cromarty O'Moore was discovered in the farm-yard, with nearly all his face cut off, and several skeen wounds in his arms and body. Early in the morning, the dead were buried without noise or disturbance, and both parties breakfasted together in perfect cordiality and good-humour: those who fell were mostly tenants of the squires. The priest, having had his burnt legs and arm dressed with chewed herbs by Jug Ogie, said a full mass, and gave all parties double absolution, as the affair was completed by the rising of the sun. The yard was cleared of blood and havock; the warders and garrison parted in perfect friendship; and the former returned to the castle, bringing back Jug Ogie to her impatient mistress. Of the warders, thirteen returned safe; six remained behind badly wounded, and six were dead. Keeran's wounds were severe, but they soon healed; and Elizabeth afterwards resided at Moret to a very late period in the reign of

[29]

George the First. Reuben soon changed its occupant, M'Mahon, who was hanged for the murder of his master; and that part of the country has since become one of the most civilized of the whole province.

I have given the foregoing little history in full, inasmuch as it is but little known, is strictly matter of fact, and exhibits a curious picture of the state of Irish society and manners in or about the year 1690.

PATRICIANS AND PLEBEIANS

I WILL now proceed to lay before the reader a brief but more general sketch of the state of Irish society at the period of my youth, reminding him of the principle which I have before assumed; namely, that of considering anecdotes, bon-mots, and such-like, valuable only as they tend to exemplify interesting facts, relative to history or manners: many such I have inserted in these fragments; and as I have been careful throughout to avoid mere inventions, my reader need not, by any means, reserve their perusal for the study of his travelling carriage.

Miss Edgeworth, in her admirable sketch of *Castle Rackrent,* gives a faithful picture of the Irish character under the circumstances which she has selected; and the account that I am about to give may serve as a kind of supplement to that little work, as well as an elucidation of the habits and manners of Irish country society about the period Miss Edgeworth alludes to, and somewhat later.

In those days, then, the common people ideally separated the gentry of the country into three classes, and treated each class according to the relative degree of respect to which they considered it was entitled.

They generally divided them thus:

1. *Half-mounted* gentlemen.
2. Gentlemen every *inch of them.*
3. Gentlemen to the *back bone.*

The first-named class formed the only species of independent yeomanry then existing in Ireland. They were the descendants of the small grantees of Queen Elizabeth,

Cromwell, and King William; possessed about 200 acres of land each, in fee farm, from the Crown; and were occasionally admitted into the society of gentlemen—particularly hunters—living at other times amongst each other, with an intermixture of their own servants, with whom they were always on terms of intimacy. They generally had good clever horses, which could leap over any thing, but had never felt the trimming-scissors or curry-comb. The riders commonly wore buck-skin breeches, and boots well greased, (blacking was never used in the country,) and carried large thong whips heavily loaded with lead at the butt-end, so that they were always prepared either to horsewhip a man or knock his brains out, as circumstances might dictate. These half-mounted gentlemen exercised the hereditary authority of keeping the ground clear at horse-races, hurlings, and all public meetings, (as the soldiers keep the lines at a review). Their business was to ride round the inside of the ground, which they generally did with becoming spirit, trampling over some, knocking down others, and slashing every body who encroached on the proper limits. Bones being but very *seldom* broken, and skulls still seldomer fractured, every body approved of their exertions, because all the by-standers gained therefrom a full view of the sport which was going forward. A shout of merriment was always set up when a half-mounted gentleman knocked down an interloper; and some of the *poets* present, if they had an opportunity, roared out their verses* by way of a song to encourage the gentlemen.

* I recollect an example of those good-humoured madrigals. A poet, called Daniel Bran, sang it aloud, as he himself lay sprawling on the grass, after having been knocked down and ridden over by old Squire Flood, who showed no mercy in the "execution of his *duty*."

"There was Despard so brave,
That son of the wave,

The second class, or gentlemen every *inch of them,* were of excellent old families;—whose finances were not in so good order as they might have been, but who were popular amongst all ranks. They were far above the first degree, somewhat inferior to the third; but had great influence, were much beloved, and carried more sway at popular elections and general county meetings than the other two classes put together.*

The third class, or gentlemen to the *back bone,* were of the oldest families and settlers, universally respected, and idolized by the peasantry, although they also were generally a little out at elbows. Their word was law; their nod would have immediately collected an army of cottagers, or colliers, or whatever the population was composed of. Men, women, and children, were always ready and willing to execute any thing "the squire" required, without the slightest consideration as to either its danger or propriety.

In travelling through Ireland, a stranger is very frequently puzzled by the singular ways, and especially by the idiomatic equivocation, characteristic of every Irish peasant. Some years back, more particularly, these men were certainly originals—quite unlike any other people whatever. Many an hour of curious entertainment has been afforded me by their eccentricities; yet, though always fond of prying into the remote sources of these national peculiarities, I must frankly confess that, with all my pains, I never was able to develop half of them, except by one sweeping observation; namely, that the brains

---

And Tom Conway, the pride of the bower;
But noble Squire Flood
Swore, G——d d——n his blood!
But he'd drown them all in the Delower."

[Barrington's footnote]

* This was Barrington's own class, as Maurice Craig has pointed out in *Dublin: 1660–1860* (London, 1952), p. 268.

and tongues of the Irish are somehow differently formed or furnished from those of other people.

One general hint which I beg to impress upon all travellers in Hibernia, is the following: that if they show a disposition towards kindness, together with a moderate familiarity, and *affect* to be *inquisitive,* whether so or not, the Irish peasant will outdo them ten-fold in every one of these dispositions. But if a man is haughty and overbearing, he had better take care of himself.

I have often heard it remarked and complained of, by travellers and strangers, that they never could get a true answer from any Irish peasant as to *distances,* when on a journey. For many years I myself thought it most unaccountable. If you meet a peasant on your journey, and ask him how far, for instance, to Ballinrobe? he will probably say it is, "*three short* miles." You travel on, and are informed by the next peasant you meet, "that it is *five long* miles." On you go, and the next will tell "your honour" it is "*four miles,* or about that same." The fourth will swear "if your honour stops at *three* miles, you'll never get there!" But, on pointing to a town just before you, and inquiring what place that is, he replies,

"Oh! plaze your honour, that's Ballinrobe, sure enough!"

"Why you said it was more than three miles off!"

"Oh yes! to be sure and sartain, that's from my *own cabin,* plaze your honour. We're no scholards in this country. Arrah! how can we tell any distance, plaze your honour, but from our own *little cabins?* Nobody but the schoolmaster knows that, plaze your honour."

Thus is the mystery unravelled. When you ask any peasant the distance of the place you require, he never computes it from where you *then are,* but from his *own cabin;* so that, if you asked twenty, in all probability you would have as many different answers, and not one of them correct. But it is to be observed, that frequently you can get no reply at all, unless you understand *Irish.*

In parts of Kerry and Mayo, however, I have met with peasants who speak Latin not badly. On the election of Sir John Brown for the County of Mayo, Counsellor Thomas Moore and I went down as his counsel. The weather was desperately severe. At a solitary inn, where we were obliged to stop for horses, we requested dinner; upon which, the waiter laid a cloth that certainly exhibited every species of dirt ever invented. We called, and remonstrating with him, ordered a clean cloth. He was a low fat fellow, with a countenance perfectly immovable, and seeming to have scarcely a single muscle in it. He nodded, and on our return to the room, (which we had quitted during the interval,) we found, instead of a clean cloth, that he had only folded up the filthy one into the thickness of a cushion. We now scolded away in good earnest. He looked at us with the greatest sang-froid, and said sententiously, *"Nemo me impune lacessit."* *

He kept his word; when we had proceeded about four miles in deep snow, and through a desperate night, on a bleak road, one of the wheels came off the carriage, and down we went! We were at least two miles from *any* house. The driver cursed, in Irish, Michael the waiter, who, he said, had put a *new* wheel upon the carriage, which had turned out to be an *old* one, and had broken to pieces.

We had to march through the snow to a wretched cottage, and sit up all night to get a genuine *new wheel* ready for the morning.

The Irish peasant, also, never answers any question directly: in some districts, if you ask him where such a gentleman's house is, he will point and reply, "Does your honour see that large house there, all amongst the trees,

---

* "No one wounds me with impunity."

with a green field before it?"—You answer, "Yes."
"Well," says he, "plaze your honour that's *not it*. But do
you see the big brick house with the cow-houses by the
side of that same, and a pond of water?"

"Yes."

"Well, plaze your honour, *that's* not it. But, if you
plaze, look quite to the right of that same house, and
you'll see the top of a castle amongst the trees there,
with a road going down to it betune the bushes."

"Yes."

"Well, plaze your honour, *that's not it* neither—but if
your honour will come down this bit of a road a couple of
miles, I'll show it you *sure enough*—and if your honour's
in a hurry, I can run on *hot foot,** and tell the squire
your honour's *galloping after* me. Ah! who shall I tell
the squire, plaze your honour, is coming to see him? he's
my own landlord, God save his honour day and night!"

---

* A figurative expression for "with all possible *speed*"—used
by the Irish peasants: by taking short cuts, and fairly hopping
along, a young peasant would beat any good traveller [Barring-
ton's footnote].

IRISH GENTRY AND
THEIR RETAINERS

THE NUMEROUS and remarkable instances, which came within my own observation, of mutual attachment between the Irish peasantry and their landlords in former times, would fill volumes. A few only will suffice, in addition to what has already been stated, to show the nature of that reciprocal good-will, which, on many occasions, was singularly useful to both: and in selecting these instances from such as occurred in my own family,—I neither mean to play the vain egotist nor to determine generals by particulars, since good landlords and attached peasantry were then spread over the entire face of Ireland, and bore a great proportion to the whole country.

I remember that a very extensive field of corn of my father's had once become too ripe, inasmuch as all the reapers in the country were employed in getting in their own scanty crops before they shedded. Some of the servants had heard my father regret that he could not by possibility get in his reapers without taking them from these little crops, and that he would sooner lose his own.

This field was within full view of our windows. My father had given up the idea of being able to cut his corn in due time. One morning, when he rose, he could not believe his sight:—he looked—rubbed his eyes—called the servants, and asked them if they saw any thing odd in the field:—they certainly did—for, on our family retiring to rest the night before, the whole body of the peasantry of the country, after their hard labour during the day, had come upon the great field, and had reaped and stacked it before dawn! None of them would even tell him who had a hand in it. Similar instances of affection repeatedly

[37]

took place; and no tenant on any of the estates of my family was ever distrained, or even pressed, for rent. Their gratitude for this knew no bounds; and the only individuals who ever annoyed them were the parsons, by their proctors, and the tax-gatherers for hearth-money; and though hard cash was scant with both landlord and tenant, and no small bank-notes had got into circulation, provisions were plentiful, and but little inconvenience was experienced by the peasantry from want of a circulating medium. There was constant residence and work: no banks and no machinery:—and though the people might not be quite so refined, most undoubtedly they were vastly happier.

But a much more characteristic proof than the foregoing of the extraordinary devotion of the lower to the higher orders in Ireland, in former times, occurred in my family, and is on record.

My grandfather, Mr. French, of County Galway, was a remarkably small, nice little man, but of an extremely irritable temperament. He was an excellent swordsman; and, as was often the case in that county, proud to excess.

Some relics of feudal arrogance frequently set the neighbours and their adherents together by the ears:— my grandfather had conceived a contempt for, and antipathy to, a sturdy *half-mounted* gentleman, one Mr. Dennis Bodkin, who, having an independent mind, entertained an equal aversion to the arrogance of my grandfather, and took every possible opportunity of irritating and opposing him.

My grandmother, an O'Brien, was high and proud— steady and sensible; but disposed to be rather violent at times in her contempts and animosities, and entirely agreed with her husband in his detestation of Mr. Dennis Bodkin.

On some occasion or other, Mr. Dennis had outdone his usual outdoings, and chagrined the squire and his

[38]

lady most outrageously. A large company dined at my grandfather's, and my grandmother launched out in her abuse of Dennis, concluding her exordium by an hyperbole of hatred expressed, but not at all meant, in these words:—"I wish the fellow's ears were cut off! that might quiet him."

It passed over as usual: the subject was changed, and all went on comfortably till supper; at which time, when every body was in full glee, the old butler, Ned Regan (who had drank enough) came in:—joy was in his eye; and whispering something to his mistress which she did not comprehend, he put a large snuff-box into her hand. Fancying it was some whim of her old domestic, she opened the box and shook out its contents:—when, lo! a considerable portion of a pair of bloody ears dropped on the table!—The horror and surprise of the company may be conceived: upon which old Ned exclaimed—"Sure, my lady, you wished that Dennis Bodkin's ears were cut off; so I told old Gahagan (the game-keeper), and he took a few boys with him, and brought back Dennis Bodkin's ears—and there they are; and I hope you are plazed, my lady!"

The scene may be imagined;—but its results had like to have been of a more serious nature. The sportsman and the boys were ordered to get off as fast as they could; but my grandfather and grandmother were held to heavy bail, and were tried at the ensuing assizes at Galway. The evidence of the entire company, however, united in proving that my grandmother never had an idea of any such order, and that it was a mistake on the part of the servants. They were, of course, acquitted. The sportsman never re-appeared in the county till after the death of Dennis Bodkin, which took place three years subsequently.*

* As Donald T. Torchiana has noted, Mrs. Yeats read selections from the *Personal Sketches* to her husband during the early

This anecdote may give the reader an idea of the devotion of servants, in those days, to their masters. The order of things is now reversed—and the change of times cannot be better proved than by the propensity servants *now* have to rob (and, if convenient, murder) the families from whom they derive their daily bread. Where the remote error lies, I know not;—but certainly the ancient fidelity of domestics seems to be totally out of fashion with those gentry at present.

1920's. When Yeats came to assess the meaning for him of Thor Ballylee in the context of Irish history, he chose this incident (which had occurred in the immediate neighborhood) for inclusion in the second stanza of part two of "The Tower." See *W. B. Yeats and Georgian Ireland* (Evanston, Ill., 1966), pp. 300–6.

IRISH DISSIPATION IN 1778

CLOSE to the kennel of my father's hounds, he had built a small cottage, which was occupied solely by an old huntsman, his older wife, and his nephew, a whipper-in. The chace, and the bottle, and the piper, were the enjoyments of winter; and nothing could recompense a suspension of these enjoyments.

My elder brother, justly apprehending that the frost and snow of Christmas might probably prevent their usual occupation of the chace, determined to provide against any listlessness during the shut-up period, by an uninterrupted match of what was called "hard going," till the weather should break up.

A hogshead of superior claret was therefore sent to the cottage of old Quin the huntsman; and a fat cow, killed, and plundered of her skin, was hung up by the heels. All the windows were closed to keep out the light. One room, filled with straw and numerous blankets, was destined for a bed-chamber in common; and another was prepared as a kitchen for the use of the servants. Claret, cold, mulled, or buttered, was to be the beverage for the whole company; and in addition to the cow above mentioned, chickens, bacon and bread were the only admitted viands. Wallace and Hosey, my father's and my brother's pipers, and Doyle, a blind but a famous fiddler, were employed to enliven the banquet, which it was determined should continue till the cow became a skeleton, and the claret should be on its stoop.

My two elder brothers;—two gentlemen of the name of Taylor (one of them afterwards a writer in India);—a Mr. Barrington Lodge, a rough songster;—Frank

Skelton, a jester and a butt;—Jemmy Moffat, the most knowing sportsman of the neighbourhood;—and two other sporting gentlemen of the county,—composed the *permanent* bacchanalians. A few visitors were occasionally admitted.

As for myself, I was too unseasoned * to go through more than the first ordeal, which was on a frosty St. Stephen's day, when the *"hard goers"* partook of their opening banquet, and several neighbours were invited, to honour the commencement of what they called their *"shut-up pilgrimage."*

The old huntsman was the only male attendant; and his ancient spouse, once a kitchen-maid in the family, now somewhat resembling the amiable Leonarda in *Gil Blas,* was the cook; whilst the drudgery fell to the lot of the whipper-in. A long knife was prepared to cut collops from the cow; a large turf fire seemed to court the gridiron; the pot bubbled up as if proud of its contents, whilst plump white chickens floated in crowds upon the surface of the water; the simmering potatoes, just bursting their drab surtouts, exposed the delicate whiteness of their mealy bosoms; the claret was tapped, and the long earthen wide-mouthed pitchers stood gaping under the impatient cock, to receive their portions. The pipers plied their chants; the fiddler tuned his cremona; and never did any feast commence with more auspicious appearances of hilarity and dissipation, appearances which were not doomed to be falsified.

I shall never forget the attraction this novelty had for my youthful mind. All thoughts but those of good cheer were for the time totally obliterated. A few curses were, it is true, requisite to spur on old Leonarda's skill, but at length the banquet entered: the luscious smoked bacon, bedded on its cabbage mattress, and partly obscured by its own savoury steam, might have tempted the most

* I.e., at eighteen.

fastidious of epicures; whilst the round trussed chickens, ranged by the half dozen on hot pewter dishes, turned up their white plump merry-thoughts exciting equally the eye and appetite: fat collops of the hanging cow, sliced indiscriminately from her tenderest points, grilled over the clear embers upon a shining gridiron, half drowned in their own luscious juices, and garnished with little pyramids of congenial shalots, smoked at the bottom of the well-furnished board. A prologue of cherry-bounce (brandy) preceded the entertainment, which was enlivened by hob-nobs and joyous toasts.

Numerous toasts, in fact, as was customary in those days, intervened to prolong and give zest to the repast—every man shouted forth his fair favourite, or convivial pledge; and each voluntarily surrendered a portion of his own reason, in bumpers to the beauty of his neighbour's toast. The pipers jerked from their bags appropriate planxties* to every jolly sentiment: the jokers cracked the usual jests and ribaldry: one songster chanted the joys of wine and women; another gave, in full glee, the pleasures of the fox-chace: the fiddler sawed his merriest jigs: the old huntsman sounded his horn, and thrusting his forefinger into his ear (to aid the quaver,) gave the *view holloa!* of nearly ten minutes' duration; to which melody *tally ho!* was responded by every stentorian voice. A fox's brush stuck into a candlestick, in the centre of the table, was worshipped as a divinity! Claret flowed—bumpers were multiplied—and chickens, in the garb of spicy spitchcocks, assumed the name of *devils* to whet the appetites which it was impossible to conquer!

My reason gradually began to lighten me of its burden, and in its last efforts kindly suggested the straw-chamber as my asylum. Two couple of favourite hounds had been introduced to share in the joyous pastime of their friends and master; and the deep bass of their

* Irish melodies, originally composed for the harp.

[43]

throats, excited by the shrillness of the huntsman's tenor, harmonized by two rattling pipers, a jigging fiddler, and twelve voices, in twelve different keys, all bellowing in one continuous unrelenting chime—was the last point of recognition which Bacchus permitted me to exercise: for my eyes began to perceive a much larger company than the room actually contained;—the lights were more than doubled, without any virtual increase of their number; and even the chairs and tables commenced dancing a series of minuets before me. A faint *tally ho!* was attempted by my reluctant lips; but I believe the effort was unsuccessful, and I very soon lost, in the straw-room, all that brilliant consciousness of existence, in the possession of which the morning had found me so happy. Just as I was closing my eyes to a twelve hours' slumber, I distinguished the general roar of *"stole away!"* which rose almost up to the very roof of old Quin's cottage.

At noon, next day, a scene of a different nature was exhibited. I found, on waking, two associates by my side, in as perfect insensibility as that from which I had just aroused. Our piper seemed indubitably dead! but the fiddler, who had the privilege of age and blindness, had taken a hearty nap, and seemed as much alive as ever. The room of banquet had been re-arranged by the old woman: spitchcocked chickens, fried rashers, and broiled marrowbones appeared struggling for precedence. The clean cloth looked, itself, fresh and exciting: jugs of mulled and buttered claret foamed hot upon the refurnished table, and a better or heartier breakfast I never in my life enjoyed.

A few members of the jovial crew had remained all night at their posts; but I suppose alternately took some rest, as they seemed not at all affected by their repletion. Soap and hot water restored at once their spirits and their persons; and it was determined that the rooms should be ventilated and cleared out for a cock-fight, to pass time till the approach of dinner. In this battle-royal, every man backed his own bird; twelve of which coura- geous animals were set down together to fight it out— the survivor to gain all. In point of principle, the battle of the Horatii and Curiatii was re-acted;* and in about an hour, one cock crowed out his triumph over the man- gled body of his last opponent;—being himself, strange to say, but little wounded. The other eleven lay dead; and to the victor was unanimously voted a writ of ease, with sole monarchy over the hen-roost for the remainder of his days; and I remember him, for many years, the proud commandant of his poultry-yard and seraglio.— Fresh visitors were introduced each successive day, and the seventh morning had arisen before the feast broke up. As that day advanced, the cow was proclaimed to have furnished her full quantum of good dishes; the claret was upon its stoop; and the last gallon, mulled with a pound of spices, was drunk in tumblers to the next merry meeting! All now returned to their *natural* rest, until the evening announced a different scene.

An early supper, to be partaken of by all the young folks, of both sexes, in the neighbourhood, was provided in the dwelling-house, to terminate the festivities. A dance, as usual, wound up the entertainment; and what was then termed a "raking pot of tea," put a finishing stroke, in jollity and good-humour, to such a revel as I never saw before, and, I am sure, shall never see again.

When I compare with the foregoing the habits of the present day, and see the grandsons of those joyous and vigorous sportsmen mincing their fish and tit-bits at their favourite box in Bond-street; amalgamating their ounce of salad on a silver saucer; employing six sauces to coax one appetite; burning up the palate to make its enjoy-

---

* In Roman legend, the three Horatii were brothers who fought with their cousins the three Curiatii brothers. In the battle, only one of the six cousins survived.

ments the more exquisite; sipping their acid claret, disguised by an olive or neutralized by a chesnut; lisping out for the scented waiter, and paying him the price of a feast for the modicum of a Lilliputian, and the pay of a captain for the attendance of a blackguard;—it amuses me extremely, and makes me speculate on what their forefathers would have done to those admirable Epicenes, if they had had them at the "Pilgrimage" in the huntsman's cot.

To these extremes of former roughness and modern affectation, it would require the pen of such a writer as Fielding to do ample justice. It may, however, afford our reader some diversion to trace the degrees which led from the grossness of the former down to the effeminacy of the latter; and these may, in a great measure, be collected from the various incidents which will be found scattered throughout these sketches of sixty solar revolutions.

Nothing indeed can better illustrate the sensation which the grandfathers, or even aged fathers, of these slim lads of the Bond-street establishments, must have felt upon finding their offspring in the occupation I have just mentioned, than a story relating to Captain Parsons Hoye, of County Wicklow, who several years since met with an instance of the kind at Hudson's, in Covent-Garden.

A nephew of his, an effeminate young fellow, who had returned from travelling, and who expected to be his heir, accidentally came into the coffee-room. Neither uncle nor nephew knew each other; but old Parsons' disgust at the dandified manners, language, and dress of the youth, gave rise to an occurrence which drew from the bluff seaman epithets rather too coarse to record:—the end of it was, that, when Parsons discovered the relationship of the stranger, he struck him out of a will which he had made, and died very soon after, as if on purpose to mortify the macaroni!

We will take this opportunity of subjoining an accurate description of the person of Captain Parsons Hoye, thereby enabling our reader to estimate the singularity of his collision with the dandy.

Commodore Trunnion was a civilized man, and a beauty (but a fool), compared to Parsons Hoye. He had a moderate hereditary property near Wicklow; had been a captain in the royal navy; was a bad farmer, a worse sportsman, and a blustering justice of peace: but great at potation! and what was called, "in the main, a capital fellow." He was nearly as boisterous as his adopted element: his voice was always as if on the quarter-deck; and the whistle of an old boatswain, who had been decapitated by his side, hung as a memento, by a thong of leather, to his waistcoat button-hole. It was frequently had recourse to, and, whenever he wanted a word, supplied the deficiency.

In form the Captain was squat, broad, and coarse:—a large purple nose, with a broad crimson chin to match, were the only features of any consequence in his countenance, except a couple of good enough bloodshot eyes, screened by most exuberant grizzle eye-lashes. His powdered wig had behind it a queue in the form of a handspike, and a couple of rolled-up paste curls, like a pair of carronades, adorned its broad-sides; a blue coat, with slash cuffs and plenty of navy buttons, surmounted a scarlet waistcoat—the skirts of which, he said, he would have of their enormous length because it assured him that the tailor had put *all the cloth in it;* a black Barcelona adorned his neck; an old round hat bordered with gold lace, pitched on one side of his head, and turned up also on one side, with a huge cockade stuck into a buttonless loop, gave him a swaggering air. He bore a shillelagh, the growth of his own estate, in a fist which would cover more ground than the best shoulder of wether mutton in a London market.* Yet the Captain had a look of generosity, good nature, benevolence and hospitality, which his features did their very best to conceal, and which none but a good physiognomist could possibly discover.

* I once saw the inconvenience of that species of fist strongly exemplified.—The late Admiral Cosby, of Stradbally Hall, had as large and as brown a fist as any admiral in His Majesty's service. Happening one day unfortunately to lay it on the table during dinner, at Colonel Fitzgerald's, Merrion Square, a Mr. Jenkins, a half-blind doctor, who chanced to sit next to the admiral, cast his eye upon the fist: the imperfection of his vision led him to believe it was a French roll of bread, and, without further ceremony, the doctor thrust his fork plump into the admiral's fist. The confusion which resulted may be easily imagined [Barrington's footnote].

MY BROTHER'S HUNTING-LODGE

I MET with a ludicrous instance of the dissipation of even later days, a few months after my marriage. Lady B—— and myself took a tour through some of the Southern parts of Ireland, and among other places visited Castle Durrow,* near which place my brother, Henry French Barrington, had built a hunting cottage, wherein he happened to have given a house-warming the previous day.

The company, as might be expected at such a place and on such an occasion, was not the most select:—in fact, they were *"hard-going"* sportsmen.

Amongst the rest, Mr. Joseph Kelly, of unfortunate fate, brother to Mr. Michael Kelly,† (who by the bye does not say a word about him in his *Reminiscences,*) had been invited, to add to the merriment by his pleasantry and voice, and had come down from Dublin for the purpose.

It may not be amiss to say something here of that remarkable person. Joe was a slender young man, remarkably handsome; but with regard to character, always what in that part of the country they emphatically styled "the *devil!*" I recollect his dancing a hornpipe in a sailor's costume most admirably upon the stage. He also sang the songs of *Young Meadows,* in "Love in a Village," extremely well, as likewise those of *Macheath* and other parts; but he could never give the *acting* any effect. He

---

* Near Durrow, County Leix.

† Musician and vocalist (1764–1826). He wrote *Reminiscences of Michael Kelly, The King's Theatre, and Theatre Royal Drury Lane* (1826).

was, strictly speaking, a bravura singer;—there was no *pathos*—nothing *touchant* in his cadences, but in drinking songs &c. he was unrivalled. Of this convivial assemblage at my brother's, he was, I suppose, the very life and soul.

The dining-room had not been finished when the day of the dinner-party arrived, and the lower parts of the walls having only that morning received their last coat of plaster, were, of course, totally wet. We had intended to surprise my brother; but had not calculated on the scene I was to witness. On driving to the cottage-door I found it open, whilst a dozen dogs, of different descriptions, showed ready to receive us not in the most polite manner. My servant's whip, however, soon sent them about their business, and I ventured into the parlour to see what cheer.—It was about ten in the morning: the room was strewed with empty bottles—some broken— some interspersed with glasses, plates, dishes, knives, spoons &c. all in glorious confusion. Here and there were heaps of bones, relics of the former day's entertainment, which the dogs, seizing their opportunity, had cleanly picked.—Three or four of the Bacchanalians lay fast asleep upon chairs—one or two others on the floor, among whom a piper lay on his back, apparently dead, with a table-cloth spread over him, and surrounded by four or five candles, burnt to the sockets; his chanter and bags were laid scientifically across his body, his mouth was quite open, and his nose made ample amends for the silence of his drone. Joe Kelly and a Mr. Peter Alley were fast asleep in their chairs, close to the wall. Had I never viewed such a scene before, it would have almost terrified me; but it was nothing more than the ordinary custom which we called *waking the piper,* when he had got too drunk to make any more music.

I went out, and sent away my carriage and its inmate to Castle Durrow, whence we had come, and afterwards proceeded to seek my brother. No servant was to be seen, man or woman. I went to the stables, wherein I found three or four more of the goodly company, who had just been able to reach their horses, but were seized by Morpheus before they could mount them, and so lay in the mangers awaiting a more favourable opportunity. Returning hence to the cottage, I found my brother, also asleep, on the only bed which it then afforded: he had no occasion to put on his clothes, since he had never taken them off.

I next waked Dan Tyron, a wood-ranger of Lord Ashbrook, who had acted as maître d'hôtel in making the arrangements, and providing a horse-load of game to fill up the banquet. I then inspected the parlour, and insisted on breakfast. Dan Tyron set to work: an old woman was called in from an adjoining cabin, the windows were opened, the room cleared, the floor swept, the relics removed, and the fire lighted in the kitchen. The piper was taken away senseless, but my brother would not suffer either Joe or Alley to be disturbed till breakfast was ready. No time was lost; and, after a very brief interval, we had before us abundance of fine eggs, and milk fresh from the cow, with brandy, sugar and nutmeg in plenty; a large loaf, fresh butter, a cold round of beef, which had not been produced on the previous day, red herrings, and a bowl dish of potatoes roasted on the turf ashes;— in addition to which, ale, whiskey, and port made up the refreshments. All being duly in order, we at length awakened Joe Kelly, and Peter Alley, his neighbour: they had slept soundly, though with no other pillow than the wall; and my brother announced breakfast with a *view holloa!*

The twain immediately started and roared in unison with their host most tremendously! it was however in a very different tone from the *view holloa,*—and perpetuated much longer.

[51]

"Come, boys," says French, giving Joe a pull—"come!"

"Oh, murder!" says Joe "I can't!"—"Murder!—murder!" echoed Peter.—French pulled them again, upon which they roared the more, still retaining their places. —I have in my lifetime laughed till I nearly became spasmodic; but never were my risible muscles put to greater tension than upon this occasion. The wall, as I said before, had only that day received a coat of mortar, and of course was quite soft and yielding when Joe and Peter thought proper to make it their pillow; it was nevertheless setting fast from the heat and lights of an eighteen hours' carousal; and, in the morning, when my brother awakened his guests, the mortar had completely set, and their hair being the thing most calculated to amalgamate therewith, the entire of Joe's stock, together with his *queue,* and half his head, was thoroughly and irrecoverably bedded in the greedy and now marble cement, so that if determined to move, he must have taken the wall along with him, for separate it would not.—One side of Peter's head was in the same state of imprisonment. Nobody was able to assist them, and there they both stuck fast.

A consultation was now held on this pitiful case, which I maliciously endeavoured to prolong as much as I could, and which was, in fact, every now and then interrupted by a roar from Peter or Joe, as they made fresh efforts to rise. At length, it was proposed by Dan Tyron to send for the stone-cutter, and get him to cut them out of the wall with a chisel. I was literally unable to speak two sentences for laughing. The old woman meanwhile tried to soften the obdurate wall with melted butter and new milk—but in vain.—I related the school story how Hannibal had worked through the Alps with hot vinegar and hot irons:—this experiment likewise was made, but Hannibal's solvent had no better success than the old crone's. Peter, being of a more passionate nature, grew ultimately

quite outrageous: he roared, gnashed his teeth, and swore
vengeance against the mason;—but as he was only held
by one side, a thought at last struck him: he asked for
two knives, which being brought, he whetted one against
the other, and introducing the blades close to his skull,
sawed away at cross corners till he was liberated, with
the loss only of half his hair and a piece of his scalp,
which he had sliced off in zeal and haste for his liberty. I
never saw a fellow so extravagantly happy! Fur was
scraped from the crown of a hat, to stop the bleeding;
his head was duly tied up with the old woman's *praskeen;**
and he was soon in a state of bodily convalescence. Our
solicitude was now required solely for Joe, whose head
was too deeply buried to be exhumated with so much
facility. At this moment, Bob Casey, of Ballynakill, a
very celebrated wig-maker, just dropped in, to see what
he could pick up honestly in the way of his profession, or
steal in the way of any thing else; and he immediately
undertook to get Mr. Kelly out of the mortar by a very
expert but tedious process, namely,—clipping with his
scissors and then rooting out with an oyster knife. He
thus finally succeeded, in less than an hour, in setting Joe
once more at liberty, at the price of his queue, which was
totally lost, and of the exposure of his raw and bleeding
occiput. The operation was, indeed, of a mongrel description—somewhat between a complete tonsure and an imperfect scalping, to both of which denominations it certainly presented claims. However, it is an ill wind that
blows nobody good! Bob Casey got the making of a
skull-piece for Joe, and my brother French had the pleasure of paying for it, as gentlemen in those days honoured
any order given by a guest to the family shop-keeper or
artizan.

I ate a hearty breakfast, returned to Durrow, and,

* A coarse *dirty* apron, worn by working women in a kitchen,
in the country parts of Ireland [Barrington's footnote].

having rejoined my companion, we pursued our journey to Waterford,—amusing ourselves the greater part of the way with the circumstances just related, which, however, I do not record merely as an abstract anecdote, but, as I observed in starting, to show the manners and habits of Irish country society and sportsmen, even so recently as thirty years ago; and to illustrate the changes of those habits and manners, and the advances towards civilization, which, coupled with the extraordinary *want* of *corresponding prosperity,* present phenomena I am desirous of impressing upon my reader's mind, throughout the whole of this miscellaneous collection of original anecdotes and observations.

RECRUITING AT CASTLEBAR

WHILE George Robert Fitzgerald was undergoing a part of his sentence in Newgate, Dublin,* his brother, Charles Lionel, got possession of the house and demesne of Turlow, near Castlebar, County Mayo—one of the most lawless places then in Ireland. George Robert had armed and organised a band of desperadoes, who knew no will but his, and had no desire but his pleasure. All men were in awe of them, and the regular army alone was then held sufficient to curb their outrages. When their leader was convicted and imprisoned their spirit was somewhat depressed; but idleness and vice were by habit so deeply engrafted in their minds, that peaceable or honest means of livelihood were scouted by them. They were at length proclaimed outlaws; the military chased them; and ultimately, a sort of treaty took place, which, like our modern diplomatic negotiations, exhibited only one party endeavouring to outwit the other. The desperadoes agreed to give up all their wild courses on a promise of pardon; a great proportion declared they would "take on" for a musket; and as the army had no objection to receive robbers and murderers to fight for their king, country, and religion, their offer was accepted.

About this time my military propensities were not

---

* Having been tried and convicted of a most *unparalleled* series of assaults upon, and imprisonment of, his own father, he was sentenced to three years' imprisonment; but, as we have before stated, was pardoned (in six months), to the disgrace of the government [Barrington's footnote].

This gentleman, though of good family and nephew of the Earl of Bristol, was a completely dissolute adventurer. He was finally executed for murder at Castlebar in 1786.

[55]

totally extinguished, but susceptible of being rekindled by proper stimuli—and Dean Coote, brother to Sir Eyre Coote, then Commander-in-chief in India, sent to my father, and made him what my family considered a magnificent offer—namely, that one of his sons should forthwith receive a captain's commission in the East India Company's service, on recruiting a hundred men for that service, and for each of which recruits, if the number were completed, twenty guineas should be paid on their being handed over to the depot in Dublin.

In acknowledgment of this flattering offer my father immediately nominated me. I now almost fancied myself a nabob, or something better, helping to plunder and dethrone a few of the native princes—then quite plentiful, and considered fair game by the Honourable Company's servants, civil and military. I with joy accepted the proposition—fully expecting, in four or five years, to return loaded with *lacs* of rupees, and carats of diamonds, and enabled to realise all my visions of ulterior happiness. The Dean also sent me the "beating order" * and instructions, with a letter of introduction, and a strong recommendation to Mr. Lionel Fitzgerald, then residing at Turlow, requesting he would aid me in enlisting his brother's outlaws for the Company's service, of whom above eighty had promised to accept the king's money on terms of pardon. All now went on prosperously; the tenants of Cullenagh brought in every shilling they could rap or run, to set the young captain a-spinning; and in a week I was on my road, through frost and snow, to the county of Mayo: my father's old huntsman, Matthew Querns, was selected to attend me as being most *sensible,* at least among the domestics of the family.

Matthew was attired in his best field clothing—namely, a green plush coat, scarlet-laced waistcoat of old times,

---

* Evidently authorization for recruitment or conscription of troops.

buckskin breeches, and a black leather hunting cap. He carried my portmanteau, with my volunteer broad-sword buckled to it, behind him, and his own hunting horn was strapped by a belt about his middle:—this he sounded at every inn door, as he said, to make us respectable.

I was mounted on a large *white* horse called Friday, after Robinson Crusoe's *black* boy. A case of huge holster pistols jogged before me, and my cavalry coat-case behind, containing my toilet, flints, a bullet mould, my flute, my beating order, with—to amuse leisure hours—a songbook, and the *Sentimental Journey* (then in high vogue, being totally new both in style and subject).* Thus caparisoned and equipped, the late Matthew Querns and the present Sir Jonah Barrington, set out, fifty years ago, for the purpose of enlisting robbers and outlaws in Mayo, to plunder gentoos in the Carnatic, and establish the Christian religion on the plains of Hindostan.

At that period of my life, cold or fatigue was nothing when I had an object in view; and at the end of the third day's trotting we arrived, through deep snow, bog roads, and after some tumbles (miserably tired), at a little cabin at Hallymount, near the plains of Kilcommon, where many a bloody battle had been fought in former times;—and as the ground was too rocky to dig graves, thousands of human skeletons had been covered up with stones—of which there is no scarcity in any, particularly that part of Ireland. Our reception was curious; and as affording an excellent idea of the species of inns and inn-keepers then prevalent in Ireland, I shall sketch one of the oddest imaginable places of "entertainment for man and horse,"—which notification was written in large let-

* As the events of this account must have taken place about 1782, it is hard to understand why Laurence Sterne's *A Sentimental Journey through France and Italy,* which had been published nearly fifteen years earlier, should have been regarded as such a novelty.

ters over the door,—and the house certainly did not belie it.

The landlord was a fat, red-nosed, pot-bellied, jovial fellow, the very emblem of goodnature and hospitality; he greeted me cordially before he knew any thing about me, and said I should have the best his house afforded, together with a hearty welcome (the welcome of an innkeeper, indeed, is generally very sincere). He also told Matthew that he never suffered his bin of oats in the stable to be closed, always leaving it to gentlemen's beasts to eat at their own discretion—as he'd engage they would stop of themselves when they had got enough; and the more they eat at one meal, the less they would eat the next—so he should be no loser.

The inn consisted of cabins on the ground-floor only, and a very good hard dry floor it certainly was. The furniture was in character: but my bed (if I were to judge from its bulk and softness) had the best feathers of five hundred geese at least in it: the curtains had obviously once been the property of some greater personage than an innkeeper, as the marks of embroidery remained (on crimson silk), which had been carefully picked out—I suppose to sell the silver. My host begged I would not trouble myself as to dinner, as he knew what was good for me after so bad a journey. He protested that, so far as poultry, game, and lobsters went, no man in Mayo could beat him; and that he had a vessel of Powldoody oysters, which was sent him by Squire Francis Macnamara, of Doolan, for old acquaintance sake.

I promptly asked for a bottle of his best wine; but he told me he never sold a *single* bottle to a gentleman, and hoped I would have no objection to two. Of course I acquiesced, though intending to dine alone and only drink the half of one. I was therefore surprised to see shortly a spruce young maid-servant lay out the table for six persons, with every thing in good order:—and on dinner coming in, my landlord introduced his old wife, two smart pretty daughters, and his son, by no means a "promising boy." He uncorked both bottles at once, and no persons ever fared more sumptuously. The wine, he said, was the finest old claret, of the "real smuggling" by Sir Neil O'Donnel's own cutter called *Paddy Whack,* from the Isle of Man;—and Sir Neil (a baronet of Newport) never sent a bad hogshead to any of his *customers:* his honour's brandy, likewise, was not a jot worse than his claret, and always tasted best of a cold morning.

We had got deep into our second bottle, of which the ladies took a glass each, while the young gentleman drank a bumper of brandy, when my host, who knew every body and every thing local, gave me the life, adventures, and character, of almost each person of note in that county, including numerous anecdotes of George Robert, which originated in, and were confined to the neighbourhood. He laughed so heartily at his own stories, that it was impossible not to join him. Tea and hot cakes followed; a roast goose, brandy punch, and old ale, made the supper, and I retired to bed hearty and careless.

Next morning I was roused rather early by a very unexpected guest, namely, a hen, which having got into my room, layed a couple of eggs at once on my coat, which lay beside me; and then, as hens accustom themselves to do, (and it is no bad practice,) she gave as loud and protracted a notice of her *accouchement* as her voice could furnish.

I immediately rose, brought out my two eggs to our breakfast-table, and was expressing my surprise at the circumstance, when Miss Betty Jennings winked, and whispered me that it was a standing joke of her father's. —The breakfast was nearly as good as the dinner had been the previous day; and on procuring my bill, I found I was charged eighteen pence for dinner, eighteen pence for claret, tenpence for my horses, sixpence for my breakfast, and nothing for the rest, though Matthew Querns had got dead drunk, my horses were nearly bursting, and I was little better myself. My host told me, when a guest who would drink with him had a bottle of claret, he always indulged in one himself; and that if I had drunk two, he should have thought it mighty uncivil if he had not done the same. I left his house with an impression that he was the most extraordinary innkeeper I had ever met with, and really bade adieu to himself and his daughters with regret.

Arriving in the course of the day at Turlow, I found that the whole family were at Castle Magarret; but Mr. Fitzgerald had got a letter about me, and all was ready for my reception. I found I was left to the care of one Hughy Hearn, who had been a serjeant of the band, but had changed sides and come over to Mr. Lionel at Turlow, after losing one of his arms in some skirmish for George Robert. I did not know who Hughy was at the time, or I should have kept aloof from him.

"Mr. Hearn," said I, next day, "have you a gun in the house? I should like to go out."

"I have, captain," said he.

"Have you powder and shot?" said I.

"No powder," said Hughy. "I fired all I had left of it last night at a man whom I saw skulking about the road after nightful."

"Did you hit him?" asked I, rather alarmed.

"I can't say," replied Hughy: "there was only one bullet *in it,* and it's not so easy to shoot a man with a single bullet when the night is very dark—and I'm hard set to aim with one arm, though I dare say I all as one as *scratcht* him, for he cried out, 'Oh! bad luck to you, Hughy!' and ran down the cross lane before I could get the other double to slap after him."

I immediately set about recruiting the outlaws with the utmost activity and success. I appointed Hughy

Hearn, who had but one arm, my drill-serjeant, and a monstrous athletic ruffian of the name of O'Mealy, my corporal, major, and inspector of recruits. I found no difficulty whatsoever in prevailing on them to take my money, clap up my cockade, get drunk, beat the towns-people, and swear "true allegiance to King George, Sir Eyre Coote, and myself," This was the oath I adminis-tered to them, as they all seemed zealous to come with me; but I took care not to tell them *where*.

The kindness and hospitality I meanwhile received at Turlow, from Mr. and Mrs. Fitzgerald, was extremely gratifying: nobody could be more interesting than the lat-ter. There I met two remarkable persons of that country —George Lyster, whose finger was broken by George Robert Fitzgerald and a little, decrepid sharp-witted dog, called George Elliston, who afterward challenged me, and threatened Counsellor Saurin, because we did not succeed in a bad cause of his in the King's Bench, wherein we had taken his briefs without fees, as a mat-ter of kindness to a pretended sufferer.

In less than a fortnight I had enlisted between fifty and sixty able, good-looking outlaws; and as my money was running low, I determined to march off my first batch of fifty men, three serjeants, and three corporals, for Dublin, and having placed them in depôt there, to return and make up my number with a replenished purse.

To give my march the greater eclat, I choose a market-day of Castlebar whereon to parade and address my com-pany. There happened to be also a fair of linen yarn, and the street was crowded with cars laden with hanks of yarn of different sizes and colours. Having drawn up my men, I ordered each one to get a bumper of whisky; after which, taking off their hats, they gave three cheers for King George, Sir Eyre Coote, and Captain Barring-ton. I then made them a speech from the top of a car. I told them we were going to a place where the halfpennys were made of gold; where plunder was permitted by the Honourable Company, and the officers taught their men how to avail themselves of this permission, where robbery and murder were not hanging matters, as in Ireland; where women were married at nine years' old, and every soldier had as many wives as he could keep from starving, with a right to rob the rich, in order to support a barrack full of them.

In short, I expatiated on all the pleasures and comforts I purposed for them; and received in return three more cheers—though neither so long or loud as I could have wished; and I perceived a good deal of whispering among my soldiers which I could not account for, save by the pain they might feel in taking leave of their fellow-robbers, as was natural enough. I was, however, soon undeceived, when, on ordering them to march, one said aloud, as if he spoke for the rest, "March *is it?* march, then, *for fat?*"

Observing their reluctance to quit Castlebar, I felt my young, slight, and giddy self swell with all the pride and importance of a martinet; I almost fancied myself a giant, and my big recruits mere pigmies. "Here, serjeant," said I arrogantly to Hughy Hearn, "draw up those *mutineers:* fall in—fall in!" but nobody fell in, and Serjeant Hearn himself fell *back.* "Serjeant," pursued I, "this moment arrest Corporal O'Mealy, he's the ringleader."

"He won't *let* me, captain," replied Serjeant Hearn.

" 'Tis your captain's command!" exclaimed I.

"He says your honour's no captain at all," said Hughy Hearn; "only a slip of a *crimp,* nothing else but a gaoler's son, that wants to sell the boys like *negers,* all as one as Hart and the green linnets in Dublin city." *

My choler could no longer be restrained:—I drew my

* Apparently a reference to a contemporary seller of caged birds in Dublin?

[62]

broadsword, and vowed I would divide the head of the first man that refused to march. "I'll teach these mutineers to obey His Majesty's commission and officer," said I.

Corporal O'Mealy and two others then took off their hats, and coming up to me, said with great good-humour and civility, "Well, captain dear, you'll forgive and forget a joke from your own boys, so you will. Sure 'twas nothin else but a parting joke for the fair, your honour! Arrah! put up that sliver of yours: sure it looks nasty in the fair, to be drawing your falchion on your own recruits, captain."

I had no suspicion; and the hanger was scarce secure in its scabbard, when some of my soldiers came behind me, and others in front, and I was completely surrounded. "I'll show you all that I am a captain, and a true captain," continued I. "Here, serjeant! bring me my beating orders."

"*Beating*—Ough! is *that* what you'd be at?" said Corporal O'Mealy, who now assumed the command. "Ough! if its 'beating' you want, by my sowl you'll be easily satisfied without Hughy Hearn's orders."

I could stand it no longer: I could not run away if I wished; a crowd was collecting around me, and so I sprang at the smallest of the recruits, whom I thought I could master, and seized him by the throat; but a smart crack given with a hank of linen yarn by some hand behind soon made me quit my prey; another crack from another quarter quickly followed. I turned round to see my executioners, when I was suddenly wheeled back by the application of a third hank. This *cracking,* like a *feu de joie,* increased every moment, and was accompanied with vociferous laughs. In short, they pounded me almost to a jelly with hanks of linen yarn, which lay ready to their hands on all the cars around us. At length, stooping down between two cars, I had the pleasure of seeing the whole of my recruits, drawn up by O'Mealy—for it appeared he was their *real captain*—march regularly by me, every fellow in turn saluting any part of me he thought proper with a hank of yarn;—and with a shout I still remember of "A George! a George! long life to our colonel!" they quitted the fair—as I learned, to take forcible possession of a house and farm from which one of them had been ejected—which feat I afterward heard they regularly performed that very night, with the addition of *roasting* the new proprietor in his own kitchen.

Though I had no bones broken, some of my flesh took pretty much the colour and consistence of what cooks call aspic jelly. I was placed on a low garron,* and returned to Turlow at night, sick, sore, and sorry. There I pretended I was only *fatigued,* and had taken cold; and after experiencing the kind hospitality of Mrs. Fitzgerald—then a most interesting young lady—on the fourth day, at an early hour of a frosty morning, old Matthew Querns and I mounted our horses, without my having obtained any thing more for my trouble, and money spent in the recruiting service, than a sound beating. A return carriage of Lord Altamont's having overtaken me on the road, I entered it, and was set down at the little inn at Hallymount, where I remained some days with Mr. Jennings and family, recovering from my bruises, and sighing over the wreck of my fondly anticipated glories as a renowned colonel at the head of my regiment, plundering a pagoda and picking precious stones out of an idol. But, alas! having lost all the remaining cash out of my pocket during the scuffle at Castlebar, instead of a *lac* of *rupees,* I found myself labouring under a complete *lack* of *guineas,* and was compelled to borrow sufficient from Candy, the innkeeper at Ballynasloe, to carry me home by easy stages. Thus did my military ardour receive its definitive cooling: no ice-

* An Irish pony, from Gaelic *gearran.*

[64]

house ever chilled champaign more effectually. I, however, got quite enough of hospitality at Turlow, and quite enough of thrashing at Castlebar, to engraft the whole circumstance on my memory.

A BARRISTER BESIEGED

THE REVEREND Mr. Thomas, whose *sobriquet* in his neighbourhood was "Long Thomas," he being nearly six feet and a half high, resided near Carlow, and once invited Curran* and myself to spend a day and sleep at his house on our return from the assizes. We accepted the invitation with pleasure, as he was an old college companion of mine—a joyous, good-natured, hospitable, hard-going divine as any in his county. The Reverend Jack Read, a three-bottle parson of Carlow, with several other jolly neighbours, were invited to meet us, and to be treated with the wit and pleasantry of the celebrated Counsellor Curran, who was often extremely fond of shining in that class of society.

We all arrived in due time;—dinner was appointed for five *precisely,* as Curran always stipulated (wherever he could make so free) for the punctuality of the dinner-bell to a single minute. The very best cheer was provided by our host: at the proper time, the dishes lay basking before the fire, in readiness to receive the several provisions all smoking for the counsellor, &c. The clock, which, to render the cook more punctual, had been that very noon regulated by the sundial, did not on its part vary one second. Its hammer and bell melodiously sounded *five,* and announced the happy signal for the banquet. All the guests assembled in the dining-room, which was, in honest Thomas's house, that apartment

* John Philpot Curran (1750–1817), perhaps the greatest lawyer of his day, and a leader in the Irish Parliament from 1783 to 1797. His daughter Sarah was the sweetheart of Robert Emmet.

[66]

which the fine people of our day would call a drawing-room—the latter being then by no means regarded as indispensable in the dwelling-house of a moderate gentleman. The family parlour, in fact, answered its purpose mighty well.

Every guest of the reverend host having now decided on his chair, and turned down his plate, in order to be as near as possible to Counsellor Curran, proceeded to whet his knife against the edge of his neighbour's, to give it a due keenness for the most tempting side of the luscious sirloin, which by anticipation frizzed upon its pewter dish. Veal, mutton, turkey, ham, duck, and partridge, all "piping hot," were ready and willing to leap from their pots and spits into their respective dishes, and to take a warm bath each in its proper gravy. The cork-screw was busily employed: the wine-decanters ornamented the four corners of the well-dressed table, and the punch, jugged, and bubbling hot upon the hearth-stone, perfumed the whole room with its aromatic potsheen odour.

Every thing bespoke a most joyous and protracted banquet;—but, meanwhile, where was the great object of the feast?—the wheedler of the petty juries, and the admonisher of the grand ones? Where was the great orator, in consequence of whose brilliant reputation such a company was collected? The fifth hour had long passed, and impatience became visible on every countenance. Each guest, who had a watch, gave his fob no tranquillity, and never were timekeepers kept on harder duty. The first half-hour surprised the company; the next quarter *astonished,* and the last *alarmed* it. The clock, by *six* solemn notes, set the whole party surmising, and the host appeared nearly in a state of stupefaction. Day had departed, and twilight was rapidly following its example, yet no tidings of the orator: never had the like been known with regard to Curran—punctuality at dinner being a portion of his very nature. There are not

more days in a leap year than there were different conjectures broached as to the cause of my friend's non-
appearance. The people about the house were sent out
on the several roads to reconnoitre. He had been seen,
certainly, in the garden at four o'clock, but never after;
—yet every now and then a message came in to announce,
that "an old man had seen *a counsellor,* as he verily believed, walking very quick on the road to Carlow."
Another reported that "a woman who was driving home
her cow met one of the counsellors going leisurely toward Athy, and that he seemed very *melancholy;* that
she had seen him at the 'sizes that blessed morning, and
the people towld her it was the great law preacher that
was in it." Another woman who was bringing home some
turf from the bog, declared before the Virgin and all the
Saints that she saw "a little man in black with a stick in
his hand going toward the Barrow;" and a collough* sitting at her own cabin door feeding the *childer,* positively
saw a "black gentleman going down to the river, and soon
afterward heard a great splash of water at the said river;"
whereupon, she went *hot-foot* to her son, Ned Coyle, to
send him thither to see if the gentleman was in the water;
but that Ned said, sure enuff nothing natural would be
after going at that time of the deep dusk to the place
where poor Armstrong's corpse lay the night he was
murthered; and he'd see all the gentlemen in the county
to the devil (God bless them!) before he'd go to the
said place till morning early."

The faithful clock now announced *seven,* and the matter became too serious to admit of any doubt as to
poor Curran having met his catastrophe. I was greatly
shocked; our only conjectures now being, not *whether,*
but *how,* he had lost his life. As Curran was known every
day to strip naked and wash himself all over with a
sponge and cold water, I conjectured, as most rational,

* An old woman, from Gaelic *cailleach.*

[68]

that he had, in lieu of his usual ablution, gone to the Barrow to bathe before dinner, and thus unfortunately perished. All agreed in my hypothesis, and hooks and a draw-net were sent for immediately to Carlow, to scour the river for his body. Nobody, whatever might have been their feelings, *said* a word about dinner. The beef, mutton, and veal, as if in grief, had either turned into broth, or dropped piecemeal from the spit; the poultry fell from their strings, and were seen broiling in the dripping-pan. The cook had forgotten her calling, and gone off to make inquiries. The stable-boy left his horses; indeed, all the domestics, with one accord, dispersed with lanterns to search for Counsellor Curran in the Barrow. The Irish cry was let loose, and the neighbourhood soon collected; and the good-natured parson, our host, literally wept like an infant. I never saw so much confusion at any *dinner-table.* Such of the guests as were gifted by Nature with keen appetites, suffered all the tortures of hunger, of which, nevertheless, they could not in humanity complain; but a stomachic sympathy of woe was very perceptible in their lamentations for the untimely fate of so great an orator.

It was at length suggested by our reverend host that his great Newfoundland dog, who was equally sagacious, if not more so, with many of the parishioners, and rivalled, in canine proportion, the magnitude of his master, was not unlikely, by driving in the Barrow, to discover where the body lay deposited—and thus direct the efforts of the nets and hookers from Carlow. This idea met with universal approbation; and every body took up his hat, to go down to the river. Mary, a young damsel, the only domestic who remained in the house, was ordered to call Diver, the dog;—but Diver was absent, and did not obey the summons. Every where resounded, "Diver! Diver!" but in vain.

New and multifarious conjectures now crossed the

[69]

minds of the different persons assembled:—the mystery thickened: all the old speculations went for nothing; it was clear that Curran and Diver had absconded together. At length, a gentleman in company mentioned the circumstance of a friend of his having been drowned while bathing, whose dog never left his clothes, on the bank, till discovered nearly dead with hunger. The conjecture founded hereon was, however, but momentary, since it soon appeared that such *could not* be the case with Curran. I knew that he both feared and hated big dogs; and besides, there was no *acquaintance* between him and the one in question. Diver had never seen the counsellor before that day, and therefore could have no personal fondness for him, not to say, that those animals have a sort of instinctive knowledge as to who likes or dislikes them, and it was more probable that Diver, if either, would be an enemy instead of a friend to so great a stranger. But the creature's absence, at any rate, was unaccountable, and the more so, inasmuch as he never before had wandered from his master's residence.

Mary, the maid, was now desired to search *all* the rooms and offices for Diver, while we sat pensive and starving in the parlour. We were speedily alarmed by a loud shriek, immediately after which Mary rushed tottering into the room, just able to articulate:—

"O, holy Virgin! holy Virgin! yes, gentlemen! the counsellor *is* dead, sure enough. And I'll die too, gentlemen! I'll never recover it!" and she crossed herself twenty times over in the way the priest had taught her.

We all now flocked round, and asked her simultaneously how she *knew* the counsellor was dead?

Crossing herself again, "I saw his *ghost,* please your reverence!" cried poor Mary, "and a frightful ghost it was! just out of the river, and not even *decent* itself. I'm willing to take my affidavy that I saw his ghost, quite *indecent,* straight forenent me."

"Where? where?" cried every body, as if with one breath.

"In the double-bedded room next to your reverence's," stammered the terrified girl.

We waited for no more to satisfy us either that she was mad, or that robbers were in the house: each person seized something by way of a weapon: one took a poker, another a candlestick, a third a knife or fire-shovel, and up stairs we rushed. Only one could go in, conveniently, abreast; and I was among the first who entered. The candles had been forgotten; but the moon was rising, and we certainly saw what, in the opinion of some present, corroborated the statement of Mary. Two or three instantly drew back in horror, and attempted to retreat, but others pressed behind; and lights being at length produced, an exhibition far more ludicrous than terrific presented itself. In a far corner of the room stood, erect and formal, and *stark naked* (as a *ghost* should be), John Philpot Curran, one of His Majesty's counsel, learned in the law,—trembling as if in the ague, and scarce able to utter a syllable, through the combination of cold and terror. Three or four paces in his front lay Diver, from Newfoundland, stretching out his immense shaggy carcase, his long paws extended their full length, and his great head lying on them with his nose pointed toward *the ghost,* as true as the needle to the pole. His hind legs were gathered up like those of a wild beast ready to spring upon his prey. He took an angry notice of the first of us that came near him, growled, and seemed disposed to resent our instrusion;—but the moment his master appeared, his temper changed, he jumped up, wagged his tail, licked the parson's hand, cast a scowling look at Curran, and then a wistful one at his master,—as much as to say, "I have done my duty, now do you yours:" he looked, indeed, as if he only waited for the word of command, to seize the counsellor by the throttle.

A blanket was now considerately thrown over Curran by one of the company, and he was *put to bed* with half a dozen more blankets heaped upon him: a tumbler of hot potsheen punch was administered, and a second worked miracles: the natural heat began to circulate, and he was in a little time enabled to rise and tell us a story which no hermit even telling his last beads could avoid laughing at. Related by *any one,* it would have been good; but as told by Curran, with his powers of description and characteristic humour, was superexcellent;—and we had to thank Diver, the water-dog, for the highest zest of the whole evening.

The fact was, that a little while previous to dinner-time, Curran, who had omitted his customary ablution in the morning, went to our allotted bed-chamber to perform that ceremony; and having stripped, had just begun to apply the sponge, when Diver, strolling about his master's premises to see if all was right, placed by chance his paw against the door, which not being fastened, it flew open, he entered unceremoniously, and observing what he conceived to be an extraordinary and suspicious figure, concluded it was somebody with no very honest intention, and stopped to reconnoitre. Curran, unaccustomed to so strange a valet, retreated, while Diver advanced, and very significantly showed an intention to seize him by the naked throat; which operation, if performed by Diver, whose tusks were a full inch in length, would no doubt have admitted an inconvenient quantity of atmospheric air into his oesophagus. He therefore crept as close into the corner as he could, and had the equivocal satisfaction of seeing his adversary advance and turn the meditated *assault* into a complete *blockade*—stretching himself out, and "maintaining his position" with scarcely the slightest motion, till the counsellor was rescued, and the siege raised.

Curran had been in hopes that when Diver had satis-

fied his *curiosity* he would retire; and with this impression, spoke kindly to him, but was answered only by a
growl. If Curran repeated his blandishments, Diver
showed his long white tusks;—if he moved his foot, the
dog's hind legs were in motion. Once or twice Curran
raised his hand: but Diver, considering that as a sort of
challenge, rose instantly, and with a low growl looked
significantly at Curran's windpipe. Curran, therefore,
stood like a *model,* if not much like a marble divinity. In
truth, though somewhat less comely, his features were
more expressive than those of the Apollo Belvedere.
Had the circumstance occurred at Athens to Demosthe-
nes, or in the days of Phidias, it is probable my friend
Curran, and Diver, would have been at this moment
exhibited in virgin marble at Florence or at the Vatican;
—and I am quite sure the *subject* would have been better
and more amusing than that of "the dying gladiator."

FORMER STATE OF MEDICINE
IN IRELAND

DOCTOR Sir Charles Morgan has given us, at the conclusion of his lady's* excellent work "Italy," the state of "medicine" in that country. Our old cookery books, in like manner, after exquisite receipts for all kinds of dainties, to suit every appetite, generally finished a luxurious volume with *remedies* for the "bite of a mad dog—for scald heads—ague—burns—St. Anthony's fire —St. Vitus's dance—the tooth-ache," &c. &c. Now, though the Doctor certainly did not take the cooks by way of precedent, that is no reason why I should not indulge my whim by citing both examples, and garnishing this volume with "the state of medicine in Ireland" fifty years ago.

I do not, however, mean to depreciate the state of medicine in these days of "new lights" and novelties, when old drugs and poisons are *nick-named,* and every recipe is a rebus to an old apothecary. Each son of Galen now strikes out his own system; composes his own syllabus; and *finishes* his patients according to his own proper fancy. When a man dies after a consultation (which is generally the case—the thing being often decided by *experiment*)—there is no particular necessity for any explanation to widows, legatees, or heirs-at-law; the death alone of any testator being a sufficient apology to his nearest and dearest relatives for the failure of a consultation—that is, if the patient left sufficient property behind him.

My state of Irish medicine, therefore, relates to those "once on a time" days, when sons lamented their fathers,

---

* Lady Sydney Morgan (ca. 1780–1859), author of *The Wild Irish Girl,* one of the most popular Irish novelists of her day.

and wives could weep over expiring husbands; when every root and branch of an ancient family became as black as rooks for the death of a blood relation, though of almost incalculable removal. In those times the medical old woman and the surgeon-farrier—the bone-setter and the bleeder—were by no means considered contemptible practitioners among the Christian population—who, in common with the dumb beasts, experience the advantages of their miscellaneous practice.

An anatomical theatre being appended to the University of Dublin, whenever I heard of a *fresh* subject, or remarkable corpse, being obtained for dissection, I frequently attended the lectures, and many were the beauteous women and fine young fellows then carved into scraps and joints *pro bono publico*. I thereby obtained a smattering of information respecting our corporeal clockwork; and having, for amusement, skimmed over Cullen's *First Lines, Every Man his Own Doctor,* Bishop Berkeley on *Tar Water,* and Sawny Cunningham on *The Virtues of Fasting Spittle,* I almost fancied myself qualified for a diploma. A Welsh aunt of mine, also, having married Doctor Burdet, who had been surgeon of the *Wasp* sloop of war, and remarkable for leaving the best stumps of any naval practitioner, he explained to me the use of his various instruments for tapping, trepanning, raising the shoulder-blades, &c. &c.: but when I had been a short time at my father's in the country, I found that the farriers and old women performed, either on man or beast, twenty cures for one achieved by the doctors and apothecaries. I had great amusement in conversing with these people, and perceived some reason in their arguments.

As to the farriers, I reflected, that as man is only a mechanical animal, and a horse one of the same description, there was no reason why a drug that was good for a pampered gelding might not also be good for the hard-goer mounted on him. In truth, I have seen instances where, in point both of intellect and endurance, there was but very little distinction between the animals—save that the beverage of the one was *water,* and that of the other was *punch*—and, in point of *quantity,* there was no great difference between them in this matter either. At that time there was seldom more than one regular doctor in a circuit of twenty miles, and a farrier never came to physic a gentleman's horse that some boxes of pills were not deducted from his bills, for the general use of the ladies and gentlemen of the family; and usually succeeded vastly better than those of the apothecary.

The class of old women called colloughs were then held in the highest estimation, as understanding the cure (that is if God pleased) of all disorders. Their *materia medica* did not consist of gums, resins, minerals, and hot iron,—as the farriers' did; but of leaves of bushes, bark of trees, *weeds* from *churchyards,* and mushrooms from *fairy grounds;* rue, garlic, rosemary, birds'-nests, foxglove, &c.: in desperate cases they sometimes found it advisable to put a *charm* into the bolus or stoop, and then it was sure to be "firm and good." I never could find out what either of their charms were. They said they should die themselves if they disclosed them to any body. No collough ever could be a *doctor* whilst she had one tooth remaining in her head, as the remedy was always reduced to a pulp or paste by her own mumbling of its materials, and the contact of an old grinder would destroy the purity of the charms and simples, and leave the cure, they would say, no better than a farrier's.

Our old collough, Jug Coyle, as she sat in a corner of the hob, by the great long turf fire in the kitchen, exactly in the position of the Indian squaws, munching and mumbling for use an apron-full of her morning's gatherings in the fields, used to talk at intervals very *sensibly* of her art. "Ough! then, my dear sowl, (said she one

[76]

evening,) what would the poor Irishers have done in owld times but for their colloughs? Such brutes as you!" continued she, (looking at Butler, the farrier of the family, who was seated fast asleep on a bench at the opposite end of the hearth,) " 'tis you, and the likes of you, a curse on you, root and branch! that starved the colloughs by giving your poisons to both cows and quality. Sure it's the farriers' and pothecaries' drugs that kills all the people—ay, and the horses and cattle too," and she shook her claw-like fist at the unconscious farrier.

"Jug Coyle," said I, "why are you so angry?"

Jug:—"Sure it's not for myself, it's for my calling," said she: "a thousand years before the round towers were built (and nobody can tell *that* time), the colloughs were greater nor any lady in the country. We had plenty of charms in those days, Master Jonah, till the farriers came, bad luck to the race! Ough! may the curse of Crummell light on yees all, breed, seed, and generation, Larry Butler! not forgetting Ned Morrisy of Clapook, the villainous cow-doctor, that takes the good from the colloughs likewise, and all—"

Here Jug Coyle stopped short, as the farrier opened his eyes, and she knew well that if Larry Butler had a sup in, he would as soon beat an old woman as any body else. She therefore resumed munching her herbs, but was totally silenced.

Larry Butler was one of the oldest and most indispensable *attachés* of our family. Though nobody remembered him a *boy,* he was as handy, as fresh, and as *rational,* perhaps more so, than half a century before. Short, broad, and bow-legged, bone and muscle kept his body together—for flesh was absent. His face, once extremely handsome, still retained its youthful colouring—though broken and divided: his sharp eye began to exhibit the dimness of age: the long white hair had deserted his high forehead, but fell, in no scanty locks, down each side of

[77]

his animated countenance. He is before my eye at this moment—too interesting, and, at the same time, odd a figure ever to be forgotten.

I had a great respect for old Butler: he was very passionate, but universally licensed: he could walk any distance, and always carried in his hand a massive firing-iron. I have thus particularly described the old man, as being one of the most curious characters of his class I ever met in Ireland.

Larry soon showed signs of relapsing into slumber; but Jug, fearing it was a *fox's sleep* (an old trick of his), did not recommence her philippic on the farriers, but went on in her simple praise of the collough practice. "Sure," said she, "God never sent any disorder into a country that he did not likewise send something to cure it with."

"Why, certainly, Jug," said I, "it would be rather bad treatment if we had no cures in the country."

"Ough! that saying is like your dear father," said she, "and your grandfather before you, and your great-grandfather who was before him agin. Moreover," pursued Jug, "God planted our cures in the fields because there was no pothecaries."

"Very true, Jug," said I.

"Well, then, Master Jonah," resumed she, "if God or the Virgin, and I'm sure I can't say which of them, planted the cures, sure they must have made people who knew how to pick them up in the fields, or what good is their growing there?"

"There's no gainsaying that, Jug," gravely observed I.

"Well, then, it was to the colloughs, sure enough, God gave the knowledge of picking the cures up—because he knew well that they were owld and helpless, and that it would be a charity to employ them. When once they learned the herbs, they were welcome every where; and there was not *one* man died in his bed (the people say) in owld times for *twenty* now-a-days."

[78]

"Of that there is no doubt, Jug," said I, "though there may be other reasons for it."

"Ough! God bless you agin, avourneen! any how," said Jug. "Well, then, they say it was Crummell and his troopers, bad luck to their sowls, the murdering villains! that brought the first farriers (and no better luck to *them!*) to Ireland, and the colloughs were kilt with the hunger. The craturs, as the owld people tell, eat grass like the beasts when the cows were all kilt by the troopers and farriers—avourneen, avourneen!"

I must here notice a revolution; namely, that of late, since farriers have got a "step in the peerage," and are made commissioned officers in the army, they think it proper to refine their pharmacopeia so as to render it more congenial to their new rank and station, and some horses are now not only theoretically but practically placed on more than a level with the persons who mount them. The practice of horse medicine is indeed so completely revolutionised, that gas, steam, and the chemistry of Sir Humphry Davy, are resorted to for the morbid affections of that animal in common with those of a nobleman. The horse, now, regularly takes his hot bath like my lord and lady, James' powders, refined liquorice, musk, calomel, and laudanum, with the most "elegant extracts" and delicate infusions. As if *Gulliver* were a prophet, he literally described, in the reign of Queen Anne, both the *English horse* and the *Irish peasant* as they exist at the present moment. If the lodging, clothing, cleaning, food, medicine, and attendance of the modern Hoynhymm, [*sic*] be contrasted with the pig-sty, rags, filth, neglect, and hunger of the Yahoo, it must convince any honest neutral that Swift (that greatest of Irishmen) did not overcharge his satire. The sum lavished upon the care of one Hoynhymm for *a single day,* with little or nothing to do, is more (exclusive of the farrier) than is now paid to five Irish Yahoos for *twelve hours'* hard labour, with to feed, clothe, lodge, and nourish *themselves,* and probably five wives and twenty or thirty children, for the same period, into the bargain.

A few very curious cases may elucidate our ancient practice of cure—a practice, I believe, never even heard of in any other part of Europe. The bite of a mad dog was to the Irish peasantry of all things the most puzzling and terrific; and I am sure I can scarcely guess what Doctor Morgan will think of my veracity when I state the two modes by which that horrible mania was neutralised or finally put an end to.

When the bite of a dog took place, every effort was made to kill the beast, and if they succeeded, it was never inquired whether he actually *was,* or (as the colloughs used to say) *pretended to be* mad: his liver was immediately taken out, dried by the fire till quite hard, then reduced to powder, and given in frequent doses with a draught of holy or blessed water, to the patient for seven days. If it happened that the saliva did not penetrate the sufferer's clothes, or if the dog was *not* actually mad, it was then considered that the patient was *cured* by drinking the dog's liver and holy water;—and if it so happened that the bite set him barking, then the priest and farrier told them it was the will of God that he should bark, and they were contented either to let him die at his leisure, or send him to heaven a little sooner than was absolutely necessary.

The herbs of the colloughs were sometimes successfully resorted to; whether accidental or actual preventives or antidotes, it is not easy to determine: but when I detail the ulterior remedy to cure the hydrophobia in Ireland, or at least to render it *perfectly innoxious,* I am well aware that I shall stand a good chance of being honoured by the periodicals with the appellation of a "bouncer," . . . but the ensuing case, as I can personally vouch for the fact, I may surely give with tolerable confidence.

Such a dread had the Irish of the bite of a mad dog, that they did not regard it as murder, but absolutely as a legal and meritorious act, to smother any person who had arrived at an advanced stage of hydrophobia. If he made a noise similar to barking, his hour of suffocation was seldom protracted.

In this mode of administering the *remedy,* it was sometimes difficult to procure proper instruments; for they conceived that *by law* the patient should be smothered between two *feather*-beds,—one being laid cleverly over him, and a sufficient number of the neighbours lying on it till he was "out of danger."

The only instance I am able to state from my own knowledge occurred about the year 1781. Thomas Palmer, of Rushhall, in Queen's County, was then my father's land-agent, and at the same time a very active and intelligent magistrate of that county. He was, *gratis,* an oracle, lawyer, poet, horse-cow-dog and man doctor, farmer, architect, brewer, surveyor, and magistrate of all work. He was friendly and good-natured, and possessed one of those remarkable figures now so rarely to be seen in society. I feel I am, as usual, digressing;—however, be the digression what it may, I cannot deny myself the pleasure of depicting my old friend, and endeavouring to render him as palpable to the vision of my reader as he is at this moment to my own.

Palmer was one of that race of giants for which the rich and extensive barony of Ossory, in Queen's County (now the estate of the Duke of Buckingham), was then and had long been celebrated. His height was esteemed the *middle* height in that county—namely, about six feet two inches; he was bulky without being fat, and strong, though not very muscular. He was, like many other giants, *split up* too much, and his long dangling limbs appeared still longer from their clothing, which was invariably the same:—a pair of strong buck-skin breeches,

[81]

never *very* greasy, but never free from grease; half jack-boots; massive, long silver spurs, either of his own or of somebody's grandfather's; a scarlet waistcoat with long skirts; and a coat with *"all the cloth* in it." These habiliments rendered him altogether a singular but not other than respectable figure. His visage made amends for both his outré boots and breeches; it was as well calculated as could be for a kind-hearted, good-humoured, convivial old man. His queue wig, with a curl at each side, had his grizzle hair combed smoothly over the front of it; and he seldom troubled the powder-puff, but when he had got the "skins whitened," in order to "dine in good company." He was the *hardest-goer* either at kettle or screw (except Squire Flood of Roundwood) of the whole grand-jury, for whose use he made a new song every summer assize: and it was from him I heard the very unanswerable argument, "that if a man fills the bottom of his glass, there can be no good reason why he should not also fill the top of it; and if he empties the top of his glass, he certainly ought in common civility to pay the bottom the same compliment:"—no man ever more invariably exemplified his own theorem.

Thomas Palmer was hale and healthy;—his fifty-seventh year had handed him over safe and sound to its next neighbour: his property was just sufficient (and no more) to gallop side by side with his hospitality. When at home, his boiler was seldom found bubbling without a corned round withinside it; and a gander or cock turkey frequently danced at the end of a string before the long turf fire. Ducks, hares, chickens, or smoked ham, often adorned the sides of his table; whilst apple-dumplings in the centre and potatoes at cross corners completed a light snack for five or six seven-feet Ossoronians, who left no just reason to the old cook and a couple of ruddy ploughmen, (who attended as *butlers,)* to congratulate themselves upon the *dainty* appetites of their masters, or the balance of nourishment left to liquidate the demand of their own stomachs. But, alas! those pleasurable specimens of solid fare have passed away for ever! As age advances, Nature diminishes her weights and measures in our *consumption,* and our early *pounds* and Scotch *pints* (*two bottles*) are at length reduced to the miserable rations of *ounces* and *glassfuls.*

At this magistrate's *cottage,* which had as stout a roof to it as any mansion in the county, I once dined, about the year 1781, when the state of medicine in Ireland was exemplified in a way that neither Cullen, Darwin, Perceval, James, or any other learned doctor ever contemplated, and which I am convinced—had it been the practice in Italy—Doctor Morgan would not have passed over in total silence.

We had scarcely finished such a meal as I have particularised, and "got into the punch," when a crowd of men, women, and children, came up to the door in great confusion, but respectfully took off their hats and bonnets, and asked humbly to speak to his worship.

Tom Palmer seemed to anticipate their business, and inquired at once "if Dan Dempsey of the Pike (turnpike) was in the same way still?"

"Ough! please your worship," cried out twenty voices together, "worse, your worship, worse nor ever, death's crawling upon him—he can't *stop,* and what's the use in leaving the poor boy in his pains any longer, your worship? We have got two good feather-beds at the Pike, and we want your worship's leave to smother Dan Dempsey, if your worship pleases."

"Ough avourneen! he growls and barks like any mastiff dog, please your worship," cried a tremulous old woman, who seemed quite in terror.

"You lie, Nancy Bergin," said her older husband, "Dan

[83]

Dempsey does *not* bark like a *mastiff;* it's for all the world like your worship's white lurcher, when she's after the rabbits, so it is!"

"He snapped three times at myself this morning," said another humane lady, "and the neighbours said it were all as one, almost, as biting me."

"Hush! hush!" said the magistrate, waving his hand: "any of you who can read and write, come in here."

"Ough! there's plenty of that sort, please your worship," said Maurice Dowling, the old schoolmaster. "Sure it's not ignorance I'd be teaching my scholars every day these forty years, except Sundays and holidays, at the Pike. There's plenty of swearing scholards here any how, your worship."

"Come in any three of you, then, who can clearly swear Dan Dempsey barks like a dog,—no matter whether like a mastiff or a lurcher—and attempts to bite."

The selection was accordingly made, and the affidavit sworn, to the effect that "Dan Dempsey had been bit by a mad dog; that he went mad himself, barked like any greyhound, and had no objection to bite whatever Christian came near him." Squire Palmer then directed them to go back to the Pike, and said they might smother Dan Dempsey if he barked any more in the morning; but told them to wait till then.

"Ah, then, at what hour, please your worship?" said Nan Bergin, accompanied by several other female voices, whose owners seemed rather impatient.

"Three hours after day-break," said the magistrate: "but take care to send to Mr. Calcut, the coroner, to come and hold his inquest after Dan's smothered. Take care of that, at your peril."

"Never fear, please your worship," said Ned Bergin.

They then gathered into a sort of consultation before the door, and bowing with the same respect as when they came, all set off, to smother Dan Dempsey of Rushhall Turnpike.

The magistrate's instructions were accurately obeyed: Daniel barked, and was duly smothered between two feather-beds, three hours after day-break next morning, by the schoolmaster's watch. Mr. Calcut came and held his coroner's inquest, who brought in their verdict that the said "Daniel Dempsey died *in consequence of a mad dog!*"

It is a singular circumstance, that the termination of poor Palmer's life resulted from his consistency in strictly keeping his own aphorism which I have before mentioned. He dined at my father's Lodge at Cullenagh; and having taken his *quantum sufficit,* (as people who dined there generally did,) became obstinate, which is frequently the consequence of being pot-valiant, and insisted on riding home, twelve or thirteen miles, in a dark night. He said he had a couple of songs to write for the high sheriff, which Mr. Boyce from Waterford had promised to sing at the assizes;—and that he always wrote best with a full stomach. It was thought that he fell asleep; and that his horse, supposing he had as much right to drink freely as his master, had quietly paid a visit to his accustomed watering-place, when, on the animal's stooping to drink, poor Palmer pitched over his head into the pond, wherein he was found next morning quite dead— though scarcely covered with water, and grasping the long branch of a tree as if he had been instinctively endeavouring to save himself, but had not strength, owing to the overpowering effect of the liquor. His horse had not stirred from his side. His loss was, to my father's affairs, irreparable.

It is very singular that nearly a similar death occurred to an attorney, who dined at my father's about a month afterward—old Allen Kelly of Portarlington, one of the

[85]

most keen though cross-grained attorneys in all Europe. He came to Cullenagh to insist upon a settlement for some bills of costs he had dotted up against my father to the tune of fifty pounds. It being generally, in those times, more convenient to country gentlemen to pay by bond than by ready money—and always more agreeable to the attorney, because he was pretty sure of doubling his costs before the judgment was satisfied, Allen Kelly said, that, out of *friendship,* he'd take a *bond and warrant of attorney* for his fifty pounds; though it was not taxed, which he declared would only *increase* it wonderfully. The bond and warrant, which he had ready filled up in his pocket, were duly executed, and both parties were pleased—my father to get rid of Allen Kelly, and Allen Kelly to get fifty pounds for the worth of ten. Of course he stayed to dine, put the bond carefully into his breeches pocket, drank plenty of port and hot punch, to keep him warm on his journey, mounted his nag, reached Portarlington, where he watered his nag (and *himself* into the bargain). Hot punch, however, is a bad balancemaster, and so Allen fell over the nag's head, and the poor beast trotted home quite lonesome for want of his master. Next day Allen was found well bloated with the Barrow water; indeed, swollen to full double his usual circumference. In his pockets were found divers documents which *had been* bonds, notes, and other securities, and which he had been collecting through the country: but unfortunately for his administrators, the Barrow had taken pity on the debtors, and whilst Allen was reposing himself in the bed of that beautiful river, her naiads were employed in picking his pocket, and there was scarcely a bill, bond, note, or any acknowledgment, where the fresh ink had not yielded up its colouring; and neither the names, sums, dates, or other written matters, of one out of ten, could be by any means decyphered. In truth few of the debtors were very desirous, on this occasion, of turning

[86]

decypherers, and my father's bond (among others) was from that day never even suggested to him by any representative of Allen Kelly, the famous attorney of Portarlington.

SKINNING A BLACK CHILD

ANOTHER, and a *not unpleasant,** because not fatal, incident may serve to illustrate the "state of medicine and surgery," between forty and fifty years ago, in Ireland. It occurred near my brother's house, at Castlewood, and the same Lieutenant Palmer, of Dureen, was a very interested party in it. The thing created great merriment among all the gossiping, tattling old folks, male and female, throughout the district.

The lieutenant having been in America, had brought home a black lad as a servant, who resided in the house of Dureen with the family. It is one of the mysteries of nature, that infants sometimes come into this world marked and spotted in diverse fantastical ways and places, a circumstance which the faculty, so far as they know any thing about it, consider as the sympathetic effect either of external touch or ardent imagination;—or, if neither of these are held to be the cause, then they regard it as a sort of *lusus* with which Dame Nature occasionally surprises, and then (I suppose) laughs at the world, for marvelling at her capriciousness,—a quality which she has, as satirists pretend, plentifully bestowed on the fairest part of the creation. Be this as it may, the incident I am about to mention is in its way unique; and whether the occasion of it proceeded from sympathy, fancy, or touch, or exhibited a regular *lusus Naturæ,* never has, and now never can be unequivocally decided.

A sister of the lieutenant, successively a very good maiden, woman, and wife, had been married to one Mr.

* Italics are the editor's. This preposterous and, to modern taste, rather sadistic story illustrates Barrington's *sang froid* on the one hand and his skill in telling tall tales on the other.

George Washington, of the neighbourhood, who, from his name, was supposed to be some distant blood relation to the celebrated General Washington; and, as that distinguished individual had no children, all the old women and other wiseacres of Durrow, Ballyragget, Ballyspellen, and Ballynakill, made up their minds that his Excellency, when dying, would leave a capital legacy in America to his blood relation, Mr. George Washington, of Dureen, in Ireland; who was accordingly advised— and, with the aid of the Rev. Mr. Hoskinson, clergyman of Durrow (father to the present Vice Provost of Dublin University), he took the advice—to write a dignified letter to his Excellency, General George Washington of Virginia, President, &c. &c. &c. stating himself to have the honour of entertaining hopes that he should be enabled to show his Excellency, by an undeniable pedigree (when he could procure it) that he had a portion of the same blood as his Excellency's running in his humble veins. The letter went on to state, that he had espoused the sister of a British officer, who had had the honour of being taken prisoner in America; and that he, the writer, having reasonable expectation of shortly fathering a young Mr. Washington, his Excellency's permission was humbly requested for the child to be named his god-son: till the receipt of which permission, the christening should be kept open by his most faithful servant and distant relation, &c.

This epistle was duly despatched to his Excellency, at Mount Vernon, in Virginia, and Mrs. George Washington, of Dureen, lost no time in performing her husband's promise. No joy ever exceeded that which seized on Mr. Washington, when it was announced that his beloved wife had been taken ill, and was in excessive torture. The entire household, master included, were just seated at a comfortable and plentiful dinner; the first slices off the round, or turkey, were cut and tasted; some respectable

[89]

old dames of the neighbourhood had just stepped in to congratulate the family on what would occur, and hear all that was going forward at this critical, cheerful, and happy moment of anticipation, when Mrs. Gregory (the *lady's doctor*), who was, in her own way, a very shrewd, humourous kind of body, and to whom most people in that country under thirty-five years of age had owed their existence, entered the apartment to announce the happy arrival of as fine a healthy little boy as could be, and that Mrs. Washington was as well, or indeed rather better, than might be expected *under the circumstances*. A general cheer by the whole company followed, and bumpers of hot punch were drunk with enthusiasm to the success and future glory of the *young* General Washington.

Mrs. Gregory at length beckoned old Mrs. Palmer to the window with a mysterious air, and whispered something in her ear; on hearing which, Mrs. Palmer immediately fell flat on the floor, as if dead. The old dames hobbled off to her assistance, and Mrs. Gregory affected to feel strongly herself about something,—ejaculating, loud enough to be generally heard, and with that sort of emphasis people use when they wish to persuade us they are praying in downright earnest, "God's will be done!"

"What about?" said the lieutenant, bristling up:—"I suppose my mother has taken a glass too much: it is not the first time!—she'll soon come round again, never fear. Don't be alarmed, my friends."

"God's will be done!" again exclaimed the oracular Mrs. Gregory.

"What's the matter? What is all this about?" grumbled the men. "Lord bless us! what can it be?" squalled the women.

"There cannot be a finer or stronger little boy in the 'varsal world," said Mrs. Gregory: "but, Lord help us!" continued she, unable longer to contain her overcharged grief, "It's—it's not so—so *white* as it should be!"

"Not white?" exclaimed every one of the company simultaneously.

"No,—O Lord, no!" answered Mrs. Gregory, looking mournfully up to the ceiling in search of heaven. Then casting her eyes wistfully around the company, she added —"God's will be done! but the dear little boy is—is— quite *black!*"

"*Black! black!*" echoed from every quarter of the apartment.

"As black as your hat, if not *blacker,*" replied Mrs. Gregory.

"Oh! Oh-h!" groaned Mr. Washington.

"Oh! Oh-h!" responded Mrs. Gregory.

"Blood and ouns!" said the lieutenant.—"See how I am shaking," said the midwife, taking up a large glass of potsheen and drinking it off to settle her nerves.

What passed afterward on that evening may be easily surmised: but the next day Mrs. Gregory, the *sage femme,* came into Castle Durrow to "prevent *mistakes,*" and tell the affair to the neighbours in her own way; that is, partly in whispers, partly aloud, and partly by nods and winks—such as old ladies frequently use when they wish to divulge more than they like to speak openly.

Sufficient could be gathered, however, to demonstrate that young Master Washington had not one white, or even *gray* spot on his entire body, and that some *frizzled* hair was already beginning to show itself on his little pate; but that no nurse could be found who would give him a drop of nourishment, even were he famishing—all the women verily believing that, as Mrs. Washington was herself an unexceptionable wife, it must be a son of the d——l by a dream, and nothing else than an imp. However, Mr. Hoskinson, the clergyman, soon contradicted this report by assuring the Protestants that the day for that sort of miracle had been for some centuries over, and that the infant was as fine, healthy, natural, and sprightly a little negro as ever came from the coast of Guinea.

Never was there such a buzz and hubbub in any neighbourhood as now took place in and about the town of Castle Durrow. Every body began to *compute periods* and form conjectures; and though it was universally known that red wine, &c. &c. cast on the mamma, often leaves marks upon children, yet censorious and incredulous people persisted in asserting, that such marks only came in spots or splashes, when the person of a lady happened to be actually touched by the colouring matter: but that no child could be black, and *all* black, unless in a *natural* way. Among the lower orders, however, the thing was settled at once in the most plausible and popular manner, and set down as downright witchcraft and nothing else: and suspicion fell on old Betty Hogan of the Seven Sisters, near Ballyspellen, who was *known* to be a witch, and able to raise the devil at Hallow Eve, to turn smocks, and tell fortunes; and she was verily seen by more than one to go into the Cave of Dunmore with a coal-black cur dog (without tail or ears) after her, the very night and minute Mrs. Washington was delivered of the devil; and nobody ever saw the cur dog before or since.

Mr. Washington and the lieutenant were, however, by no means at ease upon the subject of this freak of Nature, and were well warranted in their dissatisfaction; as at length all the old women agreed in believing, that the black lad from America was nothing else but the devil disguised, who had followed the lieutenant as a servant boy, to gain over the family, and particularly Mrs. Washington, as Satan did Eve;—and that he ought to be smothered by the priests, or at least transported out of the country, before he did any more mischief—or there would not be a white child in the whole barony the next season.

Lieutenant Palmer was of course high in blood for the

honour of his sister, and Mr. Washington cock-a-hoop for the character of his wife: and so great was their ire, that it was really believed the black boy would have been put down a draw-well, as the people threatened,—that being the approved method of getting rid of a devil whenever he showed his face in that part of the country: but as, possibly, Betty Hogan might be a better judge of him than themselves, they suspended the execution till they should bring the old witch and confront her and *the devil* together—when of course he would show his cloven foot, and they might both be put into the well, if they did not take every *taste* of the black off *Master Washington*.

The father and uncle decided more calmly and properly to lay the whole affair before a consultation of doctors, to know if it was not a regular *imagination mark* —whether a child might not be marked by mere fancy, without the marking material (such as grapes, currants, or the like,) touching the mother; and lastly, why, as children in general are only partially marked, this child was not *spotted* like others, but as black as ebony every inch of it.

All the doctors in the neighbourhood were called in to the consultation. Old Butler, the farrier (heretofore mentioned), came with all expedition to Dureen, and begged leave to give his opinion and offer his services, wishing to see Master Washington before the doctors arrived, as he had a secret for turning any skin ever so brown as white as milk!

On seeing Master Washington, however, he declared he was *too* black *entirely* for his medicines, or any body else's. "The devil so black a crethur," says he, "ever I saw, except Cornet French's *Black and all Black*,* that beat the Pandreen mare for the King's hundred at the

* This celebrated animal seems to be referred to in *Finnegans Wake* on page 59, line 4, but the meaning of the allusion remains unclear to me.

races of Gort:—the devil a white hair had *he* from muzzle to tail, good, bad, or indifferent. By my sowl! its a neat crust poor George Washington has got to mumble any how! I never saw luck or grace come of the negers, bad luck to them all!"

The day for the consultation being fixed, several apothecaries and bone-setters attended at the house of Mr. George Bathron, of Dureen, grocer, wine-merchant, surgeon, apothecary, druggist, and physician.

The first point stated and unanimously agreed on, was, "that the child was black." The reasons for that colour being universal on the young gentleman were not quite so clear. At length Dr. Bathron, finding he had the lead, and having been some years at school when a boy, and likewise apprenticed to a grocer and apothecary at Ballyragget, where he learned several technical words in the Latin tongue; finding, besides, that he had an excellent opportunity to prove his learning to those less educated, —declared with great gravity that he had read many authors upon the subject of *marks,* and could take upon himself positively to assert that the child was (according to all authority on such matters) a *casus omissus.* The others, not being exactly sure either of the shape, size, or colour, of a *casus omissus,* thought it better to *accede* to what they did not *comprehend,* and all subscribed to the opinion that the child was a *casus omissus.* It was immediately circulated outside the house, that all the doctors found the child to be a *casus omissus;* and old Skelton, who had been a trooper in Germany, declared that a doctor there told him that was the true surname of a devil incarnate. And the prevailing notion then was, that the black lad, old Betty Hogan, the witch, and Master Washington, should all be put down the draw-well together, to save the other married women of the country from bearing devils instead of children.

The *doctors,* however, having given their opinion, were

extremely ticklish in taking any step with a *casus omissus;* and not wishing to pitch themselves against any infernal personification, left future proceedings to the entire management of Dr. Bathron.

Doctor Bathron was a smart, squat, ruddy, jovial apothecary, and he was also a professed poet, who had made some celebrated odes on the birthday of Miss Flower, Lord Ashbrooke's sister, when she visited Castle Durrow; and on this occasion he required a fortnight to make up his mind as to the best proceedings to bring the skin to its proper colour. Having, by search of old bookstalls in Dublin (whither he went for the purpose), found an ancient treatise, translated from the work of the high German Doctor Cratorious (who flourished in the fourteenth century), on *skinning* certain parts of the body to change the colour or complexion, or effectually to disguise criminals who had escaped from prison;—by which means, likewise, disfiguring marks, freckles, moles, &c. might be removed,—Doctor Bathron decided, that if this could be done partially, why not on the entire body, by little and little, and not skinning one spot till the last should be healed? He therefore stated to Mr. Washington, and all the good family of Dureen, that he would take upon himself to *whiten* the child—as he was perfectly satisfied the black skin was merely the outside, or scarf-skin, and that the real skin and flesh underneath were the same as every body else's.

The mode of operating was now the subject of difficulty. It was suggested, and agreed on, to call in Mr. Knaggs, the doctor of Mount Meleck, who, though he had injured his character as a practitioner of judgment by attempting to cut off the head of Sam Doxy of the Derrys, as hereinafter mentioned,* had at the same time proved himself a skilful operator, having gashed boldly

* The anecdote referred to proved to be too sanguinary for the present editor's taste, and is therefore omitted.

into the nape of Mr. Doxy's neck without touching the spinal marrow, which a bungler needs must have done. He had also acquired the reputation of science by writing a treatise on the Spa of Ballyspellen, which the inn-keeper *there* had employed him to compose, in order to bring customers to his house to drink the waters as "a specific for numerous disorders, when mixed in due proportion with excellent wines, which might be had very reasonable at the sign of the Fox and Piper, at Ballyspellen," &c.

This man, in fine, together with Doctor Bathron, undertook to bring Master Washington to a proper hue by detaching the exterior black *pelt* which was so disagreeable to the family, and letting the natural white skin, which they had no doubt was concealed under it, come to light—thereby restoring the boy, as he ought to be, to his happy parents.

"You'll gain immortal honour," said the grandmother: "I am sure they will all be bound to pray for you!"

The state of practice in Ireland suggested but two ways of performing this notable operation—one purely surgical, the other surgico-medical; either by gradually flaying with the knife, or by blisters.

It was at length settled to begin the operation the ensuing week, previously preparing the heir-at-law by medicine to prevent inflammation; the first attempt was to be on a small scale, and the operation to be performed in Doctor Bathron's own surgery;—and he being still undecided whether the scalpel and forceps, or Spanish flies, would be the most eligible mode of skinning Master Washington, determined to try both ways at once, one on each arm, and to act in future according as he saw the skin yield easiest.

Most people conceived that, as a blister always raises the skin, it would be the readiest agent in loosening and carrying off the black one that had created so much uneasiness in the present instance:—the doctor's doubts as to which, were, that the blister alone might not rise regularly, but operate at one place better than at another —in which case the child might be *piebald,* which would make him far worse than before.

The operation at length proceeded, and Lieutenant Palmer himself recounted to me every part of the incident. A strong blister, two inches by three, was placed on the child's right arm, and being properly covered, remained there without inflicting any torture for above an hour. The left arm was reserved for the scalpel and forceps, and the operator entertained no doubt whatever of complete success.

The mode he pursued was very *scientific;* he made two parallel slashes as deep as he could in reason, about three inches down the upper part of the arm, and a cross one, to introduce the forceps and strip the loose black skin off, when he could snip it away at the bottom, and leave the white or rather red flesh underneath, to generate a new skin, and show the proper colouring for a god-child of General Washington.

All eyes were now rivetted to the spot. The women cried in an under key to Master George, who roared. "Hush, hush, my dear," said the Doctor, "you don't know what's good for you, my little innocent!" whilst he applied the forceps, to strip off the skin like a *surtout.* The skin was tight, and would not come away cleverly with the first tug, as the doctor had expected; nor did any thing *white* appear, though a sufficiency of red blood manifested itself.

The doctor was greatly surprised. "I see," said he, "it is somewhat deeper than we had conceived. We have not got deep enough." Another gash on each side; but the second gash had no better success. Doctor Bathron seemed desperate; but conceiving that in so young a subject one short cut—be it ever so deep—could do no harm, his hand shook, and he gave the scalpel its full force, till

[97]

he found it touch the bone. The experiment was now complete; he opened the wound, and starting back, affected to be struck with horror, threw down his knife, stamped and swore the child was in fact either the devil or a *lusus Naturæ,* for that he could see the very bone, and the child was actually coal-black *to* the bone, and the bone black also, and that he would not have taken a thousand guineas to have given a single gash to a thing which was clearly supernatural—actually dyed in grain. He appeared distracted; however, the child's arm was bound up, a good poultice put over it, the blister hastily removed from the other arm, and the young gentleman, fortunately for Doctor Bathron, recovered from the scarification, and lived with an old dry-nurse for four or five years. He was then killed by a cow of his *father's* horning him, and died with the full reputation of having been a devil in reality, which was fully corroborated by a white sister of his, and his mother, (as I heard,) departing about the very same time, if not on the next day. It was said he took their souls away with him, to make his peace with his master for staying so long.

Doctor George Bathron, who was the pleasantest united grocer and surgeon in the county, at length found it the best policy to tell this story himself, and by that means neutralise the ridicule of it. He often told it to me, whilst in company with Mr. Palmer; and by hearing both versions, I obtained full information about the circumstance, which I relate as a very striking example of the mode in which we managed a *lusus Naturæ* when we *caught* one in Ireland five and forty years ago.

A WEDDING IN OLDEN DAYS

THERE are few changes in the manners and customs of society in Ireland more observable than those relating to marriage. The day has been, within my recollection, when that ceremony was conducted altogether differently from the present mode. Formerly, no damsel was *ashamed,* as it were, of being married. The celebration was joyous, public, and enlivened by every species of merriment and good cheer. The bride and bridegroom, bridesmaids, and bridesmen (all dressed and decorated in gay and gallant costumes), vied in every effort to promote the pleasure they were themselves participating. When the ceremony was completed, by passing round a final and mystical word, "Amazement!"—every body kissed the bride. The company then all saluted each other: cordial congratulations went round, the music struck up, and plenty of plum cake and wine seemed to anticipate a *christening.* The bride for a moment whimpered and coloured; the mamma wept with gratification; the bridesmaids flushed with sympathy, and a scene was produced almost too brilliant for modern apathy even to gaze at. The substantial banquet soon succeeded; hospitality was all alive; the bottle circulated; the ball commenced; the bride led off, to take leave of her celibacy; men's souls were softened; maidens' hearts melted; Cupid slily stole in, and I scarce ever saw a joyous public wedding whereat he had not nearly expended his quiver before three o'clock in the morning. Every thing cheerful and innocent combined to show the right side of human nature, and to increase and perfect human happiness; a jovial hot supper gave respite to the dancers and time to escort Madam Bride to her nuptial-chamber—whither, so long as company were permitted to do so, we will attend her. The bed-curtains were adorned with festoons of ribbon. The chamber was well lighted; and the bridesmaids having administered to the bride her prescriptive refreshment of white-wine posset, proceeded to remove her left stocking and put it into her trembling hand: they then whispered anew the mystical word before mentioned; and having bound a handkerchief over her eyes, to ensure her impartiality, all the lovely spinsters surrounded the nuptial couch, each anxiously expecting that the next moment would anticipate her promotion to the same happy predicament within three hundred and sixty-five days at the very farthest. The bride then tossed the prophetic hosiery at random among her palpitating friends, and whichever damsel was so fortunate as to receive the blow was declared the next maiden in the room who would become devoted to the joys of Hymen; and every one in company—both ladies and gentlemen—afterward saluted the cheek of the lucky girl. The ball then recommenced; the *future* bride led off; night waned; —and Phoebus generally peeped again ere the company could be brought to separate. Good-humoured tricks were also on those happy occasions practised by arch girls upon the bridegroom. In short, the pleasantry of our old marriages in Ireland could not be exceeded.

How miserable has modern refinement reversed those scenes of happiness and hilarity—when the gentry of my native land were married in warm, cheerful chambers, and in the midst of animated beings, beloving and beloved! No gloom was there: every thing seemed to smile; and all thoughts of death or memoranda of mortality were discarded.

Now, those joyous scenes are shifted by sanctity and *civilisation*. Now, the female soul almost shudders—and it well may—on reaching the site of the connubial cere-

Moret Castle, Queens County, from *Antiquities of Ireland*, 1791.
Photograph courtesy of the National Library of Ireland

Donnybrook Fair. Photograph courtesy of the National Library of Ireland

mony. The long, chilling aisle, ornamented only by sculp-
tured tablets and tales of death and futurity, is terminated by the sombre chancel—whence the unpupilled eye
and vacant stare of cold marble busts glare down on
those of youth and animation, seeming to say, "Vain, hap-
less couple! see me—behold your fate!—the time is running now, and will not stop its course a single moment
till you are *my* companions!" Under such auspices, the
lovers' vows are frozen ere they can be registered by the
recording angel.

The cheerless ceremony concluded, the bridegroom solemnly hands the silent bride into her travelling chariot;
hurries her to some country inn, with her pretty maid—
perhaps destined to be a future rival; they remain there
a few days, till yawning becomes too frequent, and the
lady then returns to town a listless matron—to receive,
on her couch of *ennui*, a string of formal congratulations,
and predictions of connubial comfort, few of which are
doomed to be so *prophetic* as the *bridal stocking* of her
grandmother.

In those days, so soon as an elder son came of age, the
father and he united to raise money to pay off all family
incumbrances. The money certainly was raised, but the
incumbrances were so lazy, that in general they remained
in statu quo. The estates were soon clipped at both ends;
the father nibbling at one, the son pilfering at the other,
and the attorney at both. The rent-roll became short;
and it was decided that the son must marry to "sow his
wild oats," and make another settlement on younger
children. Money, however, was not always the main object of Irish marriages:—first, because it was not always
to be had; and next, because if it was to be had, it would
so soon change masters, that it would be all the same after a year or two. Good family, good cheer, and beauty,
when they could find it, were the chief considerations
of a country gentleman, whose blood relatives, root and

branch (as is still the case on the continent), generally attended the act of alliance, with all the splendour their tailors, milliners, and mantua-makers could or would supply.

My eldest brother . . . was an officer of that once magnificent regiment the Black Horse, and fell most vehemently in love with the sister of a brother-officer, afterward Colonel E—— of Old Court, County Wicklow. . . . Alicia was just eighteen: she had no regular feature: her mouth was disproportionately large; her lips were coral; her eyes destitute of fire—but they were captivating tell-tales; her figure was rather below the middle height, but without an angle; and the round, graceful delicacy of her limbs could not be surpassed. It was, however, the unrivalled clearness of her pellucid skin that gave a splendour and indescribable charm to the contour of Alicia's animated face. I may be considered as exaggerating when I declare that her countenance appeared nearly transparent, and her hands were more clear than may well be imagined. Her address was still more engaging than her person.

It being determined that the wedding should be upon a public and splendid scale, both families prepared to act fully up to that resolution. The proper trades-people were set to work; ribbon favours were woven on a new plan; in fact, all Dublin heard of the preparations from the busy milliners, &c.; and on the happy day, a crowd of neighbours collected about my father's house in Clare Street, to see the cavalcade, which was to proceed to Old Court House, near the Dargle, where the ceremony was to be performed.

The dress of those days on such occasions was generally splendid; but our garments "out-Heroded-Herod." The bridegroom, cased in white cloth with silver tissue, belaced and bespangled, glittered like an eastern caliph. My mother, a woman of high blood and breeding, and just pride, was clad in what was called a *manteau* of silvered satin: when standing direct before the lights, she shone out as the reflector of a lamp; and as she moved majestically about the room, and curtseyed *à la Madame Pompadour,* the rustling of her embroidered habit sounded like music appropriate to the flow of compliments that enveloped her. My father, one of the handsomest men of his day, was much more plainly dressed than any of us.

The gilded coach of ceremony . . . was put in requisition; and its four blacks, Bully, Blackbird, the colt, and Stopfour (fourteen years of age), were all as sleek and smooth as if cut out of ebony. Tom White and Keeran Karry (postilions), with big Nicholas (the footman), sported appropriate costumes; and the whole was led by Mr. Mahony, the butler, mounted on Brown Jack, my father's hunter.

The cavalcade started off at a hand-gallop for Bray, accompanied by the benediction of old Sarah the cook, and Judy Berger the hereditary house-keeper, who stood praying meanwhile and crossing their foreheads, at the door. An old travelling chaise of no very prepossessing appearance (which had been rescued from the cocks and hens in the country out-house), with a pair of hacks, was driven by Matthew Querns the huntsman, and contained the residue of the party—namely, my two other brethren and self.

The more particular description of our attire may strike certain *moderns* as somewhat ridiculous; but that attire was in the *goût* of the day, and covered as good proportions as those of the new gentry who may deride it. The men wore no stays; the ladies covered their shoulders; and the first were to the full as brave, and the latter at least as modest, as their successors. *Our* wedding suits were literally thus composed. The blue satin vests and inexpressibles were well laced and spangled wherever there was any room for ornament. The coats were of white cloth with blue capes. Four large paste curls, white as snow with true rice powder, and scented strong with real bergamot, adorned our heads. My third brother, Wheeler Barrington, had a coat of scarlet cloth, because he was *intended* for the army.

In truth, greater luminaries never attended a marriage festivity. Our equipage, however, by no means corresponded with our personal splendour and attractions; and I thought the contrast would be too ridiculous to any observing spectator who might know the family. I therefore desired Matthew to take a short turn from the great rock road to avoid notice as much as possible; which caution being given, we crowded into the tattered vehicle, and trotted away as swiftly as one blind and one lame horse could draw such magnificoes. There were (and are) on the circular road by which I had desired Matthew Querns to drive us, some of those nuisances called turnpikes. When we had passed the second gate, the gatekeeper, who had been placed there recently, of course demanded his toll. "Pay him, French," said I to my brother. "Faith," said French, "I changed my clothes, and I happen to have no money in my pocket." "No matter," answered I, "Wheeler, give the fellow a shilling." "I have not a rap," said Wheeler.—"I lost every halfpenny I had yesterday at the royal cockpit in Essex Street."

By a sort of instinct I put my hand into my own pocket; but instinct is not money, and *reality* quickly informed me that I was exactly in the same situation. However, "no matter," again said I; so I desired old Matthew Querns to pay the turnpike. "Is it me pay the pike?" said Matthew—"me? the devil a cross of wages I got from the master this many a day; and if I did, do you think, Master Jonah, the liquor would not be after having it out of me by this time?" and he then attempted to drive on *without* paying, as he used to do at Cullenaghmore. The man however grappled the blind horse, and gave us a full quantum of abuse, in which his wife, who issued forth at the sound, vociferously joined. Matthew began to whack him and the horses alternately with his thong whip; my brother French struggled to get out, and beat the pike-man; but the door would not open readily, and I told him that if he beat the turnpike man properly, he'd probably bleed *a few* himself; and that a single drop of blood on his fine clothes would effectually exclude him from society. This reasoning succeeded; but the blind horse not perceiving what was the matter, supposed something worse had happened, and began to plunge and break the harness. "You d———d gilt vagabonds," said the turnpike man, "such fellows should be put into the stocks or ducked at the broad stone beyond Kilmainham. Oh! I know you well enough! (looking into the carriage window:) what are yees but stage-players that have run away from Smock Alley,* and want to impose upon the country-folk!—But I'll neither let yees back or forward, by ———, till you pay me a *hog* for the pike, and two and eightpence-halfpenny for every wallop of the whip that the ould green mummer there gave me, when I only wanted my honest dues."

I saw fighting was in vain; but courtesy can do any thing with an Irishman. "My honest friend," said I, (to soften him,) "you're right; we are poor stage-players sure enough: we have got a loan of the clothes from Mr. Ryder†—may Heaven bless him! and we're hired out to play a farce for a great wedding that's to be performed at Bray to-night. When we come back with our money we'll pay you true and fair, and drink with you till you're stiff, if you think proper."

* One of the earliest theaters in Dublin, first opened in 1662.
† Thomas Ryder was manager of the Smock Alley Theatre from 1772 to 1781.

On this civil address the pike-man looked very kind: "Why, then, by my sowl its true enough," said he, "ye can't be very rich till ye get your entrance money; but sure I won't be out of pocket for all that. Well, faith and troth, ye look like decent stage-players; and I'll tell you what, I like good music, so I do. Give me a new song or two, and d——mme but I'll let you off, you poor craturs, till you come back agin. Come, give us a chaunt, and I'll help you to mend the harness too!"

"Thank you, sir," said I humbly. "I can't sing," said my brother French, "unless I'm drunk!" "Nor I, drunk or sober," said Wheeler. "You *must* sing for the *pike,*" said I to French; and at length he set up his pipes to a favourite song, often heard among the half-mounted gentlemen in the country when they were drinking; and as I shall never forget any incident of that (to me) eventful day, and the ditty is quite characteristic both of the nation generally and the half-mounted gentlemen in particular, (with whom it was a sort of charter song,) I shall give it.

> D——n money—its nothing but trash:
> We're happy though ever so poor!
> When we have it we cut a great dash,
> When it's gone, we ne'er think of it more.
> Then let us be wealthy or not,
> Our spirits are always the same;
> We're free from every dull thought,
> And the "Boys of old Ireland's" our name!

I never saw a poor fellow so pleased as the pike-man; the words hit his fancy: he shook us all round, most heartily, by the hand; and running into his lodge, brought out a pewter pot of frothing beer, which he had just got for himself, and insisted on each of us taking a drink. We of course complied. He gave Matthew a drink too, and desired him not to be so handy with his whip to other pike-men, or they'd *justice* him at Kilmainham. He then helped up our traces; and Matthew meanwhile, who, having had the last draught, had left the pot no further means of exercising its hospitality—enlivened by the liquor and encouraged by the good-nature of the pike-man, and his pardon for the *walloping*—thought the least he could do in gratitude was to give the honest man a sample of his own music, vocal and instrumental: so taking his hunting horn from under his coat (he never went a yard without it) and sounding his best "Death of Reynard," he sang a stave which was then the charter song of *his* rank, and which he roared away with all the graces of a view holloa:

> Ho! ro! the sup of good drink!
> And it's ho! ro! the heart wou'dn't think!
> Oh! had I a shilling lapp'd up in a clout,
> 'Tis a sup of good drink that should wheedle it out.
> And it's ho! ro! &c. &c.

The man of the pike was delighted. "Why, then, by my sowl, you ould mummer," said he, "it's a pity the likes of you should *want* a *hog*. Arrah! here (handing him a shilling), maybe your whistle would run dry on the road, and you'll pay me when you come back, won't you? Now all's settled, off wid yees! Success!—success!" And away we went, as fast as the halt and blind could convey us. We arrived safe and in high glee, just as the prayer-book was getting ready for the ceremony.

I will here state, by way of episode, that great difficulties and delays, both of law and equity, had postponed the matrimonial connexion of my brother, Major Barrington (he bore that rank in the old Volunteers), for a considerable time. There was not money enough *afloat* to settle family incumbrances, and keep the younger children from starving. A temporary suspension was of course put to the courtship. My brother in consequence grew nearly outrageous, and swore to me that he had not slept a wink for three nights, considering what species of *death* he should put himself to. Strong, and young, (though tolerably susceptible myself,) my heart was at that time my own, and I could not help laughing at the extravagance of his passion. I tried to ridicule him out of it. "Heavens!" said I. "Jack, how can you be at a loss on *that* score? You know I am pretty sure that, by your intended suicide, I shall get a step nearer Cullenaghmore. Therefore, I will remind you that there are a hundred very *genteel* ways by which you may despatch yourself without either delay or expense."

He looked at me quite wildly. In fact he was distractedly in love. Alicia was eternally on his lips, and I really believe, if his head had been cut off like the man's in *Alonzo de Cordova*,* it would have continued pronouncing "Alicia," till every drop of blood was clean out of it. Reasoning with a mad lover is in vain, so I still pursued ridicule. "See," said I, "that marble chimneypiece at the end of the room; suppose, now, you run headforemost against it,—in all human probability you'll knock your brains out in a novel and not at all a vulgar way."

I spoke in jest, but found my hearer jested not. Before I could utter another word, he bent his head forward, and with might and main rushed plump at the chimneypiece, which he came against with a crash that I had no doubt must have finished him completely. He fell back and lay without a struggle; the blood gushed, and I stood petrified. The moment I was able I darted out of the room, and calling for aid, his servant Neil came. I told him that his master was dead.

"Dead!" said Neil, "By ——— he is, and *double dead* too! Ah! then, who *kilt* the major?"

He took him up in his arms, and laid him on a sofa. My brother, however, soon gave Neil the "retort courteous." He opened his eyes, groaned, and appeared any

* Probably an inaccurate allusion to John Home's *Alonzo* (1773).

thing but *dying*. My fright ceased; he had been only stunned, and his head cut, but his brains were safe in their case. He had luckily come in contact with the *flat* part of the marble: had he hit the *moulding,* he would have ended his love and misfortunes together, and given me, as I had said, a step toward Cullenaghmore. The cut on his head was not material, and in a few days he was tolerably well again. This story, however, was not to be divulged; it was determined that it should remain with us a great secret. Neil, his servant, we swore on a Bible not to say a word about it to any body; but the honest man must have practised some mental reservation, as he *happened* just only to *hint* it to his sweetheart, Mary Donnellan, my mother's maid, and she in a tender moment told the postilion Keeran, for whom she had a regard. Keeran never kept a secret in all his life; so he told the dairy-maid, Molly Coyle, whom he preferred to Mary Donnellan. And the dairy-maid told my father, who frequented the dairy, and delighted to see Molly Coyle a-churning. The thing at length became quite public, and my brother, to avoid raillery, set off to his regiment at Philipstown, whither I accompanied him. He still raved about taking the first favourable *opportunity* of putting himself to death, if the courtship were much longer suspended; and spoke of gallantly throwing himself off his charger at full gallop, previously fastening his foot in the stirrup. The being dragged head downwards over a few heaps of paving stones would certainly have answered his deadly purpose well enough; but I dissuaded him without much difficulty from that species of self-murder, by assuring him that every body, in such a case, would attribute his death to *bad horsemanship,* which would remain, on the records of the regiment, an eternal disgrace to his professional character. Many other projects he thought of; but I must here make one remark, which perhaps may be a good one in general—namely, that every one of those projects *happened* to originate *after dinner*—a period when Irishmen's chivalric fancies are at their most enthusiastic and visionary height.

At length, a happy letter reached the major, signifying that all parties had agreed, and that his Alicia, heart and hand, was to be given up to him for life, as his own private and exclusive property—"to have and to hold, for better for worse," &c. &c. This announcement rendered him almost as wild as his despair had done previously. When he received the letter, he leaped down a flight of stairs at one spring, and in five minutes ordered his charger to be saddled for himself; his hunter, "Mad Tom," for me; and his chesnut, "Rainbow," for Neil. In ten minutes we were all mounted and in full gallop toward Dublin, which he had determined to reach that night after one short stoppage at Kildare, where we arrived (without slackening rein) in as short a time as if we had rode a race. The horses were fed well, and drenched with hot ale and brandy; but as none of them were in love, I perceived that they would willingly have deferred the residue of the journey till the ensuing morning. Indeed, my brother's steed conceiving that *charges* of such rapidity and length were not at all military, unless in *running away,* determined practically to convince his master that such was his notion. We passed over the famous race-ground of the Curragh in good style; but, as my brother had not given his horse time to lie down gently and rest himself in the ordinary way, the animal had no choice but to perform the feat of lying down whilst in full gallop—which he did very expertly just at the Curragh stand-house. The only mischief occurring herefrom was, that the drowsy charger stripped the skin, like rags, completely off both his knees, scalped the top of his head, got a hurt in the back sinews, and (no doubt without intending it) broke both my brother's collarbones. When we came up (who were a few hundred yards behind him), both man and beast were lying very quietly, as if asleep;—my brother about five or six yards before the horse, who had cleverly thrown his rider far beyond the chance of being tumbled over by himself. The result was, as usual on similar occasions, that the horse was led limping and looking foolish to the first stable, and committed to all the farriers and grooms in the neighbourhood. My brother was carried flat on a door to the nearest ale-house; and doctors being sent for, *three* (with bags of instruments) arrived from different places before night, and, after a good deal of searching and fumbling about his person, one of them discovered that both collar-bones were smashed, as aforesaid, and that if either of the broken bones or splinters thereof turned *inward* by his stirring, it might run through the lobes of his lungs, and very suddenly end all hopes of ever completing his journey: his nose had likewise taken a different turn from that it had presented when he set out:—and the palms of his hands fully proved that they could do without any skin, and with a very moderate quantity of flesh.

However, the bones were well arranged, a pillow strapped under each arm, and another at his shoulder-blades. All necessary comforts were procured, as well as furniture from Mr. Hamilton, whose house was near. I did not hear a word that night about Alicia; but in due time the major began to recover once more, and resumed his love, which had *pro tempore* been literally knocked out of him. It was announced by the doctor that it would be a long time before he could use his hands or arms, and that removal or exercise might produce a new fracture, and send a splinter or bone through any part of his interior that might be most handy.

Though I thought the blood he had lost, and the tortures the doctor put him to, had rendered his mind a good deal tamer than it was at Maryborough, he still talked much of Alicia, and proposed that I should write to her,

[111]

on his part, an account of his misfortunes; and the doctor in attendance allowing him the slight exertion of signing his name and address in his own handwriting, I undertook to execute my task to the utmost of my skill, and certainly performed it with great success. I commenced with due warmth, and stated that the "accident he had met with only retarded the happiness he should have in making her his wife, which he had so long burned for, but which circumstances till then had prevented," &c. &c. (The words I recollect pretty well, because they afterward afforded me infinite amusement.) The letter was sealed with the family arms and crest.

"Now, Jonah," said my brother, "before I marry I have a matter of some importance to arrange, lest it should come to the ears of my Alicia, which would be my ruin; and I must get you to see it settled for me at Philipstown, so as to prevent any thing exploding." He went on to give me the particulars of a certain *liaison* he had formed with a young woman there, an exciseman's daughter, which he was now, as may be supposed, desirous of breaking; and (though protesting that interference in such matters was not at all to my taste) I consented to write, at his dictation, a sort of compromise to the party, which he having signed, both epistles were directed at the same time, and committed to the post-office of Kilcullen bridge.

The amorous and fractured invalid was now rapidly advancing to a state of convalescence. His nose had been renovated with but an inconsiderable partiality for the left cheek; his collar-bones had approximated to a state of adhesion; and he began impatiently to count the days and nights that would metamorphose his Alicia from a spinster to a matron.

The extravagance of his flaming love amused me extremely: his aerial castles were built, altered, and demolished with all the skill and rapidity of modern architecture; while years of exquisite and unalloyed felicity arose before his fancy, of which they took an immovable grasp.

We were busily engaged one morning in planning and arranging his intended establishment, on returning to the sports and freaks of a country gentleman (with the addition of a terrestrial angel to do the honours), when, on a sudden, we heard rather a rough noise at the entrance of the little chamber wherein the invalid was still reclining upon a feather-bed, with a pillow under each arm to keep the bones in due position. Our old fat landlady, who was extremely partial to the cornet,* burst in with her back toward us, endeavouring to prevent the entrance of a stranger, who, however, without the least ceremony, giving her a hearty curse, dashed into the centre of the room in a state of bloated rage scarcely conceivable—which was more extraordinary as the individual appeared to be no other than Captain Tennyson Edwards, of the 30th regiment, third brother of the beloved Alicia. Of course we both rose to welcome him most heartily: this however he gave us no opportunity of doing; but laying down a small mahogany case, which he carried in his hand, putting his arms akimbo, he loudly exclaimed without any exordium, "Why, then, Cornet Jack Barrington, are you not the greatest scoundrel that ever disgraced civilised society?"

This quere of course was not answered in the affirmative by either of us; and a scene of astonishment on the one side and increasing passion on the other, baffled all common-place description: I must therefore refer it to the imagination of my readers. The retort courteous was over and over reiterated on both sides without the slightest attempt at any *éclaircissement*.

At length the captain opened his mahogany case, and exhibited therein a pair of what he called his "barking

* My brother's *actual* rank in *the army* [Barrington's footnote].

[113]

irons," bright and glittering as if both able and willing to commit most expertly any murder or murders they might be employed in.

"You scoundrel!" vociferated the captain to the cornet, "only that your bones were smashed by your horse, I would not leave a whole one this day in your body. But I suppose your brother here will have no objection to exchange shots *for* you, and not keep me waiting till you are well enough to be *stiffened!* Have you any objection (turning to me) 'to take a *crack?*' "

"A very considerable objection," answered I; "first, because I never fight without knowing *why;* and secondly, because my brother is not in the habit of fighting by proxy."

"Not know why?" roared the captain. "There! read that! Oh! I wish you were hale and whole, cornet, that I might have the pleasure of a *crack* with *you.*"

I lost no time in reading the letter; and at once perceived that my unlucky relative had, in the flurry of his love, misdirected each of the two epistles just now spoken of, and consequently informed "the divine Alicia" that he could hold no further intercourse with her, &c.

A fit of convulsive laughter involuntarily seized me, which nothing could restrain; and the captain meanwhile, nearly bursting with rage, reinvited me to be shot at. My brother stood all the time like a ghost, in more pain, and almost in as great a passion as our visitor. He was unable to articulate; and the pillows fixed under each arm rendered him one of the most grotesque figures that a painter could fancy.

When I recovered the power of speaking (which was not speedily), I desired Tennyson to follow me to another room: he took up his pistol-case, and expecting I was about to indulge him with a *crack* or two, seemed somewhat easier in mind and temper. I at once explained to him the curious mistake, and without the least hesitation the captain burst into a much stronger paroxysm of laughter than I had just escaped from. Never did any officer in the king's service enjoy a victory more than Captain Edwards did this strange blunder. It was quite to his taste, and on our proposing to make the invalid as happy as exhaustion and fractures would admit of, a new scene, equally unexpected, but of more serious consequences, turned up.

A ruddy, active and handsome country girl came to the door, and sprang with rapidity from a pillion on which she had been riding behind a good-looking rustic lad. Our landlady greeted her new customer with her usual urbanity. "You're welcome to these parts, miss," said Mrs. Mahony: "you stop to-night—to be sure you do:—what do you choose, miss?—Clean out the settle-bed parlour: —the chickens and rashers, miss, are capital, so they are. —Gassoon, do run and howld the lady's beast; go, avourneen, carry him in and wipe him well—do you hear? and throw a wisp of hay before the poor brute. You rode hard, miss, so you did!"

"Oh! where's the cornet?" cried the impatient maiden, totally disregarding Mrs. Mahony: for it was Jenny —————— herself, who had come speedily from Philipstown to forestall the happy moments which my bewildered brother had, in his letter to his Alicia, so delightfully anticipated. Nothing could restrain her impatience; she burst into the little parlour full on the astounded invalid, who was still standing bolt upright, like a statue, in the very position wherein we had left him. His loving Jenny, however, unconscious that his collar-bones had been disunited, rushed into his arms with furious affection. "Oh! my dearest Jack!" cried she, "we *never* part *no* more! no, never—never!" and tight, indeed, was the embrace wherewith the happy Jenny now encircled the astonished cornet; but, alas! down came one of the pillows! the arm, of course, closed; and one half of the left collar-bone being as ignorant as its owner of the cause of so obstreperous an embrace, and, wishing as it were to see what matter was going forward in the world, instantly divorced itself from the other half, and thrusting its ivory end through the flesh, skin, and integuments (which had obstructed its egress), quickly appeared peeping through the lover's shirt.

The unfortunate inamorato could stand these accumulated shocks no longer, and sank upon the feather-bed in a state of equal astonishment and exhaustion, groaning piteously.

Here I must again apply to the imagination of my reader for a true picture of the succeeding scene. Fielding alone could render a detail palatable; the surgeons were once more sent for to reset the collar: an energetic kiss, which his Jenny had imprinted on the cornet's nose, again somewhat disturbed its new position, and conferred a pain so acute, as to excite exclamations, by no means gentle in their nature, from the unresisting sufferer. Suffice it to say, Jenny was with much difficulty at length forced away from her Jack, if not in a dead *faint,* at least in something extremely *like* one. An *éclaircissement* took place so soon as she came round; and the *compromise,* before hinted at, was ultimately effected.

Edwards asked a hundred pardons of my poor brother, who, worn out, and in extreme pain, declared he would as soon die as live. In fine, it was nearly a month more ere the cornet could travel to Dublin, and another before he was well enough to throw himself at the feet of his Dulcinea: which ceremony was in due season succeeded by the wedding I have already given my account of.

II

LIFE IN TOWN

MY EDUCATION

MR. GEORGE LODGE had married a love-daughter of old Stephen Fitzgerald, Esq. of Bally Thomas, who by affinity was a relative of the house of Cullenaghmore, and from this union sprang Mr. Michael Lodge.

I never shall forget his figure!—he was a tall man with thin legs and great hands, and was generally biting one of his nails whilst employed in teaching me. The top of his head was half bald: his hair was clubbed with a rose-ribbon; a tight stock, with a large silver buckle to it behind, appeared to be almost choking him: his chin and jaws were very long—and he used to hang his under jaw, shut one eye, and look up to the cieling, when he was thinking or trying to recollect anything.

Mr. Michael Lodge had been what is called a Matross* in the artillery service. My grandfather had got him made a gauger; but he was turned adrift for letting a poor man do something wrong about distilling. He then became a land-surveyor and architect for the farmers:— he could farry, cure cows of the murrain, had numerous secrets about cattle and physic, and was accounted the best bleeder and bone-setter in that county—all of which healing accomplishments he exercised gratis. He was also a famous brewer and accountant—in fine, was every thing at Cullenagh: steward, agent, caterer, farmer, sportsman, secretary, clerk to the colonel as a magistrate, and also clerk to Mr. Barret as the parson: but he would not sing a stave in church, though he'd chant indefatigably in

---

* According to the *O.E.D.,* "a soldier next in rank below the gunner in a train of artillery, who acted as a kind of assistant or mate."

the hall. He had the greatest contempt for women, and used to beat the maid-servants; whilst the men durst not vex him, as he was quite despotic! He had a turning-lathe, a number of grinding-stones, and a carpenter's bench, in his room. He used to tin the saucepans, which act he called *chymistry;* and I have seen him, like a tailor, putting a new cape to his riding-coat! He made all sorts of nets, and knit stockings; but above all he piqued himself on the variety and depth of his *learning.*

Under the tuition of this Mr. Michael Lodge, who was surnamed the "wise man of Cullenaghmore," I was placed at four years of age, to learn as much of the foregoing as he could teach me in the next five years: at the expiration of which period he had no doubt of my knowing as much as himself, and then (he said) I should go to school *"to teach the master."*

This idea of teaching the master was the greatest possible incitement to me; and as there was no other child in the house, I never was idle, but was as inquisitive and troublesome as can be imagined. Every thing was explained to me; and I not only got on surprisingly, but my memory was found to be so strong, that Mr. Michael Lodge told my grandfather *half learning* would answer me as well as *whole learning* would another child. In truth, before my sixth year, I was making a very great hole in Mr. Lodge's stock of information (fortification and gunnery excepted), and I verily believe he only began to learn many things himself when he commenced teaching them to me.

He took me a regular course by Horn-book, Primer, Spelling-book, Reading-made-Easy, Æsop's Fables, &c.: but I soon aspired to such of the old library books as had pictures in them; and particularly, a very large History of the Bible with cuts was my constant study. Hence I knew how every saint was murdered; and Mr. Lodge not only told me that each martyr had a painter to take his likeness before death, but also fully explained to me how they had all sat for their pictures, and assured me that most of them had been murdered by the *Papists*. I recollect at this day the faces of every one of them at their time of martyrdom; so strongly do youthful impressions sink into the mind, when derived from objects which at the time were viewed with interest.

Be this as it may, however, my wise man, Mr. Michael Lodge, used his heart, head, and hands, as zealously as he could to teach me most things that he did know, and many things he did not know; but with a skill which none of our schoolmasters practise, he made me think he was only amusing instead of giving me a task. The old man tried to make me inquisitive, and inclined to ask about the thing which he wanted to explain to me; and consequently, at eight years old I could read prose and poetry, write text,—draw a house, a horse, and a gamecock, tin a copper saucepan, and turn my own tops. I could do the manual exercise with my grandfather's crutch; and had learnt, besides, how to make bullets, pens, and black-ball; to dance a jig, sing a cronane, and play the Jew's harp. Michael also showed me, out of Scripture, how the world stood stock still whilst the sun was galloping round it; so that it was no easy matter at college to satisfy me as to the Copernican system. In fact, the old Matross gave me such a various and whimsical assemblage of subjects to think about, that my young brain imbibed as many odd, chivalrous, and puzzling theories as would drive some children out of their senses; and, truly, I found it no easy matter to get rid of several of them when it became absolutely necessary, whilst *some* I shall certainly retain till my death's day.

This course of education I most sedulously followed, until it pleased God to suspend my learning by the death of my grandfather, on whom I doated. He had taught me the broad-sword exercise with his cane, how to snap a pistol, and shoot with the bow and arrow; and had bespoken a little quarter-staff to perfect me in that favourite exercise of his youth, by which he had been enabled to knock a gentleman's brains out for a wager, on the ridge of Maryborough, in company with the grandfather of the present Judge Arthur Moore, of the Common Pleas of Ireland. It is a whimsical gratification to me, to think that I do not at this moment forget much of the said instruction which I received either from Michael Lodge, the Matross, or from Colonel Jonah Barrington,— though after a lapse of nearly sixty years!

A new scene was now to be opened to me. I was carried to Dublin, and put to the famous schoolmaster of that day, Dr. Ball,* of St. Michael-a-Powell's, Ship-street;— and here my puzzling commenced in good earnest. I was required to learn the English Grammar in the Latin tongue; and to translate languages without understanding any of them. I was taught prosody without verse, and rhetoric without composition; and before I had ever heard any oration except a sermon, I was flogged for not minding my emphasis in recitation. To complete my satisfaction,—for fear I should be idle during the course of the week, castigation was regularly administered every Monday morning, to give me, by anticipation, a sample of what the repetition-day might produce.

However, notwithstanding all this, I worked my way, got two premiums, and at length was reported fit to be placed under the hands of a private tutor, by whom I was to be *finished* for the University.

That tutor was well known many years in Diggesstreet, Dublin, and cut a still more extraordinary figure than the Matross. He was the Rev. Patrick Crawly, Rector of Killgobbin, whose son, my schoolfellow, was hanged

* Some other famous students of Dr. Ball include Lord Clare, John Forster, last Speaker of the Irish Parliament, and Henry Grattan.

a few years ago for murdering two old women with a shoemaker's hammer. My tutor's person was, in my imagination, of the same genus as that of Caliban. His feet covered a considerable space of any room wherein he stood, and his thumbs were so large that he could scarcely hold a book without hiding more than half the page of it: —though bulky himself, his clothes doubled the dimensions proper to suit his body; and an immense frowzy wig, powdered once a week, covered a head which, for size and form, might vie with a quarter-cask.

Vaccination not having as yet plundered horned cattle of their disorders, its predecessor had left evident proofs of attachment to the rector's countenance. That old Christian malady, the small-pox, which had resided so many centuries amongst our ancestors, and which modern innovations have endeavoured to undermine, had placed his features in a perfect state of compactness and security—each being screwed quite tight to its neighbour, and every seam appearing deep and gristly, so that the whole visage appeared to defy alike the edge of the sharpest scalpel and the skill of the most expert anatomist.

Yet this was as good-hearted a parson as ever lived:— affectionate, friendly, and, so far as Greek, Latin, Prosody, and Euclid went, excelled by few: and under him I acquired, in one year, more classical knowledge, than I had done during the former six, whence I was enabled, out of thirty-six pupils, early to obtain a place in the University of Dublin.

The college course, at that time, though a very learned one, was ill arranged, pedantic, and totally out of sequence. Students were examined in Locke *On the Human Understanding,* before their own had arrived at the first stage of maturity; and Euclid was pressed upon their reason before any one of them could comprehend a single problem. We were set to work at the most abstruse sciences before we had well digested the simpler ones, and posed ourselves at optics, natural philosophy, ethics, astronomy, mathematics, metaphysics, &c &c. without the least relief from belles-lettres, modern history, geography, or poetry; in short, without regard to any of those acquirements—the classics excepted, which form essential parts of a gentleman's education.

Nevertheless, I jogged on with *bene* for the classics—*satis* for the sciences—and *mediocriter* for mathematics. I had, however, the mortification of seeing the stupidest fellows I ever met, at school or college, beat me out of the field in some of the examinations, and very justly obtain premiums for sciences which I could not bring within the scope of my comprehension. My consolation is, that many men of superior talent to myself came off no better; and I had the *satisfaction* of knowing that some of the most erudite, studious, and distinguished of my contemporary collegians, went raving—and others melancholy—mad; and I do believe, that there are at this moment five or six of the most eminent of my academic rivals roaring in asylums for lunatics.

The death of my grandmother, which now took place, made a very considerable change in my situation, and I had sense enough, though still very young, to see the necessity of turning my mind towards a preparation for some lucrative profession—either law, physic, divinity, or war.

I debated on all these, as I thought, with great impartiality:—the pedantry of college disgusted me with clericals; wooden legs put me out of conceit with warfare; the horror of death made me shudder at medicine; and whilst the law was but a lottery-trade, too precarious for my taste, manufacture was too humiliating for my pride. Nothing, on the other hand, could induce me to remain a walking gentleman: and so, every occupation that I could think of having its peculiar disqualification, I remained a considerable time in a state of great uncertainty and disquietude.

Meanwhile, although my choice had nothing to do with the matter, I got almost imperceptibly engaged in that species of *profession* exercised by a young sportsman, whereby I was initiated into a number of *accomplishments* ten times worse than the negative ones of the walking gentleman:—namely, riding, drinking, dancing, carousing, hunting, shooting, fishing, fighting, racing, cockfighting, &c. &c.

CHOICE OF PROFESSION

M Y VEERING opinion as to a choice of profession was nearly decided by that military ardour which seized all Ireland, when the whole country had entered into resolutions to free itself for ever from English domination. The entire kingdom took up arms—regiments were formed in every quarter—the highest, the lowest, and the middle orders, all entered the ranks of freedom, and every corporation, whether civil or military, pledged life and fortune to attain and establish Irish independence.

My father had raised and commanded two corps—a dragoon regiment called the Cullenagh Rangers, and the Ballyroan Light Infantry. My elder brother commanded the Kilkenny Horse, and the Durrow Light Dragoons. The general enthusiasm caught me, and before I well knew what I was about, I found myself a military martinet and a red-hot patriot. Having been a university man, I was also considered to be of course a *writer,* and was accordingly called on to draw up resolutions for volunteer regiments all over the county. This was the first tirade I ever attempted on a political subject, and it being quite short enough and warm enough to be comprehended by all the parties, it was unanimously adopted—every man swearing, as he kissed the blade of his sword, that he would adhere to these resolutions to the last drop of his blood, which he would by no means spare, till we had finally achieved the independence of our country. We were very sincere, and, really I think, determined to perish, if necessary, in the cause—at least, I am sure, I was so.

The national point was gained, but not without much

difficulty and danger. The Irish parliament had refused to grant supplies to the Crown for more than six months. The people had entered into resolutions to prevent the importation of any British merchandise or manufactures. The entire kingdom had disavowed all English authority or jurisdiction, external or internal; the judges and magistrates had declined to act under British statutes:—the flame had spread rapidly, and had become irresistible.

The British Government saw that either temporising or an appeal to force would occasion the final loss of Ireland: 150,000 independent soldiers, well armed, well clothed, and well disciplined, were not to be coped with, —and England yielded. Thus the volunteers kept their oaths: they redeemed their pledge, and did not lay down their arms until the independence of Ireland had been pronounced from the throne, and the distinctness of the Irish nation promulgated in the government gazette of London.

Having carried our point with the English, and having proposed to prove our independence by going to war with Portugal about our linens, we completely set up for ourselves, except that Ireland was bound, constitutionally and irrevocably, never to have any king but the King of Great Britain.

We were now, in fact, regularly in a fighting mood: and being quite in good humour with England, we determined to fight the French, who had threatened to invade us; and I recollect a volunteer belonging to one of my father's corps, a school-master of the name of Beal, proposing a resolution to the Ballyroan Infantry, which purported, "that they would never stop fighting the French till they had flogged every man of them into mincemeat!" This magnanimous resolution was adopted with cheers, and was, as usual, *sworn to,* each hero kissing the muzzle of his musket.

I am not going any further into a history of those

times, to which I have alluded in order to mention what, for the moment, excited my *warlike ardour,* and fixed my determination, although but temporarily, to adopt the military profession.

On communicating this decision to my father, he procured me, from a friend and neighbour, General Hunt Walsh, a commission in that officer's own regiment, the 30th. The style of the thing pleased me very well:—but, upon being informed that I should immediately join the regiment, in America, my heroic tendencies received a serious check. I had not contemplated transatlantic emigration, and feeling that I could get my head broken just as well in my own country, I, after a few days' mature consideration, perceived my military ardour grow cooler and cooler every hour—until, at length, it was obviously defunct. I therefore wrote to the General a most thankful letter, but at the same time, "begging the favour of him to present my commission in his regiment to some hardier soldier, who could serve His Majesty with more vigour; as I, having been brought up by my grandmother, felt as yet too *tender* to be any way effective on foreign service—though I had no objection to fight as much as possible in Ireland, if necessary." The general accepted my resignation, and presented my commission to a young friend of his, whose brains were blown out in the very first engagement.

Having thus rejected the military, I next turned my thoughts to that very opposite profession—the clerical. But though preaching was certainly a much safer and more agreeable employment than bush-fighting, yet a curacy and a wooden leg being pretty much on a parallel in point of remuneration, and as I had the strongest objection to be half starved in the service of either the king or the altar, I also declined the cassock, assuring my father that "I felt I was not steady enough to make an 'exemplary parson;' and as any other kind of parson generally did more harm than good in a country, I could not, in my conscience, take charge of the morals of a flock of men, women, and children, when I should have quite enough to do to manage my own; and I should therefore leave the church to some more orthodoxical graduate."

Medicine, therefore, was the next in the list of professions to which I had, abstractedly, some liking. I had attended several courses of anatomical lectures at Dublin, and, although with some repugnant feelings, I had studied that most sublime of all sciences, human organization, by a persevering attention to the celebrated wax-works of that university. But my horror and disgust of *animal putridity* in all its branches was so great, inclusive even of stinking venison, (which most people admire,) that all surgical practice by me was necessarily out of the question; and medicine without surgery presenting no better chance than a curacy, it shared an equally bad fate with the sword and the pulpit.

Of the liberal and learned professions, there now remained but one, namely, the law. Now, as to this, I was told by several old practitioners, who had retired into the country, (from having no business to do in town), that if I was even as wise as Alfred, or as learned as Lycurgus, nobody would give me sixpence for all my law (if I had a hundred weight of it), until I had spent at least ten years in watching the manufacture. However, they consoled me by saying, that if I could put up with light eating and water-drinking during that period, I might then have a very reasonable chance of getting some briefs, particularly after having a gang of attornies to dine with me. Here I was damped again! and though I should have broken my heart if condemned to remain much longer a walking gentleman, I determined to wait a while, and see if nature would open my propensities a little wider, and give me some more decisive indication of what she thought me fittest for.

Whilst in this comfortless state of indecision, my father, like other country gentlemen, to gratify his lady under the shape of educating his children, gave his consent to be launched into the new scenes and pleasures of a city residence. He accordingly purchased an excellent house in Clare-street, Merrion-square; left a steward in the country to *mis*manage his concerns there; made up new wardrobes for the servants; got a fierce three-cocked hat for himself; and removed his establishment (the hounds excepted) to the metropolis of Ireland.

Here my good and well-bred mother (for such she was) had her Galway pride revived and gratified; the green coach *de cérémonie* was regilt and regarnished, and four black horses, with two postilions and a sixteen-stone footman, completed her equipage.

I had my bit of blood in the stable; my elder brother, who had been in the 1st Horse, had plenty of them:—my father had his old hunter, "Brown Jack;" and we set out at what is commonly called a *great rate*—but which great rates are generally, like a fox-chase, more hot than durable. However, the thing went on well enough; and during our city residence many pleasurable and many whimsical incidents occurred to me and other individuals of my family; one of which was most interesting to myself, and will form a leading feature in my subsequent Memoirs.

A DUBLIN BOARDING-HOUSE

O^N MY return to Dublin from London,* before I could suit myself with a residence to my satisfaction, I lodged at the house of Mr. Kyle, in Frederick-street, uncle to the present provost of Dublin University. Mrs. Kyle was a remarkably plain woman, of the most curious figure, being round as a ball; but she was as good as she was ordinary. This worthy creature, who was a gentlewoman by birth, had married Kyle, who, though of good family, had been a trooper. She had lived many years, as companion, with my grandmother, and in fact regarded me as if I had been her own child.

In her abode so many human curiosities were collected, and so many anecdotes occurred, that, even at this distance of time, the recollection of it amuses me. Those who lodged in the house dined in company: the table was most plentifully served, and the party generally comprised from eight to ten select persons. I will endeavour to sketch the leading members of the society there at the period of which I speak; and first on the list I will place the late Lord Mountmorris, of celebrated memory. He was a very clever and well-informed, but eccentric man; —one of the most ostentatious and at the same time parsimonious beings in the world. He considered himself by far the greatest orator and politician in Europe; and it was he who sent a florid speech, which he *intended* to have spoken in the Irish House of Lords, to the press:— the debate on which it was to be spoken did not ensue; but his lordship having neglected to countermand the pub-

* That is, after completing his law studies in England. Curiously, Barrington has very little to say about this period in his life.

[131]

lication, his studied harangue appeared next day in the Dublin newspapers with all the supposititious *cheerings,* &c. duly interposed! I believe a similar *faux pas* has been committed by some English legislator.

His Lordship, at the period in question, was patronizing what is commonly ycleped a *Led Captain*—one Lieutenant Ham or Gam Johnson, of the Royal Navy, brother to the two judges, and the attorney, of whom I shall speak hereafter. Without being absolutely disgusting, Lieut. Johnson was certainly the ugliest man in Christendom. It was said of him that he need never fire a shot, since his countenance was sufficient to frighten the bravest enemy. His bloated visage, deeply indented by that cruel ravager of all comeliness, the small-pox, was nearly as large as the body which supported it, and that was by no means diminutive. Yet the man was civil and mild, and had, withal, much higher character as an officer than his Captain in the Artois frigate, Lord Charles Fitzgerald, who, it was at that time thought, preferred a sound nap to a hard battle.

Next in the company came Sir John O'Flaherty, Bart. and Lady O'Flaherty his *sposa.* He was a plain, agreeable country gentlemen. Her Ladyship was to the full as *plain,* but not quite so agreeable. However, it was (as Mrs. Kyle said) *respectable,* at a boarding-house, to hear— "Sir John O'Flaherty's health!"—and "Lady O'Flaherty's health!"—drunk or hobnobbed across the table.— They formed, indeed, excellent make-weights to cram in between Lord Mountmorris and the *canaille.*

Lady Barry, widow of the late Sir Nathaniel Barry, Bart. and mother of Sir Edward, (who was also an occasional guest,) follows in my catalogue, and was as valuable a curiosity as any of the set.

Mrs. Wheeler, the grandmother of Sir Richard Jonah Denny Wheeler Cuffe, gave up her whole attention to lap-dogs; and neither she nor the last-mentioned dowager

The Right Honourable John Philpot Curran, engraved by H. Meyer from an original painting by Sir Thomas Lawrence. Photograph courtesy of the National Library of Ireland

Archibald Hamilton Rowan. Photograph courtesy of the National
Library of Ireland

were by any means averse to the fermented grape—though we never saw either of them "*very* far gone."

Lady Barry's only daughter, afterwards the unfortunate Mrs. Baldwin, was also of the party. Though this young female had not a beautiful face, it was yet peculiarly pleasing, and she certainly possessed one of the finest figures,—tall, and slender in its proportions, and exquisitely graceful,—I had ever seen. Her father, Sir Nathaniel Barry, many years the principal physician of Dublin, adored his daughter, and had spared no pains nor expense on her education. She profited by all the instruction she received, and was one of the most accomplished young women of her day.

But unfortunately he had introduced her to the practice of one very objectionable accomplishment,—calculated rather to give unbounded latitude to, than check, the light and dangerous particles of a volatile and thoughtless disposition. He was himself enthusiastically fond of *theatricals,* and had fitted up a theatre in the upper story of his own house.—There the youthful mind of his hitherto untainted daughter was first initiated into all the schemes, the passions, the arts and the deceptions of lovers and of libertines!—the close mimicry of which forms the very essence of dramatic perfection. At sixteen, with all the warmth of a sensitive constitution, she was taught to personify the vices, affect the passions, and assume the frivolities of her giddy sex!

Thus, through the folly or vanity of her father, she was led to represent by turns the flirt, the jilt, the silly wife, the capricious mistress and the frail maiden,—before her understanding had arrived at sufficient maturity, or his more serious instructions had made sufficient impression,—to enable her to resist voluptuous sensations. She had not penetration enough (how could she have?) to perceive that a moral may be extracted from almost every crime, and that a bad example may sometimes be more preservative against error, (from exhibiting its ruinous consequences,) even than a good one. She was too young, and too unsteady, to make these subtle distinctions. She saw the world's pleasures dancing gaily before her, and pursued the vision—until her mimicry, at length, became nature, and her personification identity. After two or three years, during which this mistaken course was pursued, Sir Nathaniel died, leaving his daughter in possession of all the powers of attraction without the guard of prudence. In the dance—in declamation—in music—in the languages—she excelled: but in those steady and solid qualities which adapt women for wedlock and domesticity, she was altogether deficient. Her short-sighted father had been weak enough to deck her with the gaudy qualifications of an actress at the expense of all those more estimable acquirements which her mind and her genius were equally susceptible of attaining.

The misfortunes which ensued should therefore be attributed rather to the folly of the parent than to the propensities of the child. Her heart once sunk into the vortex of thoughtless variety and folly, her mother was unable to restrain its downward progress; and as to her weak dissipated brother, Sir Edward, I have myself seen him, late at night, require her to come from her chamber to sing, or play, or spout, for the amusement of his inebriated companions;—conduct which the mother had not sufficient sense nor resolution to control. However, good fortune still gave Miss Barry a fair chance of rescuing herself, and securing complete comfort and high respectability. She married well, being united to Colonel Baldwin, a gentleman of character and fortune:—but alas! that delicacy of mind which is the best guardian of female conduct had been irrecoverably lost by her pernicious education, and in a few years she sank beyond the possibility of regaining her station in society.

Long after the period of her unhappy fall, I saw Mrs.

Baldwin at the house of a friend of mine, into which she had been received, under an assumed name, as governess. This effort, on her part, could not be blamed: on the contrary, it was most commendable; and it would have been both cruel and unjust, by discovering her, to have thwarted it. Though many years had elapsed, and her person had meanwhile undergone total alteration,—her size being doubled, and her features grown coarse and common,—I instantly recognised her as one whom I had known long before, but whose name I could not recollect. I had tact enough to perceive that she courted concealment, and, in consequence, I carefully abstained from any pointed observation. The mother of the children subsequently told me that her governess was an admirable musician, and took me to the door of her room to hear her play. She was sitting alone, at the piano. I listened with an anxiety I cannot describe nor indeed scarcely account for. She sang not with superiority, but in plaintive tones, which I was confident I had heard before, yet could not remember where,—when an air which, from a very peculiar cause, had in early days impressed itself *indelibly* on my memory, brought Miss Barry at once to my recollection. Her image swam into my mind as she appeared when youth, grace, innocence and accomplishments made her a just subject for general admiration, and had particularly attracted a friend of mine, Mr. Vicars, the brother of Mrs. Peter Latouche, who loved her to distraction.

Her secret I kept inviolably:—but some person, I believe, was afterwards less considerate, and she was discovered. Had I supposed it possible she could have then enfeebled the morals, or injured the habits, of my friend's children, I should myself have privately given her a hint to change her situation;—but I never should have *betrayed* the poor creature.—However, I conceived her at that time to be trustworthy in the execution of the

[135]

duties she had undertaken. She had suffered amply. Her own daughter resided with her, and scarcely ever left her side. No longer a subject for the irregular passions, she had just lived long enough, and felt keenly enough, to render her early follies a warning for her later years, and even to cause her to entertain disgust for those errors which had led her to destruction:—and I then believed, nor have I now any reason to question the solidity of my judgment, that she was on the direct road to prudence and good conduct.

I have related these events, as I confess myself to be an avowed enemy to a dramatic education. That sexual familiarity which is indispensable upon the stage under-mines, and is, in my opinion, utterly inconsistent with, the delicacy of sentiment, the refinement of thought, and reserve of action, which constitute at once the surest guards and the most precious ornaments of female char-acter. Strong minds and discriminating understandings may occasionally escape; but, what a vast majority of Thalia's daughters fall victims to the practices of their own calling!

But let us return to Kyle's boarding-house. The differ-ent pursuits adopted by these curious members of the society assembled there were to me subjects of constant entertainment. I stood well with all parties.

One day, after dinner, Lord Mountmorris seemed rather less communicative than usual, but not less cheer-ful. He took out his watch; made a speech, as customary; drank his *tipple* (as he denominated the brandy and water); but seemed rather impatient. At length, a loud rap announced somebody of consequence, and the Mar-quis of Ely was named.

Lord Mountmorris rose with his usual ceremony, made a very low bow to the company, looked again at his watch, repeated his congé, and made his exit. He entered the coach where Lord Ely was waiting, and away they drove. Kyle (a most curious man) instantly decided that a duel was in agitation, and turned pale at the dread of losing so good a lodger. Lieutenant Gam Johnson was of the same opinion, and equally distressed by the fear of losing his Lordship's interest for a frigate. Each snatched up his beaver, and with the utmost expedition, pursued the coach. I was also rather desirous to see *the fun,* as Gam (though with a sigh!) called it; and made the best of my way after the two mourners, not, however, hurrying myself so much—as, whilst they kept the coach in view, I was contented with keeping them within sight. Our pursuit exceeded a mile; when, in the distance, I perceived that the coach had stopped at Donnybrook-fair green, where, on every eighth of June, many an eye seems to mourn for the broken skull that had protected it from expulsion. I took my time, as I was now sure of my game, and had just reached the field when I heard the firing. I then ran behind a large tree, to observe further.

Gam and Kyle had flown towards the spot, and nearly tumbled over my Lord, who had received a bullet from the Hon. Francis Hely Hutchinson, (late Collector for Dublin,) on the right side, directly under his Lordship's pistol arm. The peer had staggered and measured his length on the greensward, and I certainly thought it was all over with him. I stood snugly all the while behind my tree, not wishing to have any thing to do at the coroner's inquest, which I considered inevitable. To my astonishment, however, I saw my Lord arise! and, after some colloquy, the combatants bowed to each other and separated; my Lord got back to his coach, with aid, and reached Frederick-street, if not in quite as good health, certainly with as high a character for bravery, as when he had left it. In fact, never did any person enjoy a wound more sincerely! He kept his chamber a month, and was inconceivably gratified by the number of inquiries daily made respecting his health—boasting ever after of the profusion of *friends* who thus proved their solicitude. His answer from first to last was—*"no better."*—To speak truth, one-half of the querists were sent in jest by those whom his singularity diverted.

ENTRANCE INTO PARLIAMENT

THE DAY on which I first took my seat in the Irish Parliament for the City of Tuam, I still reflect on as one of the most gratifying of my life. The circumstance, abstractedly, was but of secondary consideration; but its occurrence brought back to my mind the events of past ages, and the high respectability of the race from which I sprang. I almost fancied, as I entered the House, that I could see my forefathers, ranged upon those seats which they had so long and so honourably occupied in the senate of their country, welcoming their descendant to that post which had not for a few years past been filled by any member of the family. In fact, the purer part of my ambition was hereby gratified. I felt myself an entirely independent representative of an equally independent nation—as a man assuming his proper station in society, not acquiring a new one.

I confess I always had, and still continue to have, and to nourish, the pride which arises from having been born a gentleman. I am aware that wealth, and commerce, and perhaps talent, have, in modern times, occasioned family pride to be classed in the rank of follies, but I feel it, nevertheless, most strongly:—and if it be even a crime, I am culpable; if a folly, I submit to be regarded as imbecile. The sensations I experienced were indeed altogether delightful upon finding myself seated under that grand and solemn dome:—I looked around me, and saw the most dignified men of that day,—the ablest orators of the period,—many of the best-bred courtiers, and some of the most unsophisticated patriots, in the Empire! These, including a few friends and intimates of my family, were mingled, here and there, in amicable groups, and by turns kindly encouraged a young barrister, of only two years' practice, without patronage or party, as a fair aspirant to rank and eminence.

I was very greatly moved and excited: but it was not excitement of an ephemeral or feverish character; on the contrary, my emotions had their source in a tranquil, deep-seated, perhaps proud, satisfaction, impossible to be felt by any but such as might be placed in circumstances precisely similar.

There were members present, I have already said, with whom I was personally acquainted. My friend, Sir John Parnel,* partly, I am sure, on my account, and partly, no doubt, with a view to the service of government, lost no time in introducing me to many of his own particular friends.

I dined with him on that day: he was then Chancellor of the Exchequer. The entire party I do not recollect; but I remember perfectly those individuals of it with whom I subsequently cultivated acquaintance. Amongst them were Major Hobart (since Lord Buckinghamshire), Isaac Corry, Sir John (since Lord) De Blacquiere, Robert Thoroton, White, Marcus Beresford (Lord Clare's nephew), the present Lord Oriel (then Speaker), Thomas Burgh, of Bert, Sir Hercules Langreish, and James Cuffe, (since Lord Tyrawley). The scene was new to me:—hitherto, my society in Dublin had naturally fallen amongst the members of my own profession; we were all barristers, and I felt myself but a barrister: and though certainly we formed at that time the second-best society in Ireland, it was inferior to that of which I had now become a member. I found myself, in fact, associated as an equal in a circle of legislators whose good-breeding,

---

* Second Baronet; Chancellor of Exchequer, 1787; Lord of the Treasury, 1793; great-grandfather of Charles Stewart Parnell.

wit, and conviviality were mingled with political and general information. The first steps of the ladder were mounted; and as meanwhile Sir John's champaign was excellent, and quickly passed round, my spirits rose to a pitch far higher than in the morning, and any talent for conversation or anecodote which I might possess involuntarily coming out, Sir John Parnel, shaking his fat sides with laughter, according to his usual custom, said to me, before we broke up, "Barrington, you'll do!" upon which, Sir Hercules Langreish, who had very much the tone of a Methodist preacher, yet was one of the wittiest men in Ireland, immediately said,—"No—we must have another trial" and a day was fixed to dine with him.

My acquaintance soon augmented to a degree almost inconvenient. My *friendship* I limited to such men as I held to possess congeniality of sentiment; and before any long time had elapsed, I was not only the frequent guest of many of the distinguished characters of Ireland, but was considered as an early and favoured candidate for any professional promotion which the shortness of my standing at the Bar would admit of.

Reflecting, soon after I had taken my seat, on the novel nature of my situation, I felt that it was beset by considerable difficulties. I allude to the decision necessary for me to come to with respect to the line of politics I meant to pursue. I was not a *new* man, by whom any course might be taken, without exciting comment or question. On the contrary, I was of an old family, the importance and influence of which I was desirous to revive, and hence it became requisite that I should weigh my actions well, and avoid precipitancy.

Political parties at that time ran high, though but little individual hostility existed. Grattan, the two Ponsonbys, Curran, Brownlow, Forbes, Bowes, Daly, Connolly, Arthur Brown, and numerous other most respectable personages were then linked together in a phalanx of opposition which, under the name of Whiggery, not only assailed the government upon every feasible occasion, but was always proposing measures which under the then existing system were utterly inadmissible. The opposition had the advantage in point of ability, and, therefore, nothing but supreme talent had any chance, amongst them, of rendering its possessor useful or valued. Though my nature was patriotic, I ever respected the aristocracy, which, whilst the democracy exhibits a people's general character and energy, tends to embellish the state, and to give it an imposing grandeur.

The supporters of the Irish government, as I have said, were certainly inferior, except in patronage and power, to the opposition by which they were assailed. But they lived socially: there was a sort of convivial union amongst them, which, whether in high or low life, is, of all other ties, for a while most binding upon my countrymen. It was therefore rather inconsistent in Lord Clare* to give offence, as he did, to many of the most respectable gentlemen of Ireland by calling the Whigs an "eating and drinking club," since the sarcasm might, at least with equal justice, have been retorted on the supporters of His Majesty's government. All the great constitutional questions were, in 1790, supposed to have been arranged. Still the opposition sought a more radical reform, to which the government would not accede. They wrangled, in fact, about every trifle—and that at a time when the local concerns of the country were advancing to the highest pitch of prosperity. To neither party, however, attached any dishonourable stigma, which should prevent an honest man from joining their ranks; and meanwhile, I sought celebrity and advancement. The coast was clear before me. I was my own mas-

* John Fitzgibbon, Earl of Clare (1749–1802), Lord Chancellor of Ireland during the final years of the eighteenth century.

ter, and free to choose my own course. In case of my connecting myself with the Whigs, I saw that I must play but a very inferior part in their game. I felt that amidst such an assemblage of talent, I had but little right to expect eminence, and still less probability of acquiring professional advancement, even if my friends should become victorious. But, above all, I reflected that what at first view had appeared to me a blaze of constitutional patriotism, dwindled, on a closer inspection, into what is generally called party.

The country had prospered beyond all possible anticipation, and was still further advancing in prosperity, under the then existing system of administration. I did not perceive that any immediate change of men or of measures was at all in prospect, nor that it was at that moment necessary, or even desirable. My immediate personal connexions were on the side of the government. I had always doubted the sincerity of the Whigs: my doubts were now realized, and, on the whole consideration, I determined to attach myself to the administration. I had previously voted with them on the choice of a Speaker; but that I did not consider as constituting any pledge as to my future conduct. I voted for Mr. Forster, as the friend of Sir John Parnel, and because I considered him more fitting for the station than his opponent, Mr. William Ponsonby.

Thus my mind being at length made up, I determined to render myself of some importance to the side I had adopted. The common course of desultory debate, (even conquest over declaimers of my own calibre,) would have led to no distinction. I decided either to rise or fall; and with this view, resolved to fly at once at the highest game, in which attempt even if I should not succeed, the trial itself would be honourable. My earliest effort was therefore directed against the two most celebrated speakers of that period, Grattan and Curran; and on the first day I rose, I exhibited a specimen of what I may now call true arrogance. The novelty of such unexpected effrontery surprised the House, and afterwards surprised myself. It was a species of bold hardihood, which, I believe, no person who had a just sense of his own inferiority would have ventured on without great hesitation.—I launched into a strong philippic on the conduct of the most able and respectable opposition that Ireland had ever possessed. I followed and traced the Whigs, as I thought, through all their meanderings and designs. In a word, I surpassed the boundaries, not only of what I had myself resolved, but of what common prudence and propriety should have dictated. The government party, at the same time, was evidently not gratified. Its members, no doubt, considered me as a lost partizan, who had courted and called for my own suppression; and with some portion of the same feeling myself, I sat down almost ashamed of my forwardness, and awaiting, if not with resignation, at least with certainty, a just although cruel chastisement. How then must I have been surprised, and how wofully rebuked, by the mild and gentlemanly retorts which I received from Grattan! whilst Curran's good temper never showed itself more conspicuously than in his treating me merely with wit and facetiousness. I was abashed and mortified on contrasting the forbearance of those great men with my own intemperance. Had I perceived anything like contempt in that forbearance, I really believe I should have found it difficult to resume my spirits in the House; but no such feeling appeared towards me, and it is most singular to say, that some incidents which sprang from that very night's debate gave rise both to the friendship of Mr. Grattan, with which I was afterwards honoured, and to the close intimacy between me and Mr. Curran, which was never after interrupted.

I had the good fortune, on that occasion, to make one

fair hit as to Grattan, which he afterwards told me he was much pleased by. It came across me at the moment—in fact, most of the speeches I ever made have been literally *impromptu*. I never studied a set speech in my life, except on law cases; and perhaps to this circumstance I may honestly attribute an incorrectness of language that frequently attended my best efforts.

Grattan had repeatedly assailed our side of the house, as "a side from which all public virtues had long been banished." I observed, "that the right honourable gentleman had proved unequivocally the falsehood of his own assertion, that public virtue was confined to *one* side of the House—for I had had the honour of seeing the right honourable gentleman himself on *both*." I alluded to his having supported government against Mr. Flood, after the vote of £50,000 by Parliament. This joke was loudly cheered, and perhaps somewhat contributed to save me from discomfiture.

From that day I attached myself zealously and sincerely to the administration of Lord Westmoreland. I became more or less intimate with almost every member of my party in Parliament. I formed close and lasting friendships with Edward Cooke, the unfortunate and lamented Robert Thoroton, Isaac Corry, and Sir John De Blacquiere; and it was not very long before the opposition also opened their convivial ranks to receive me. Curran and Arthur Brown were the earliest of my intimates on that side the house; and before 1792 had expired, I felt myself as happy on all points, and as much befriended, as any man of my standing who had preceded me.

Before I went into Parliament, I had become acquainted with Mr. R. Thoroton, who had come over to Ireland with the Duke of Rutland. He had the manner of a coxcomb, but the heart of a friend and the sentiments of a gentleman. He was clerk of the House of Commons; and being by no means a common man, formed a necessary part of all our societies. He and I lived much together: and I found the intercourse very advantageous, since my friend knew every thing that was going forward, and, under the rose, set me right on many occasions. At the same time, I was aware that circumstances existed which were the cause, to him, of great anxiety; and, finally, a most unexpected event,—namely, the death of Mr. Thoroton by his own hand,—deprived me of one of the sincerest and most useful friends I ever possessed.

But amongst the foremost of all those persons who, from first to last, endeavoured to do me service, was a man universally esteemed for his gentlemanly manners, and as universally abused for public jobbing. As to the latter, it concerned not me; whilst his friendship was of the greatest advantage.

Sir John (afterwards Lord) De Blacquiere (I believe of Swiss descent,) had been colonel of a regiment of heavy cavalry in Ireland; had acted as Secretary of Legation in France with Lord Harcourt, and, having succeeded him there for a short time as Minister, came to Ireland with his Lordship as principal Secretary, and becoming a permanent resident, attached himself to that side of politics whence only he could derive the great object of his exertions,—a revenue sufficiently ample to enable him to entertain his friends as well, and far more agreeably, than any other person I had previously met. Nobody ever understood eating and drinking better than Sir John De Blacquiere; and no man ever was better seconded in the former respect than he was by his cook, Mrs. Smith, whom he brought from Paris, after he had been Minister there. His company seldom exceeded ten in number, but so happily was it selected, that I never yet saw a person rise from his table who did not feel gratified. Sir John was one of the old school; and with all the playful good-breeding by which it was distinguished, he had nothing of that starch pride which, in more recent times, has supplanted conviviality without making men either wiser, better, or happier.

Sir John certainly was a *pluralist,* enjoying, at one time, the first, the middle, and the last pension on the Irish civil list. He was Director of the Public Works in Dublin; and to his *jobbing* is that capital indebted for its wide streets, paving, lighting, and convenient fountains. He made as much as he could of these works, it is true; but every farthing he acquired in Ireland he expended in it. If his money came from the public purse, it was distributed to the public benefit: if he received pensions from the Crown, butchers, bakers and other tradesmen pocketed every shilling of it. He knew employment to be the best species of charity. In short, Sir John De Blacquiere was as much abused, and as much regarded, as any public character of any period.

THE LAW OF LIBEL

IN THE early part of my life, the Irish press, though supposed to be under due restraint, was in fact quite uncontrolled. From the time of Dean Swift, and *Draper's Letters* [*sic*], its freedom had increased at intervals not only as to public but private subjects. This was attributable to several curious causes, which combined to render the law of libel, although stronger in theory, vastly feebler in practice than at the present day; and whoever takes the trouble of looking into the Irish newspapers about the commencement of the American revolution, and in 1782, will find therein some of the boldest writing and ablest *libels* in the English language. Junius was the pivot on which the liberty of the press at one moment vibrated: liberty was triumphant; but if that precedent were to prevail to the same extent, I am not sure it did not achieve too much.

The law of libel in Ireland was formerly very loose and badly understood, and the courts there had no particular propensity for multiplying legal difficulties on ticklish subjects. The judges were then dependent; a circumstance which might have partially accounted for such causes being less frequent than in later times: but another reason, more extensively operating, was that in those days men who were libelled generally took the law into their own hands, and eased the King's Bench of great trouble by the substitution of a small-sword for a declaration, or a case of pistols for a judgment;—and these same articles certainly formed a greater check upon the propagation of libels than the twelve judges and thirty-six jurors, altogether, at the present day; and gave rise to a code of laws very different from those we call municipal. A third consideration is, that scolding-matches and disputes among soldiers were then never made matters of legal inquiry. Military officers are now, by statute, held unfit to remain such if they fight one another, whilst formerly they were thought unfit to remain in the army if they did not: formerly, they were bound to fight in person; now they can fight by proxy, and in Ireland may lure champions to contest the matter for them every day in the week, (Sunday excepted) and so decide their quarrels without the least danger or one drop of bloodshed. A few able lawyers, armed with paper and parchment, will fight for them all day long, and, if necessary, all night likewise; and that, probably, for only as much recompense as may be sufficient to provide a handsome entertainment to some of the spectators and to their pioneer attorney, who is generally bottle-holder on these occasions.

Another curious anomaly is become obvious. If *lawyers* now refuse to pistol each other, they may be scouted out of society, though duelling is *against* the *law!* but if military officers take a shot at each other, they may be dismissed from the army, though fighting is the essence and object of their profession: so that a civilian, by the new lights of society, changes places with the soldier;— the soldier is bound to be peaceable, and the civilian is forced to be pugnacious—*cedent arma togæ*. It is curious to conjecture what our next metamorphosis may be!

The late Lord Clonmell's heart was nearly broken by vexations connected with his public functions. He had been in the habit of holding parties to excessive bail in libel cases on his own fiat, which method of proceeding was at length regularly challenged and brought forward; and, the matter being discussed with asperity in Parliament, his Lordship was, to his great mortification, restrained from pursuing such a course for the future.

He had in the Court of King's Bench used rough language towards Mr. Hackett, a gentleman of the bar, the members of which profession considered themselves as all assailed in the person of a brother barrister. A general meeting was therefore called by the father of the bar; a severe condemnation of his Lordship's conduct voted, with only one dissentient voice; and an unprecedented resolution entered into, that "until his Lordship publicly apologised, no barrister would either take a brief, appear in the King's Bench, or sign any pleadings for that court."

This experiment was actually tried:—the judges sat, but no counsel appeared; no cause was prepared, the attorneys all vanished, and their Lordships had the court to themselves. There was no alternative; and next day, Lord Clonmell published a very ample apology, by advertisement in the newspapers, and, with excellent address, made it appear as if written on the evening of the offence, and therefore voluntary.

This nobleman had built a beautiful house near Dublin, and walled in a deer-park to operate medicinally, by inducing him to use more riding exercise than he otherwise would take. Mr. Magee, printer of the *Dublin Evening Post,* (who was what they call a little cracked, but very acute,) one of the men whom his Lordship had held to excessive bail, had never forgiven it, and purchased a plot of ground under my Lord's windows, which he called "Fiat-hill:" there he entertained the populace of Dublin, once a week, with various droll exhibitions and sports:—such, for instance, as asses dressed up with wigs and scarlet robes; dancing dogs, in gowns and wigs, as barristers; soaped pigs, &c. These assemblies, although productive of the greatest annoyance to his Lordship, were not sufficiently riotous to be termed a public nuisance, being solely confined to Magee's own field, which his Lordship had unfortunately omitted to purchase when he built his house.

The Earl, however, expected at length to be clear of his tormentors' feats—at least for awhile; as Magee was found guilty on a charge of libel, and Lord Clonmell would have no qualms of conscience in giving *justice* full scope by keeping him under the eye of the marshal, and consequently an absentee from "Fiat-hill," for a good space of time.

Magee was brought up for judgment, and pleaded himself, in mitigation, that he was ignorant of the publication, not having been in Dublin when the libel appeared; which fact, he added, Lord Clonmell well knew. He had been, indeed, entertaining the citizens under the Earl's windows, and saw his Lordship peeping out from the side of one of them the whole of that day; and the next morning he had overtaken his Lordship riding into town. "And by the same token," continued Magee, "your Lordship was riding *cheek by jowl* with your own brother, Matthias Scott, the tallow-chandler,* from Waterford, and audibly discussing the price of fat, at the very moment I passed you."

There was no standing this:—a general laugh was inevitable; and his Lordship, with that address for which he was so remarkable, (affecting to commune a moment with his brother judges) said,—"it was obvious, from the poor man's manner, that he was not just then in a state to receive definitive judgment; that the paroxysm should be permitted to subside before any sentence could be properly pronounced. For the present, therefore, he should only be given into the care of the marshal, till it

* Lord Clonmell and Matthias Scott vied with each other which had the largest and most hanging pair of cheeks—vulgarly called *jowls*. His Lordship's chin was a treble one, whilst Matthias's was but doubled;—but then it was broader and hung deeper than his brother's [Barrington's footnote].

[151]

was ascertained how far the state of his intellect should regulate the court in pronouncing its judgment." The marshal saw the crisis, and hurried away Magee before he had further opportunity of incensing the Chief-Justice.

Theophilus Swift, who, though an Irishman, practised at the English bar, gave rise to one of the most curious libel cases that ever occurred in Ireland, and which involved a point of very great interest and importance.

Theophilus had two sons. In point of figure, temper, disposition, and propensities, no two brothers in the whole kingdom were so dissimilar. Dean Swift, the eldest, was tall, thin, and gentlemanly, but withal an unqualified reformer and revolutionist: the second, Edmond, was broad, squat, rough, and as fanatical an ultra-royalist as the king's dominions afforded. Both were clever men in their way.

The father was a free-thinker in every respect;—fond of his sons, although materially different from either, but agreeing with the younger in being a professed and extravagant loyalist. He was bald-headed, pale, slender, and active—with gray eyes, and a considerable squint: an excellent classic scholar, and versed likewise in modern literature and belles lettres. In short, Theophilus Swift laid claim to the title of a sincere, kind-hearted man; but was, at the same time, the most visionary of created beings. He saw every thing whimsically—many things erroneously—and nothing like another person. Eternally in motion,—either talking, writing, fighting, or whatever occupation came uppermost, he never remained idle one second whilst awake, and I really believe was busily employed even in his slumbers.

His sons, of course, adopted entirely different pursuits; and, though affectionate brothers, *agreed* in nothing save a love for each other and attachment to their father. They were both writers, and good ones; both speakers and bad ones.

Theophilus had a competent private fortune; but as such men as he must somehow be always dabbling in what is called in Ireland "a bit of a law-suit," a large percentage of his rents never failed to get into the pockets of the attorneys and counsellors; and . . . he determined to change his site, settle in his native country, and place his second son in the University of Dublin.

Suffice it to say, that he soon commenced a fracas with *all* the Fellows of the University, on account of their "not doing justice somehow," as he said, "to the cleverest lad in Ireland!" and, according to his usual habit, he determined at once to punish several of the offenders by penmanship, and regenerate the great university of Ireland by a powerful, pointed, personal, and undisguised libel against its Fellows.

Theophilus was not without some plausible grounds to work upon; but he never considered that a printed libel did not admit of any legal justification. He at once put half a dozen of the Fellows *hors de société,* by proclaiming them to be perjurers, profligates, impostors, &c. &c.; and printed, published, and circulated this his *eulogium* with all the activity and zeal which belonged to his nature, working hard to give it a greater circulation than almost any libel published in Ireland, and that is saying a great deal!—but the main tenor of his charge was a most serious imputation and a very home one.

By the statutes of the Irish university,* strict celibacy is required; and Mr. Swift stated "that the Fellows of that university, being also clergy-men, had sworn on the Holy Evangelists, that they would strictly obey and keep sacred these statutes of the university, in manner, form, letter, and spirit, as enjoined by their charter from the

* That is, Trinity College, Dublin.

Virgin Queen. But that, notwithstanding such their solemn oath, several of these Fellows and clergymen, flying in the face of the Holy Evangelists and of Queen Elizabeth; and forgetful of morality, religion, common decency, and good example, had actually taken to themselves each one woman, (at least) who went by the name of *Miss Such-a-one,* but who, in fact, had, in many instances, undergone, or was supposed to have undergone, the ceremony and consummation of marriage with such and such a perjured Fellow and parson of Dublin University: and that those who had not so married, had done worse! and that, thereby, they all had so perjured themselves and held out so vicious a precedent to youth, that he was obliged to take away his son, for fear of contamination, &c. &c."

It is easy to conceive that this publication, from the pen of a very gentlemanly, well-educated barrister . . . naturally made no small bustle and fuss amongst a portion of the University-men. Those who had kept out of the scrape were not reported to be in any state of deep mourning on the subject, as their *piety* was the more conspicuous; and it could not hurt the feelings either of them to reflect that he might possibly get a step in his promotion, on account of the defection of those seniors whose hearts might be broken, or removal made necessary, by the never-ending perseverance of this tremendous barrister, who had christened his son *Dean* Swift, that he might appear a relative of that famous churchman, the patron and idol of the Irish people.*

The gentlemen of the long robe were, of course, delighted with the occurrence: they had not for a long time met with so full and fair an opportunity of expending

---

* This is a little unfair. In the first place, Theophilus Swift was actually related to Jonathan Swift, and, in the second place, Theophilus named his son for an illustrious ancestor, Admiral Deane.

every sentence of their wit, eloquence, law, and logic, as in taking part in this celebrated controversy. I was greatly rejoiced at finding on my table a retainer against the Fellows and parsons of Trinity College, whom I had always considered as a narrow-minded and untalented body of men, getting from £1000 to £1500 a year each for teaching several hundred students how to remain ignorant of most of those acquirements that a well-educated gentleman ought to be master of: it is true, the students had a fair chance of becoming good Latin scholars, of gaining a little Greek and Hebrew, and of understanding several books of Euclid, with three or four chapters of Locke's *On the Human Understanding,* and a sixpenny treatise on logic written by a very good divine, (one of the body) to prove clearly that sophistry is superior to reason. This being my opinion of them, I felt no qualms of conscience in undertaking the defence of Theophilus Swift, Esq. though most undoubtedly a libeller. It is only necessary to say, that Lord Clonmell, who had been (I believe) a sizer* himself in that university, and in truth, all the judges, (and with good reason) felt indignant at Theophilus Swift's so violently assailing and disgracing, in the face of the empire, the only university in Ireland.

The trial at length came on, and there were decidedly more parsons present than I believe ever appeared in any court of justice of the same dimensions. The court set out full gallop against us: nevertheless, we worked on—twice twelve judges could not have stopped us! I examined the most learned man of the whole university, Dr. Barret,†

* More properly "sizar"—what would be called nowadays a scholarship student.
† John Barrett (1753-1821), one of the great Irish eccentrics, Vice Provost of Trinity College 1807–21. Maurice Craig says of him: "He rarely ventured further than the Bank of Ireland across the street, where he used to lodge immense sums saved by paring candle-ends. But he once saw the sea at Clontarf, and described

a little, greasy, shabby, croaking, round-faced vice-provost: he knew of nothing on earth, save books and guineas—never went out, held but little intercourse with men, and none at all with women. I worked at him unsuccessfully for more than an hour; not one decisive sentence could I get him to pronounce: at length, he grew quite tired of me, and I thought to conciliate him by telling him that his father had christened me. "Indeed!" exclaimed he: "Oh! I did not know you were a Christian!" At this unexpected repartee, the laugh was so strong against me, that I found myself muzzled. My colleagues worked as hard as I: but a seventy-horse power could not have moved the court. It was, however, universally admitted that there was but one little point against us out of a hundred which the other side had urged: that point too had only three letters in it: yet it upset all our arguments: that talismanic word "law" was more powerful than two speeches of five hours each;—and, by the unanimous concurrence of the court and jury, Theophilus Swift was found guilty of writing, publishing, and undoubtedly *proving,* that certain parsons, Fellows of Dublin University, had been living (conjugally) with certain persons of an entirely different sex: and, in consequence, he was sentenced to twelve months' imprisonment in His Majesty's gaol of Newgate, where he took up his residence with nearly two hundred and forty felons and handy pick-pockets.

My poor visionary friend was in a sad state of depression: but heaven had a banquet in store for him which more than counterbalanced all his discomfitures:—an incident that I really think even the oracle of Delphos never would have thought of predicting.

The Rev. Doctor Burrows was, of all, the most in-

---

it thus: 'A broad flat superficies, like Euclid's definition of a line expanding itself into a surface, and blue, like Xenophon's plain covered with wormwood' " (*Dublin,* p. 185).

veterate enemy and active prosecutor of my friend Theophilus: he was one of those who, in despite of God and
Queen Elizabeth, had fallen in love, and indulged his
concupiscence by uniting his fortunes and person with
the object of it—and thereby got within the circle of
Swift's anti-moralists. This reverend person determined
to make the public hate Theophilus, if possible, as much
as he did himself; and forgetting, in his zeal, the doctrine
of libel, and the precedent which he had himself just
helped to establish, set about to slay the slayer, and write
a *quietus* for Theophilus Swift (as he supposed) during the rest of his days! Thus, hugging himself in all
the luxury of complete revenge on a fallen foe, Dr. Burrows produced a libel at least as unjustifiable against the
prisoner, as the prisoner had promulged against him: and
having printed, published, and circulated the same, his
Reverence and Madam conceived they had executed full
justice on the enemy of marriage and the clergy. But, alas!
they reckoned without their host: no sooner had I received a copy of this redoubtable pamphlet, than I
hastened to my friend Theophilus, whom, from a state of
despondency and unhappiness, I had the pleasure, in half
an hour, of seeing at least as happy and more pleased
than any king in Europe. It is unnecessary to say more
than that I recommended an immediate prosecution of
the Rev. Doctor Burrows, for a false, gross, and malicious
libel against Theophilus Swift, Esq. Never was any
prosecution better founded, or more clearly and effectually supported; and it took complete effect. The
reverend prosecutor, now culprit in his turn, was sentenced to one-half of Swift's term of imprisonment, and
sent off to the same gaol.

The learned Fellows were astounded; the university so
far disgraced; and Theophilus Swift immediately published both trials, with observations, notes critical and
historical, &c.

But, alas! the mortification of the reverend Fellow did not end here. On arriving at Newgate (as the governor informed me) the Doctor desired a room as high up as could be had, that he might not be disturbed whilst remaining in that mansion. The governor informed him, with great regret, that he had not even a pigeonhole in the gaol unoccupied at the time, there being two hundred and forty prisoners, chiefly pick-pockets, many of whom were waiting to be transported; and that, till these were got rid of, he had no private room that would answer his reverence: but there was a very neat and good chamber in which were only two beds—one occupied by a respectable and polite gentleman; and if the Doctor could manage in this way meanwhile, he might depend on a preference the moment there should be a vacancy. Necessity has no law; and the Doctor, forced to acquiesce, desired to be shown to the chamber. On entering, the gentleman and he exchanged bows—but in a moment both started involuntarily at sight of each other. On one was to be seen the suppressed smile of mental triumph, and on the other the grin of mortification. But Swift (naturally the *pink* of politeness) gave no reason for an increase of the Doctor's chagrin. As the sunbeams put out a fire, so did a sense of his folly flash so strong upon the Doctor's reason, that it extinguished the blaze of his anger; and the governor having left them, in a short time an *éclaircissement* took place between these two fellow-lodgers in a room fourteen feet by twelve! I afterwards learned that they jogged on very well together till the expiration of their sentences, and I never heard of any libel published by either the Doctor or Swift afterwards.

DR. ACHMET BORUMBORAD*

UNTIL England dragged the sister kingdom with herself into the ruinous expenses of the American War, Ireland owed no public debt.—There were no taxes, save local ones: the Parliament, being composed of resident gentlemen, interested in the prosperity and welfare of their country, was profuse in promoting all useful schemes; and no projector, who could show any reasonable grounds for seeking assistance, had difficulty in finding a patron. On these points, indeed, the gentlemen who possessed influence, were often unguarded, and sometimes extravagant.

Amongst other projectors, whose ingenuity was excited by this liberal conduct, was one of a very singular description—a Turk who had come over, or (as the *on-dit* went,) had *fled* from Constantinople. He proposed to establish, what was greatly wanted at that time in the Irish metropolis, "Hot and Cold Sea-water Baths;" and by way of advancing his pretensions to public encouragement, offered to open free baths for the poor, on an extensive

* This story has all the earmarks of a "tall tale." Yet Maurice Craig, who alone of Dublin's historians gives Barrington very much credit for authenticity, comments: "What is the truth of this matter? No other writer, that I know of, mentions this excellent anecdote: the Charlemont papers seem to be silent about Borumborad. But in 1771 the *House of Commons Journals* reveal financial support given to 'Dr. Achmet' for his baths, and so for several following years also. To sniff at Barrington as an historical authority seems to me the very nadir of ingratitude" (*Dublin,* pp. 271–72).

Since Barrington is the sole chronicler of this anecdote, the mention of "Afamado Hairductor Achmed Borumborad, M.A.C.A." on page 492 of *Finnegans Wake* makes it certain that Joyce was familiar with the *Sketches.*

plan—giving them, as a Doctor, attendance and advice gratis, every day in the year. He spoke English very intelligibly; his person was extremely remarkable; and the more so, as he was the first *Turk* who had ever walked the streets of Dublin in his native costume. He was in height considerably above six feet, rather pompous in his gait, and apparently powerful; an immense black beard covering his chin and upper lip. There was, at the same time, something cheerful and cordial in the man's address; and, altogether, he cut a very imposing figure. Every body liked Doctor Achmet Borumborad: his Turkish dress, being extremely handsome without any approach to the tawdry, and crowned with an immense turban, drew the eyes of every passer-by; and I must say that I have never myself seen a more stately-looking Turk since that period.*

The eccentricity of the Doctor's appearance was, indeed, as will readily be imagined, the occasion of much idle observation and conjecture. At first, whenever he went abroad, a crowd of people, chiefly boys, was sure to attend him—but at a respectful distance; and if he turned to look behind him, the gaping boobies fled, as if they conceived even his looks to be mortal. These fears, however, gradually wore away, and were entirely shaken off, on the fact being made public, that he meant to attend the poor; which undertaking was, in the usual spirit of exaggeration, soon construed into an engagement, on the part of the Doctor, to cure *all disorders whatever!* and hence he quickly became as much admired and respected as he had previously been dreaded.

My fair readers will perhaps smile, when I assure them that the persons who seemed to have the least apprehension of Doctor Borumborad, or rather to think

* Note that, although this whole chapter has the air of being an eyewitness account, Barrington could not have been more than eleven years old when the "baths" were subsidized. See preceding footnote.

him "a very *nice* Turk!" were the ladies of the metropolis. Many a smart, snug little husband, who had been heretofore considered "quite the thing,"—despotic in his own house, and peremptory commandant of his own family, was now regarded as a wretched, contemptible, close-shaven pigmy, in comparison with the immensity of the Doctor's figure and whiskers; and, what is more extraordinary, his good humour and engaging manners gained him many friends even among the husbands themselves! he thus becoming, in a shorter period than could be imagined, a particular favourite with the entire city, male and female.

Doctor Achmet Borumborad, having obtained footing thus far, next succeeded surprisingly in making his way amongst the Members of Parliament. He was full of conversation, yet knew his proper distance; pregnant with anecdote, but discreet in its expenditure; and he had the peculiar talent of being humble without the *appearance* of humility. A submissive Turk would have been out of character, and a haughty one excluded from society: the Doctor was aware of this, and regulated his demeanour with remarkable skill upon every occasion (and they were numerous) whereon (as a *lion*) he was invited to the tables of the great. By this line of conduct, he managed to warm those who patronized him into becoming violent partizans; and accordingly little or no difficulty was experienced in getting a grant from Parliament for a sufficient fund to commence his great metropolitan undertaking.

Baths were now planned after Turkish models. The money voted was most faithfully appropriated; and a more ingenious or useful establishment could not be formed in any metropolis. But the cash, it was soon discovered, ran too short to enable the Doctor to complete his scheme; and, on the ensuing Session, a further vote became necessary, which was by no means opposed, as the institution was good, fairly executed, and charitably applied. The worthy Doctor kept his ground: session after session he petitioned for fresh assistance, and never met with refusal: his profits were good, and he lived well; whilst the baths proved of the utmost benefit, and poor received attention and service from his establishment, without cost. An immense cold bath was constructed, to communicate with the river: it was large and deep, and entirely renewed every tide. The neatest lodging rooms, for those patients who chose to remain during a course of bathing, were added to the establishment, and always occupied. In short, the whole affair became so popular, and Dr. Achmet acquired so many friends, that the annual grants of Parliament were considered nearly as matters of course.

But alas! fortune is treacherous, and prosperity unstable. Whilst the ingenious Borumborad was thus rapidly flourishing, an unlucky though most ludicrous incident threw the poor fellow completely a-back; and, without any fault on his part, nearly ruined both himself and his institution.

Preparatory to every Session, it was the Doctor's invariable custom to give a grand dinner, at the baths, to a large number of his patrons, Members of Parliament, who were in the habit of proposing and supporting his grants. He always, on these occasions, procured some professional singers, as well as the finest wines in Ireland; endeavouring to render the parties as joyous and convivial as possible. Some nobleman, or commoner of note, always acted for him as chairman, the Doctor himself being quite unassuming.

At the last commencement of a Session, whereupon he anticipated this patronage, it was intended to increase his grant, in order to meet the expenses of certain new works, &c. which he had executed on the strength of the ensuing supply; and the Doctor had invited nearly thirty of the leading members to a grand dinner in his spacious saloon.

[162]

The singers were of the first order; the claret and champagne excellent; and never was the Turk's hospitality shown off to better advantage, or the appetites of his guests administered to with greater success. The effects of the wine, as usual on all such meetings in Ireland, began to grow obvious. The elder and more discreet members were for adjourning; whilst the juveniles declared they would stay for another dozen! and Doctor Borumborad accordingly went down himself to his cellar, to select and send up a choice dozen by way of *bonne bouche* for *finishing* the refractory Members of Parliament.

In his absence, Sir John S. Hamilton, though a very *dry* Member, took it into his head that he had taken enough, and rose to go away, as is customary in these days of freedom when people are so circumstanced: but at that period men were not always their own masters on such occasions, and a general cry arose of—"Stop, Sir John!—stop him!—the bonne bouche!—the bonne bouche!"—The carousers were on the alert instantly: Sir John opened the door and rushed out; the ante-chamber was not lighted; some one or two-and-twenty staunch Members stuck to his skirts; when *splash* at once comes Sir John, not into the street, but into the great *cold bath*, the door of which he had retreated by, in mistake! The other Parliament-men were too close upon the baronet to stop short (like the horse of a Cossack): in they went, by fours and fives; and one or two, who, on hearing the splashing of the water, cunningly threw themselves down on the brink to avoid popping in, operated directly as stumbling blocks to those behind, who thus obtained their full share of a *bonne bouche* none of the parties had bargained for.

When Doctor Borumborad re-entered, ushering a couple of servants laden with a dozen of his best wine, and missed all his company, he thought some devil had carried them off; but perceiving the door of his noble,

[163]

deep, cold salt-water bath open, he with dismay rushed thither, and espied eighteen or nineteen Irish Parliamentmen either floating like so many corks upon the surface, or scrambling to get out like mice who had fallen into a bason! The Doctor's *posse* of attendants were immediately set at work, and every one of the Honorable Members extricated: the quantity of salt-water, however, which had made its way into their stomachs, was not so easily removed, and most of them carried the beverage home to their own bed-chambers.

It was unlucky, also, that as the Doctor was a Turk, he had no Christian wardrobe to substitute for the well-soaked garments of the Honorable Members. Such dresses, however, as he had, were speedily put into requisition; the bathing attendants furnished their quota of dry apparel, and all was speedily distributed amongst the swimmers, some of whom exhibited in Turkish costume, others in bathing shifts; and when the clothes failed, blankets were pinned around the rest. Large fires were made in every room; brandy and mulled wine liberally resorted to; and as fast as sedan-chairs could be procured, the Irish Commoners were sent home, cursing all Turks and infidels, and denouncing a crusade against anything coming from the same quarter of the globe as Constantinople.

Poor Doctor Achmet Borumborad was distracted and quite inconsolable! Next day he duly visited every suffering Member, and though well received, was acute enough to see that the ridicule with which they had covered themselves was likely to work out eventually his ruin. His anticipations were well-founded; though the Members sought to hush up the ridiculous parts of the story, they became, from that very attempt, still more celebrated. In fact, it was too good a joke to escape the embellishments of Irish humour; and the statement universally circulated was—that "Doctor Borumborad had

nearly drowned nineteen Members of Parliament, because they would not promise to vote for him!"

The poor Doctor was now assailed in every way.
Among other things, it was asserted that he was the
Turk who had strangled the Christians in the Seven
Towers at Constantinople!—Though every body laughed
at *their own* inventions, they believed those of *other
people;* and the conclusion was, that no more grants
could be proposed, since not a single Member was stout
enough to mention the name of Borumborad! the laugh,
indeed, would have overwhelmed the best speech ever
delivered in the Irish Parliament.

Still, the new works must be paid for, although no
convenient vote came to make the necessary provision: the
poor Doctor was therefore cramped a little; but notwithstanding his embarrassment, he kept his ground well,
and lost no private friends except such as the wearing-off
of novelty estranged. He continued to get on; and at
length a new circumstance intervened to restore his happiness, in a way as little to be anticipated by the reader
as was his previous discomfiture.

Love had actually seized upon the Turk above two
years before the accident we have been recording. A respectable surgeon of Dublin, of the name of Hartigan,
had what might be termed a very "neat" sister; and this
lady had made a lasting impression on the heart of
Borumborad, who had no reason to complain of his suit
being treated with disdain, or even indifference. On the
contrary, Miss H. liked the Doctor vastly! and praised
the Turks in general, both for their dashing spirit and
their beautiful whiskers. It was not, however, consistent
either with her own or her brother's Christianity, to
submit to the Doctor's tremendous beard, or think of
matrimony, till—"he had shaved the chin at least, and
got a parson to turn him into a Christian, or something of
that kind." Upon those terms only would she surrender

[165]

her charms and her money—for some she had—to Doctor Achmet Borumborad, however amiable.

The Doctor's courtship with the Members of Parliament having now terminated, so far at any rate as further grants were concerned, and a *grant* of a much more tender nature being now within his reach, he began seriously to consider if he should not at once capitulate to Miss H., and exchange his beard and his Alcoran for a razor and the New Testament. After weighing matters deliberately, love prevailed, and he intimated by letter, in the proper vehemence of Asiatic passion, his determination to turn Christian, discard his beard, and, throwing himself at the feet of his beloved, vow eternal fidelity to her in the holy bands of matrimony. He concluded by requesting an interview in the presence of the young lady's confidant, a Miss Owen, who resided next door. His request was granted, and he repeated his proposal, which was duly accepted, Miss Hartigan stipulating that he should never see her again until the double promise in his letter was fully redeemed; upon which he might mention his own day for the ceremony. The Doctor having engaged to comply, took leave.

On the evening of the same day, a gentleman was announced to the bride-elect, with a message from Doctor Achmet Borumborad. Her confidential neighbour was immediately summoned; the gentleman waiting meantime in a coach at the door. At length Miss Hartigan and her friend being ready to receive him, in walked a Christian gallant, in a suit of full-dress black, and a very tall, fine-looking Christian he was! Miss H. was surprised; she did not recognise her lover, particularly as she thought it impossible he could have been made a Christian before the ensuing Sunday! He immediately, however, fell on his knees, seized and kissed her lily hand, and on her beginning to expostulate, cried out at once, "Don't be angry, my dear creature! to tell the honest truth, I am as good a Christian as the Archbishop; I'm your own countryman,

sure enough! Mr. Patrick Joyce* from Kilkenny county:
—the devil a Turk any more than yourself, my sweet
angel!" The ladies were astonished; but astonishment
did not prevent Miss Hartigan from keeping her word,
and Mr. and Mrs. Joyce became a very loving and happy
couple.

The Doctor's great skill, however, was supposed to lie
in his beard and faith;—consequently, on this *denouement*, the baths declined. But the honest fellow never had
done any discreditable or improper act; none indeed was
ever laid to his charge: he fully performed every engagement with the Parliament whilst he retained the
power to do so.

His beauty and portly appearance were considerably
diminished by his change of garb. The long beard and
picturesque dress had been half the battle; and he was,
after his transformation, but a plain, rather coarse, but
still brave-looking fellow. An old memorandum-book reminded me of these circumstances, as it noted a payment
made to him by me on behalf of my elder brother, who
had been lodging in the bathhouse at the time of the
swimming match.

I regret that I never inquired as to Joyce's subsequent
career, nor can I say whether he is or not still in the land
of the living. This little story shows the facility with which
public money was formerly voted, and at the same time
the comparatively fortunate financial state of Ireland at
that period, when the public purse could afford a multiplicity of such supplies without any tax or imposition
whatsoever being laid upon the people to provide for
them! How very different were the measures of that
Parliament even ten years afterwards!

---

* The reference to Borumborad-Joyce in *Finnegans Wake* (see
earlier footnote) takes on typical resonance with this revelation.
Joyce has himself in mind, as well as Borumborad, and also *Doctor
Patrick W. Joyce, M.R.I.A.* the well-known nineteenth-century
Irish antiquarian.

DONNYBROOK FAIR

THE SITE of the fair is a green flat of no great extent, about a mile from Dublin city, and on the banks of a very shallow stream that runs dribbling under a high bridge:—fancy irregular houses on one side, and a highroad through the middle, and you will have a pretty good idea of that plain of festivity.

Many and of various proportions were the tents which, in time past, composed the encampment upon the plains of Donnybrook; and if persevering turbulence on the part of the Emeralders should ever put it into the heads of the members of His Majesty's government to hire a few bands of *Cossacks* to keep them in order, (and I really believe they are the only folks upon earth who could frighten my countrymen,) the model of a Donnybrook tent will be of great service to the Don-Russian auxiliaries —the materials being so handy and the erection so *facile*. I shall therefore describe one accurately, that the Emperor Nicholas and his brother Michael, who has seen something of Ireland already, may, upon any such treaty being signed, perceive how extremely well his Imperial Majesty's Tartars will be accommodated.

Receipt for a Donnybrook Tent.

Take eight or ten long wattles, or any indefinite number, according to the length you wish your tent to be (whether two yards, or half a mile, makes no difference as regards the architecture of construction). Wattles need not be provided by purchase and sale, but may be readily procured any dark night by cutting down a sufficient number of young trees in the demesne or plantation of any gentleman in the neighbourhood—a prescriptive *privilege* or rather *practice,* time immemorial, throughout all Ireland.

Having procured the said wattles *one way or other,* it is only necessary to stick them down in the sod in two rows, turning round the tops like a woodbine arbour in a lady's flower-garden, tying the two ends together with neat ropes of hay, which any gentleman's farm-yard can (during the night time, as aforesaid) readily supply,—then fastening long wattles in like manner lengthways at top from one end to the other to keep all tight together; and thus the "wooden walls" of Donnybrook are ready for roofing in; and as the building materials cost nothing but *danger,* the *expense* is very trivial.

A tent fifty feet long may be easily built in about five minutes, unless the builders should adopt the old mode of *peeling* the wattles; and when once a wattle is stripped to its *buff,* he must be a wise landlord indeed who could swear to the identity of the timber—a species of evidence nevertheless that the Irish wood-rangers are extremely expert at. This precaution will not however be necessary for the Don Cossacks, who being educated as highway robbers by the Emperor of all the Russias, and acting in that capacity in every country, cannot of course be called to account for a due exercise of their vocation.

The covering of the tents is now only requisite; this is usually done according to fancy; and being unacquainted with the taste of the Russian gentlemen on that head, I shall only mention the general mode of *clothing* the wattles used in my time—a mode that, from its singularity, had a far more imposing appearance than any encampment ever pitched by His Majesty's regular forces, horse, foot, or artillery. Every cabin, alehouse, and other habitation wherein quilts or bedclothes were used, or could be procured by *civility* or *otherwise* (except *money,* which was not current for such purposes), was ransacked for *apparel* wherewith to cover the wattles. The favourite covering was *quilts,* as long as such were forthcoming; and when not, old winnowing sheets, sacks ripped open, rugs, blankets, &c. &c.—Every thing, in fact, was expended in the *bed* line (few neighbours using that accommodation during the fair)—and recourse often had to women's apparel, as old petticoats, praskeens, &c. &c.

The covering being spread over the wattles as tightly and snugly as the materials would admit, all was secured by hay ropes and pegs. When completed, a very tall wattle with a dirty birch-broom, the hairy end of an old sweeping brush, a cast-off lantern of some watchman, rags of all colours made into streamers, and fixed at the top by way of sign, formed the invitation to *drinking;*—and when *eating* was likewise to be had, a rusty tin saucepan, or piece of a broken iron pot, was hung dangling in front, to crown the entrance and announce good cheer.

The most amusing part of the coverings were the quilts, which were generally of patchwork, comprising scraps of all the hues in the rainbow—cut into every shape and size, patched on each other, and quilted together.

As to furniture, down the centre doors, old or new, (whichever were most handy to be *lifted,*) were stretched from one end to the other, resting on hillocks of clay dug from underneath, and so forming a capital table with an agreeable variety both as to breadth and elevation. Similar constructions for benches were placed along the sides, but not so steady as the table; so that when the liquor got the mastery of one convivial fellow, he would fall off, and the whole row generally following his example, perhaps ten or even twenty gallant *shamrocks* were seen on their backs, kicking up their heels, some able to get up again, some lying quiet and easy, singing, roaring, laughing, or cursing; while others, still on their legs, were drinking and dancing, and setting the whole tent in motion, till all began to long for the open air, and a little wrestling, leaping, cudgelling, or fighting upon the green grass. The tent was then cleaned out and prepared for a new company of the shillelah boys.

The best tents, that supplied "neat victuals," had a pot boiling outside on a turf fire, with good fat lumps of salt beef and cabbage, called "spooleens," always ready simmering for such customers as should like a *sliver*. The potatoes were plentiful, and salt Dublin-bay herrings also in abundance. There was, besides, a cold round or rump of beef at double price for the *quality* who came to see the *curiosities*.

Except toys and trinkets for children, merchandise of any sort they seemed to have a contempt for; but these were bought up with great avidity; and in the evening, when the parents had given the *childer* a glass each of the *cratur* (as they called whisky), "to keep the cowld out of their little stomachs," every trumpet or drum, fiddle, whistle, or pop-gun, which the fond mothers had bestowed, was set sounding (all together) over the green, and chimed in with a dozen fiddlers and as many pipers jigging away for the dance,—an amalgamation of sounds among the most extraordinary that ever *tickled* the ear of a musician. Every body, drunk or sober, took a share in the *long* dance, and I have seen a row of a hundred couple labouring at their jig steps till they fell off actually breathless, and rather *wetter* than if they had been river deities of the Donnybrook.

This however must be remarked as constituting a grand distinction between the beloved St. Bartholomew of the cockneys and the Emeralders' glory;—that at the former, robbers, cheats, gamblers, and villains of every description collect, and are most active in their respective occupations; whilst at the latter, no gambling of any sort existed;—nor were thieves, pickpockets or swindlers often there: for a good reason—because there was no money worth stealing, and *plenty* of *emptiness* in the

[171]

pockets of the amateurs. However, love reigned in all its glory, and Cupid expended every arrow his mother could make for him: but with this difference, that love is in general represented as discharging his shafts into people's hearts, whereas, at Donnybrook, he always aimed at their *heads;* and before it became quite dusk he never failed to be very successful in his archery. It was after sunset, indeed, that sweethearts made up their matches; and a priest (Father Kearny of Liffy Street, a good *clergy*) told me that more marriages were celebrated in Dublin the week *after* Donnybrook fair, than in any two months during the rest of the year: the month of June being warm and *snug* (as he termed it), smiled on every thing that was good, and helped the *liquor* in making arrangements; and with great animation he added, that it was a gratifying sight to see his young parishioners who had made up their matches at Donnybrook coming there in a couple of years again, to buy whistles for their children.

The *horse* part of the fair was not destitute of amusement—as there was a large ditch with a drain, and a piece of a wall, which the sellers were always called upon to "leather their horses over" before any body would bid for them; and the tumbles which those venturous jockies constantly received, with the indifference wherewith they mounted and began again, were truly entertaining.

The common Irish are the most heroic horsemen I ever saw :—it was always one of their attributes. They ride on the horse's bare back with rapidity and resolution; and coming from fairs, I have often seen a couple or sometimes three fellows riding one bare-backed horse as hard as he could go, and safely—not one of whom, if they were on their own legs, could stand perpendicular half a minute.

It is a mistake to suppose that Donnybrook was a remarkable place for fighting, or that much blood was ever drawn there. On the contrary, it was a place of good-humour. Men, to be sure, were knocked down now and then, but there was no malice in it. A head was often cut, but quickly tied up again. The women first parted the combatants and then became mediators; and every fray which commenced with a knock-down, generally ended by shaking hands, and the parties getting dead drunk together.

That brutal species of combat, *boxing,* was never practised at our fairs; and that savage nest and hot-bed of ruffians called the "Ring," so shamefully tolerated in England, was unknown among the Emeralders. With the shillelah, indeed, they had great skill, but it was only like sword exercise, and did not appear savage. Nobody was disfigured thereby, or rendered fit for a doctor. I never saw a bone broken or any dangerous contusion from what they called *"whacks"* of the shillelah (which was never too heavy) : it was like fencing: a cut on the skull they thought no more of than we should of the prick of a needle: of course, such accidents frequently occurred, and (I believe very well for them) let out a little of their blood, but did not for a single moment interrupt the song, the dance, the frolicking and good-humour.

THE FIRE-EATERS

IT MAY be objected that anecdotes of duelling have more than their due proportion of space in these sketches, and that no writer should publish feats of that nature (if feats they can be called), especially when performed by persons holding grave offices, or by public functionaries. These are very plausible, rational observations, and are now anticipated for the purpose of being answered.

It might be considered a sufficient excuse, that these stories refer to events long past; that they are amusing, and the more so as being matters of fact, (neither romance nor exaggeration,) and so various that no two of them are at all similar. But a much better reason can be given;—namely, that there is no other species of detail or anecdote which so clearly brings in illustration before a reader's eye the character, genius, and manners of a country, as that which exemplifies the distinguishing propensities of its population for successive ages. Much knowledge will necessarily be gained by possessing such a series of anecdotes, and by then going on to trace the decline of such propensities to the progress of civilization in that class of society where they had been prevalent.

As to the objection founded on the rank or profession of the parties concerned, it is only necessary to subjoin the following *short* abstract from a long list of official duellists who have figured [fired?] away in my time, and some of them before my eyes.—The number of grave personages who appear to have adopted the national taste, (though in most instances it was undoubtedly before their elevation to the bench that they signalised themselves in single combat,) removes from me all imputation

[174]

of pitching upon and exposing any unusual frailty; and I think I may challenge any country in Europe to show such an assemblage of gallant *judicial* and *official* antagonists at fire and sword as is exhibited even in the following list.

The Lord Chancellor of Ireland, Earl Clare, fought the Master of the Rolls, Curran.

The Chief Justice K.B. [King's Bench] Lord Clonmell, fought Lord Tyrawley, (a Privy Counsellor,) Lord Llandaff, and two others.

The Judge of the County of Dublin, Egan, fought the Master of the Rolls, Roger Barrett, and three others.

The Chancellor of the Exchequer, the Right Honourable Isaac Corry, fought the Right Honourable Henry Grattan, a Privy Counsellor, and another.

A Baron of the Exchequer, Baron Medge, fought his brother-in-law and two others.

The Chief Justice C.P. [Common Pleas], Lord Norbury, fought Fire-eater Fitzgerald, and two other gentlemen, and frightened Napper Tandy and several besides: one hit only.

The Judge of the Prerogative Court, Doctor Duigenan, fought one barrister and frightened another on the ground.—N.B. The latter case a curious one.

The Chief Counsel to the Revenue, Henry Deane Grady, fought Counsellor O'Mahon, Counsellor Campbell, and others: all hits.

The Master of the Rolls fought Lord Buckinghamshire, the Chief Secretary, &c.

The Provost of the University of Dublin, the Right Honourable Hely Hutchinson, fought Mr. Doyle, Master in Chancery, (they went to the plains of Minden to fight,) and some others.

The Chief Justice C.P., Patterson, fought three country gentlemen, one of them with swords, another with guns, and wounded all of them.

[175]

The Right Honourable George Ogle, a Privy Counsellor, fought Barney Coyle, a distiller, because he was a Papist.—They fired eight shots and no hit; but the second broke his own arm.

Thomas Wallace, K.C. [King's Counsel] fought Mr. O'Gorman, the Catholic Secretary.

Counsellor O'Connell fought the Orange chieftain: fatal to the champion of Protestant ascendency.

The Collector of the Customs of Dublin, the Honourable Francis Hutchinson, fought the Right Honourable Lord Mountmorris.

The reader of this dignified list (which, as I have said, is only an abridgment*) will surely see no great indecorum in an Admiralty judge† having now and then exchanged broadsides, more especially as they did not militate against the law of nations.

However, it must be owned that there were occasionally very peaceable and forgiving instances amongst the barristers. I saw a very brave King's Counsel, Mr. Curran, horse-whipped most severely in the public street, by a very savage nobleman, Lord Clanmorris; and another barrister was said to have had his eye saluted by a moist messenger from a gentleman's lips (Mr. May's) in the body of the House of Commons. Yet, both those little *incivilities* were arranged very amicably, in a private manner, and without the aid of any deadly weapon whatsoever, I suppose for variety's sake. But the people of Dublin used to observe, that a judgment came upon Counsellor O'Callaghan, for having kept Mr. Curran quiet in the horse-whipping affair, inasmuch as his own brains were literally scattered about the ground by an attorney very soon after he had turned pacificator.

* Two hundred and twenty-seven memorable and official duels have actually been fought during my grand climacteric [Barrington's footnote].
† I.e., Barrington himself.

In my time, the number of killed and wounded amongst the bar was very considerable. The other learned professions suffered much less.

It is, in fact, incredible what a singular passion the Irish gentlemen (though in general excellent-tempered fellows) formerly had for fighting each other and immediately making friends again. A duel was indeed considered a necessary piece of a young man's education, but by no means a ground for future animosity with his opponent.

Within my recollection, this national propensity for fighting and slaughtering was nearly universal, originating in the spirit and habits of former times. When men had a glowing ambition to excel in all manner of feats and exercises, they naturally conceived that manslaughter in an *honest* way (that is, not knowing *which* would be slaughtered,) was the most chivalrous and gentlemanly of all their accomplishments; and this idea gave rise to an assiduous cultivation of the arts of combat, and dictated the wisest laws for carrying them into execution with regularity and honour.

About the year 1777, the *Fire-eaters* were in great repute in Ireland. No young fellow could finish his education till he had exchanged shots with some of his acquaintances. The first two questions always asked as to a young man's respectability and qualifications, particularly when he proposed for a lady-wife, were,—"What family is he of?"—"Did he ever blaze?"

Tipperary and Galway were the ablest schools of the duelling science. Galway was most scientific at the sword: Tipperary most practical and prized at the pistol: Mayo not amiss at either: Roscommon and Sligo had many professors and a high reputation in the leaden branch of the pastime. When I was at the university, Jemmy Keogh, Buck English, Cosey Harrison, Crowe Ryan, Reddy Long, Amby Bodkin, Squire Falton, Squire Blake, Amby

[177]

Fitzgerald, and a few others, were supposed to understand the points of honour better than any men in Ireland,
and were constantly referred to.

In the North, the Fallows and the Fentons were the
first hands at it; and most counties could have then
boasted their regular *point-of-honour* men. The present
Chief Justice of the Common Pleas was supposed to
have understood the thing as well as any gentleman in
Ireland. In truth, these oracles were in general gentlemen
of good connexions and most respectable families, otherwise nobody would fight or consult them.

Every family then had a case of hereditary pistols,
which descended as a heir-loom, together with a long
silver-hilted sword, for the use of their posterity. Our
family pistols, denominated *pelters,* were brass (I believe my second brother has them still) : the barrels were
very long and *point-blankers*. They were included in the
armoury of our ancient castle of Ballynakill* in the reign
of Elizabeth, (the stocks, locks, and hair triggers were,
however, modern,) and had descended from father to
son from that period: one of them was named "sweet
lips," the other "the darling." The family rapier was
called "skiver the pullet" by my grand-uncle, Captain
Wheeler Barrington, who had fought with it repeatedly
and run through different parts of their persons several
Scots officers, who had challenged him all at once for
some national reflection. It was a very long, narrow-
bladed, straight cut-and-thrust, as sharp as a razor, with
a silver hilt, and a guard of buff leather inside it. I kept
this rapier as a curiosity for some time; but it was stolen
during my absence at Temple.

I knew Jemmy Keogh extremely well. He was considered in the main a peace-maker, for he did not like to
see any body fight but himself; and it was universally admitted that he never killed any man who did not well

* In County Galway.

deserve it. He was a plausible, although black-looking fellow, with remarkably thick, long eye-brows closing with a tuft over his nose. He unfortunately killed a cripple in the Phoenix Park, which accident did him great mischief. He was land-agent to Bourke of Glinsk, to whom he always officiated as second.

At length, so many quarrels arose without sufficiently *dignified* provocation, and so many things were considered as quarrels *of course,* which were not quarrels at all,—that the principal fire-eaters of the South saw clearly disrepute was likely to be thrown both on the science and its professors, and thought it full time to interfere and arrange matters upon a proper, steady, rational, and moderate footing; and to regulate the time, place, and other circumstances of duelling, so as to govern all Ireland on one principle—thus establishing a uniform, national code of the *lex pugnandi;* proving, as Hugo Grotius did, that it was for the benefit of all belligerents to adopt the same code and regulations.

In furtherance of this object, a branch society had been formed in Dublin termed the "Knights of Tara," which met once a month at the theatre, Capel-street, gave premiums for fencing, and proceeded in the most laudably systematic manner. The amount of the admission-money was laid out on silver cups, and given to the best fencers, as prizes, at quarterly exhibitions of pupils and amateurs.

Fencing with the small-sword is certainly a most beautiful and noble exercise: its acquirement confers a fine bold manly carriage, a dignified mien, a firm step, and graceful motion. But, alas! its practisers are now supplanted by contemptible groups of smirking quadrillers with unweaponed belts, stuffed breasts, and strangled loins!—a set of squeaking dandies, whose sex may be readily mistaken, or, I should rather say, is of no consequence.

The theatre of the Knights of Tara, on these occa-

[179]

sions, was always overflowing:—the combatants were dressed in close cambric jackets, garnished with ribbons, each wearing the favourite colour of his fair one: bunches of ribbons also dangled at their knees, and roses adorned their morocco slippers, which had buff soles, to prevent noise in their lunges. No masks or visors were used as in these more timorous times; on the contrary, every feature was uncovered, and its inflections all visible. The ladies appeared in full morning dresses, each handing his foil to her champion for the day, and their presence animating the singular exhibition. From the stage-boxes the prizes likewise were handed to the conquerors by the fair ones, accompanied each with a wreath of laurel, and a smile then more valued than a hundred victories! The tips of the foils were blackened, and therefore instantly betrayed the hits on the cambric jacket, and proclaimed without doubt the successful combatant. All was decorum, gallantry, spirit, and good temper.

The Knights of Tara also had a select committee to decide on all actual questions of honour referred to them: —to reconcile differences, if possible; if not, to adjust the terms and continuance of single combat. Doubtful points were solved generally on the peaceable side, provided women were not insulted or defamed; but when that was the case, the knights were obdurate, and blood must be seen. They were constituted by ballot, something in the manner of the Jockey Club; but without the possibility of being dishonourable, or the opportunity of cheating each other.

This most agreeable and useful association did not last above two or three years. I cannot tell why it broke up: I rather think, however, the original fire-eaters thought it frivolous, or did not like their own ascendency to be rivalled. It was said that they threatened direct hostilities against the knights; and I am the more disposed to believe this, because, soon after, a comprehensive code of the laws and points of honour was issued from the Southern fire-eaters, with directions that it should be strictly observed by all gentlemen throughout the kingdom, and kept in their pistol-cases, that ignorance might never be pleaded. This code was not circulated in print, but very numerous written copies were sent to the different county clubs, &c. My father got one for his sons; and I transcribed most (I believe not all) of it into some blank leaves. These rules brought the whole business of duelling into a focus, and have been much acted upon down to the present day. They called them in Galway "the thirty-six commandments."

As far as my copy went, they appear to have run as follows:—

The practice of duelling and points of honour settled at Clonmell summer assizes, 1777, by the gentlemen delegates of Tipperary, Galway, Mayo, Sligo, and Roscommon, and prescribed for general adoption throughout Ireland.

[Here follows a list of rules covering the fine points of dueling. This list, of which Rule 22—"Any wound sufficient to agitate the nerves and necessarily make the hand shake, must end the business for *that* day"—is typical, occupies eight pages of the original edition.]

These rules and resolutions of the "Fire-eaters" and "Knights of Tara" were the more deeply impressed on my mind, from my having run a great chance of losing my life, when a member of the university, in consequence of the strict observance of one of them. A young gentleman of Galway, Mr. Richard Daly, then a Templar, had the greatest predilection for single combat of any person (not a society fire-eater) I ever recollect: he had fought sixteen duels in the space of two years: three with swords and thirteen with pistols;—yet, with so little skill or so much good fortune, that not a wound worth mentioning occurred in the course of the whole. This gentleman after-

[181]

wards figured for many years as patentee of the Theatre Royal, Dublin, and had the credit of first introducing that superior woman and actress, Mrs. Jordan,* then Miss Francis, on the Dublin boards.

I was surprised one winter's evening at college by receiving a written challenge in the nature of an *invitation*, from Mr. Daly, to fight him early the ensuing morning. I never had spoken a word to him in my life and scarcely *of* him, and no possible cause of quarrel that I could guess existed between us: however, it being then a decided opinion that a first overture of that nature could *never* be declined, I accepted the *invitation* without any inquiry; writing, in reply, that as to place, I chose the field of Donnybrook fair as the fittest spot for *all* sorts of *encounters*. I had then to look out for a second, and resorted to a person with whom I was very intimate, and who, as he was a curious character, may be worth noticing. He was brother to the unfortunate Sir Edward Crosby, Bart. who was *murdered* by a court-martial at Carlow, May, 1798. My friend was afterwards called "Balloon Crosby," being the first aeronaut who constructed an Hibernian balloon, and ventured to take a journey into the sky from Ireland.†

* Dorothea Jordan (1762–1816), a famous actress. She later became a close friend of Barrington, and an even closer friend of the Duke of Clarence (William IV), by whom she had ten children.

† And a most unfortunate journey it was for the spectators! The ascent was from the Duke of Leinster's lawn, Merrion-square: the crowds outside were immense, and so many squeezed together and leaned against a thick parapet wall fronting the street, that it yielded to the weight and pressure, and the spectators and parapet wall came tumbling down together a great depth. Several were killed and many disabled; whilst Crosby sailed quietly over their heads, in all human probability, to be drowned before an hour had expired [Barrington's footnote].

Barrington's friend was Richard Crosbie (b. 1755). He made two flights in 1785—the first on January 19, which concluded with a landing on the North Strand. The second ascent, to which Barrington here refers, took place on July 19. On this occasion he

Crosby was of immense stature, being above six feet three inches high: he had a comely-looking, fat, ruddy face, and was, beyond all comparison, the most ingenious mechanic I ever knew. He had a smattering of all sciences, and there was scarcely an art or a trade of which he had not some practical knowledge. His chambers at college were like a general workshop for all kinds of artizans: he was very good tempered, exceedingly strong, and as brave as a lion—but as dogged as a mule: nothing could change a resolution of his, when once made; and nothing could check or resist his perseverance to carry it into execution. He highly approved of my promptness in accepting Daly's invitation, but I told him that I unluckily had no pistols, and did not know where to procure any against the next morning. This puzzled him: but on recollection, he said he had no complete pistols neither; but he had some old *locks, barrels, and stocks,* which, as they did not originally belong to each other, he should find it very difficult to make any thing of: nevertheless, he would fall to work directly. He kept me up till late at night in his chambers to help him in filing the old locks and barrels, and endeavouring to patch up two or three of them so as to go off and answer that individual job. Various trials were made: much filing, drilling, and scanning were necessary. However, by two o'clock in the morning, we had completed three entire pistols, which, though certainly of various lengths and of the most ludicrous workmanship, struck their fire *right well,* and that was all we wanted of them,—symmetry (as he remarked) being of no great value upon *these* occasions.

It was before seven o'clock on the twentieth of March,*

---

came down in the Irish Sea, but was rescued and received a hero's welcome. See J. T. Gilbert's *A History of the City of Dublin* (Dublin, 1861), III, 279–82, for details.

* Another example of Barrington's maddening habit of omitting the full date. Presumably the year is about 1780.

with a cold wind and a sleety atmosphere, that we set out on foot for the field of Donnybrook fair, after having taken some good chocolate and a plentiful draught of cherry brandy, to keep the cold wind out. On arriving, we saw my antagonist and his friend (Jack Patterson, nephew to the Chief Justice) already on the ground. I shall never forget Daly's figure. He was a very fine-looking young fellow, but with such a squint that it was totally impossible to say what he looked at, except his nose, of which he never lost sight. His dress (they had come in a coach) made me ashamed of my own: he wore a pea-green coat; a large tucker with a diamond brooch stuck in it; a three-cocked hat with a gold button-loop and tassels; and silk stockings; and a *couteau-de-chasse* hung gracefully dangling from his thigh. In fact, he looked as if already standing in a state of triumph, after having vanquished and trampled on his antagonist. I did not half like his steady position, showy surface, and mysterious squint; and I certainly would rather have exchanged *two* shots with his slovenly friend, Jack Patterson, than *one* with so magnificent and overbearing an adversary.

My friend Crosby, without any sort of salutation or prologue, immediately cried out "Ground, gentlemen! ground, ground! damn measurement!" and placing me on his selected spot, whispered into my ear "*Medio tutissimus ibis:** never look at the head or the heels: *hip* the maccaroni! the hip for ever, my boy! hip, hip!"—when my antagonist's second, advancing and accosting mine, said, Mr. Daly could not think of going any further with the business; that he found it was totally a mistake on his part, originating through misrepresentation, and that he begged to say he was extremely sorry for having given

---

* This phrase is taken directly from Ovid, *Metamorphoses*, Book II, lines 136–37. It might be best translated as, "You're safest going for the middle."

[184]

Mr. Barrington and his friend the trouble of coming out, hoping they would excuse it and shake hands with him. To this arrangement, I certainly had no sort of objection; but Crosby, without hesitation, said, "We cannot do that *yet,* sir: I'll *show* you we *can't:* (taking a little manuscript book out of his breeches pocket,) there's the *rules!*—look at that, sir," continued he, "see No. 7:—no apology can be received *after* the parties meet, *without a fire.* You see, there's the rule," pursued Crosby, with infinite self-satisfaction; "and a young man on his *first blood* cannot break rule, particularly with a gentleman so used to the sport as Mr. Daly. Come, gentlemen, proceed! proceed!"

Daly appeared much displeased, but took his ground, without speaking a word, about nine paces from me. He presented his pistol instantly, but gave me most gallantly a full front.

It being, as Crosby said, my first blood, I lost no time, but let fly without a single second of delay, and without taking aim: Daly staggered back two or three steps; put his hand to his breast; cried, "I'm hit, sir!" and did not fire. Crosby gave me a slap on the back which staggered me, and a squeeze of the hand which nearly crushed my fingers. We got round him: his waistcoat was opened, and a black spot, about the size of a crown-piece, with a little blood, appeared directly on his breast-bone. I was greatly shocked: fortunately, however, the ball had not penetrated; but his brooch had been broken, and a piece of the setting was sticking fast in the bone. Crosby stamped, cursed the damp powder or under-loading, and calmly pulled out the brooch: Daly said not a word; put his cambric handkerchief doubled to his breast, and bowed. I returned the salute, extremely glad to get out of the scrape, and so we parted without conversation or ceremony; save that when I expressed my wish to know the cause of his challenging me, Daly replied that he would *now* give no such explanation, and *his* friend then produced his book of rules, quoting No. 8 :—"If a party challenged accepts the challenge without asking the reason of it, the challenger is never bound to divulge it afterwards."

My friend Crosby, as I have mentioned, afterwards attempted to go off from Dublin to England in a balloon of his own making, and dropped between Dublin and Holyhead into the sea, but was saved. The poor fellow, however, died far too early in life for the arts and sciences, and for friendship, which he was eminently capable of exciting. I never saw two persons in face and figure more alike than Crosby and my friend Daniel O'Connell: but Crosby was the taller by two inches, and it was not *so* easy to discover that he was an Irishman.

DUELLING EXTRAORDINARY

OUR ELECTIONS were more prolific in duels than any other public meetings: they very seldom originated at a horse-race, cock-fight, hunt, or at any place of amusement: folks then had pleasure in view, and "something else to do" than to quarrel: but at all elections, or at assizes, or, in fact, at any place of business, almost every man, without any very particular or assignable reason, immediately became a violent partisan, and frequently a furious enemy to somebody else; and gentlemen often got themselves shot before they could tell what they were fighting about.

At an election for Queen's County, between General Walsh and Mr. Warburton, of Garryhinch, about the year 1783, took place the most curious duel of any which have occurred within my recollection. A Mr. Frank Skelton, one of the half-mounted gentlemen described [earlier],—a boisterous, joking, fat young fellow,—was prevailed on, much against his grain, to challenge the exciseman of the town for running the butt-end of a horse-whip down his throat the night before, whilst he lay drunk and sleeping with his mouth open. The exciseman insisted that snoring at a dinner-table was a personal offence to every gentleman in company, and would therefore make no apology.

Frank, though he had been nearly choaked, was very reluctant to fight; he said "he was sure to die if he did, as the exciseman could snuff a candle with his pistol-ball; and as he himself was as big as a hundred dozen of candles, what chance could he have?" We told him jocosely to give the exciseman no time to take aim at him, by which means, he might perhaps hit his adversary first, and thus survive the contest. He seemed somewhat encouraged and consoled by the hint, and most strictly did he adhere to it.

Hundreds of the towns-people went to see the fight on the green of Maryborough. The ground was regularly measured; and the friends of each party pitched a ragged tent on the green, where whiskey and salt beef were consumed in abundance. Skelton having taken his ground, and at the same time two heavy drams from a bottle his foster-brother had brought, appeared quite stout till he saw the balls entering the mouths of the exciseman's pistols, which shone as bright as silver, and were nearly as long as fusils. This vision made a palpable alteration in Skelton's sentiments: he changed colour, and looked about him as if he wanted some assistance. However, their seconds, who were of the same rank and description, handed to each party his case of pistols, and half-bellowed to them—"blaze away, boys!"

Skelton now recollected his instructions, and *lost no time:* he cocked *both* his pistols at once; and as the exciseman was deliberately and most scientifically coming to his "dead level," as he called it, Skelton let fly.

"Holloa!" said the exciseman, dropping his level, "I'm battered, by Jasus!"

"The devil's cure to you!" said Skelton, instantly firing his second pistol.

One of the exciseman's legs then gave way, and down he came on his knee, exclaiming "Holloa! holloa! you blood-thirsty villain! do you want to take my life?"

"Why, to be sure I do!" said Skelton. "Ha! ha! have I *stiffened* you, my lad?" Wisely judging, however, that if he staid till the exciseman recovered his legs, he might have a couple of shots to stand, he wheeled about, took to his heels, and got away as fast as possible. The crowd shouted; but Skelton, like a hare when started, ran the faster for the shouting.

Jemmy Moffit, his own second, followed, overtook, tripped up his heels, and cursing him for a disgraceful rascal, asked "why he ran away from the exciseman?"

"Ough thunther!" said Skelton, with his chastest brogue, "how many holes did the villain want to have drilled into his carcase? Would you have me stop to make a *riddle* of him, Jemmy?"

The second insisted that Skelton should return to the field, to be shot at. He resisted, affirming that he had done *all* that *honour* required. The second called him *"a coward!"*

"By my sowl," returned he, "my dear Jemmy Moffit, may be so! you may call me a coward, if you please; but I did it all for *the best*."

"The *best!* you blackguard?"

"Yes," said Frank: "sure it's *better* to be a *coward* than a *corpse!* and I must have been either *one* or *t'other* of them."

However, he was dragged up to the ground by his second, after agreeing to fight again, if he had another pistol given him. But, luckily for Frank, the last bullet had struck so fast between the bones of the exciseman's leg that he could not stand. The friends of the latter then proposed to strap him to a tree, that he might be able to shoot Skelton; but this being positively objected to by Frank, the exciseman was carried home: his first wound was on the side of his thigh, and the second in his right leg; but neither proved at all dangerous.

The exciseman, determined on *haling* Frank, as he called it, on his recovery challenged Skelton in his turn. Skelton accepted the challenge, but said he was *tould* he had a right to choose his own weapons. The exciseman, knowing that such was the law, and that Skelton was no swordsman, and not anticipating any new invention, acquiesced. "Then," said Skelton, "for my weapons, I choose my *fists:* and, by the powers, you gauger, I'll give you such a *basting* that your nearest relations shan't know you." Skelton insisted on his right, and the exciseman not approving of this species of combat, got nothing by his challenge; the affair dropped, and Skelton triumphed.

There could not be a better elucidation of Rule No. 5, of the code of honour, than an anecdote of Barry Yelverton,* second son of Lord Avonmore, Baron of the Exchequer.—Barry was rather too odd a fellow to have been accounted at all times perfectly *compos mentis.* He was a barrister. In a ball-room on circuit, where the officers of a newly arrived regiment had come to amuse themselves and set the Munster lasses agog, Barry, having made too many libations, let out his natural dislike to the military, and most grossly insulted several of the officers; abusing one, treading on the toes of another, jostling a third, and so forth, till he had got through the whole regiment. Respect for the women, and the not choosing to commit themselves with the black gowns on the first day of their arrival, induced the insulted parties to content themselves with only requiring Barry's address, and his hour of being seen the next morning. Barry, with great satisfaction, gave each of them his card, but informed them that sending to him was unnecessary;— that he was *his own second,* and would meet every man of them at eight o'clock next morning, in the ball-room; concluding by desiring them to bring their swords, as that was always his weapon. Though this was rather a curious rendezvous, yet, the challenged having the right to choose

* It is from this gentleman, or from his father (who had the same name), that Joyce derives the name of one of Leopold Bloom's accusers in the Circe sequence of *Ulysses:* "Mrs. Yelverton Barry." Note that the latter's husband is also a barrister "in the North Riding of Tipperary on the Munster circuit" (*Ulysses,* Random House 1961 edition, p. 465).

his weapon, and the place being *à propos,* the officers all attended next day punctually, with the surgeon of the regiment and a due proportion of small-swords, fully expecting that some of his brother gownsmen would join in the rencontre. On their arrival, Barry requested to know how many gentlemen had done him the honour of giving him the invitation, and was told their names, amounting to nine. "Very well, gentlemen," said Yelverton, "I am well aware I abused some of you, and gave others an offence equivalent to a blow,—which latter being the greatest insult, we'll dispose of those cases first, and I shall return in a few minutes fully prepared."

They conceived he had gone for his sword, and friends. But Barry soon after returned alone, and resumed thus: —"Now, gentlemen, those to each of whom I gave an equivalent to a blow, will please step forward:"—four of them accordingly did so, when Barry took from under his coat a bundle of switches, and addressed them as follows:—"Gentlemen, permit me to have the honour of handing each of you a switch (according to the rule No. 5. of the Tipperary Resolutions,) wherewith to return the blow, if you feel any particular desire to put that extremity into practice: I fancy, gentlemen, that settles *four* of you; and as to the rest, here, (handing one of his cards to each, with *I beg your pardon* written above his name) that's agreeable to No. 1." (reading the Rule) "Now I fancy *all* your cases are disposed of; and having done my duty according to the Tipperary Resolutions, which I will never swerve from,—if, gentlemen, you are not satisfied, I shall be on the bridge to-morrow morning, with a case of *barking-irons*." The officers stared, first at him, then at each other: the honest, jolly countenance and drollery of Barry were quite irresistible; first a smile of surprise, and then a general laugh, took place, and the catastrophe was their asking Barry to dine with them at the mess, where his eccentricity and good humour delighted the whole regiment. The poor fellow grew quite deranged at last, and died, I believe, in rather unpleasant circumstances.

Leonard M'Nally, well known both at the English and Irish bars,* and in the dramatic circles as the author of that popular little piece "Robin Hood," &c. was one of the strangest fellows in the world. His figure was ludicrous; he was very short, and nearly as broad as long: his legs were of unequal length, and he had a face which no washing could clean: he wanted one thumb, the absence of which gave rise to numerous expedients on his part; and he took great care to have no nails, as he regularly eat every morning the growth of the preceding day: he never wore a glove, lest he should appear to be guilty of affectation in concealing his deformity. When in a hurry, he generally took two thumping steps with the short leg, to bring up the space made by the long one; and the bar, who never missed a favourable opportunity of nicknaming, called him accordingly "one *pound* two." He possessed, however, a fine eye, and by no means an ugly countenance; a great deal of middling intellect; a shrill, full, good bar voice; great quickness at cross-examination, with sufficient adroitness at defence; and in Ireland was the very staff and standing-dish of the criminal jurisdictions: in a word, M'Nally was a good-natured, hospitable, talented, dirty fellow, and had, by the latter qualification, so disgusted the circuit bar, that they refused to receive him at their mess—a cruelty I set my face against, and every summer circuit endeavoured to vote him into

* Leonard MacNally or McNally (1752–1820) was indeed well known at the bar for his defense of Thomas Emmet, Napper Tandy, Wolfe Tone, and other rebels. He was one of the original members of the United Irishmen. After his death, it became known that he had for many years served as a spy for the Castle (that is, the British Government), especially during the 1790's. See W. J. Fitzpatrick's *The Secret Service under Pitt* (London, 1892), chap. xiv.

the mess, but always ineffectually, his neglect of his person, the shrillness of his voice, and his frequenting low company, being assigned as reasons which never could be set aside.

M'Nally had done something in the great cause of Napper and Dutton, which brought him into still further disrepute with the bar.* Anxious to regain his station by some act equalizing him with his brethren, he determined to offend or challenge some of the most respectable members of the profession, who, however, showed no inclination to oblige him in that way. He first tried his hand with Counsellor Henry Deane Grady, a veteran, but who, upon this occasion, refused the combat. M'Nally, who was as intrepid as possible, by no means despaired; he was so obliging as to honour me with the next chance, and in furtherance thereof, on very little provocation, gave me the retort *not* courteous in the court of King's Bench.†

I was well aware of his object; and, not feeling very comfortable under the insult, told him (taking out my watch) "M'Nally, you shall meet me in the Park in an hour."

The little fellow's eyes sparkled with pleasure at the invitation, and he instantly replied, "In *half an hour,* if you please," comparing, at the same moment, his watch with mine:—"I hope you won't disappoint me," continued he, "as that ——— Grady did."

* McNally had been counsel for Napper Tandy in a case against the Viceroy in 1792, and it is believed that McNally was even then disclosing secret information to the Crown.

† Fitzpatrick gives an interesting sidelight on this duel: "McNally, irrespective of the knowledge he possessed as counsel for the rebels, was himself a 'United Irishman.' An organ of that body, the *Northern Star,* on March 3, 1797, proudly describes him as such in connection with the fact that he challenged and fought Sir Jonah Barrington for having used disparaging language toward the United Irishmen" (*The Secret Service under Pitt,* p. 177). The duel itself apparently took place in 1794.

"Never fear, Mac," answered I, "there's not a gentleman at the bar but will fight you *tomorrow,* provided you live so long, which I can't promise."

We had no time to spare, so parted, to get ready. The first man I met was Mr. Henry Harding, a huge, wicked, fighting King's County attorney. I asked him to come out with me: to him it was fine sport. I also summoned Rice Gibbon, a surgeon, who being the most ostentatious fellow imaginable, brought an immense bag of surgical instruments, &c. from Mercers Hospital. In forty-five minutes we were regularly posted in the middle of the review-ground in the Phoenix-park, and the whole scene, to any person not so seriously implicated, must have been irresistibly ludicrous. The sun shone brightly; and Surgeon Gibbon, to lose no time in case of a hit, spread out all his polished instruments on the grass, glittering in the light on one side of me. My second having stepped nine paces, then stood at the other side, handed me a case of pistols, and desired me to "*work* away by J——s." M'Nally stood before me, very like a beer-barrel on its stilling, and by his side were ranged three unfortunate barristers, who were all soon afterwards hanged and beheaded for high-treason; namely, John Sheers, (who was his second, and had given him his *point-blanks,*) with Henry Sheers and Bagenal Harvey, who came as amateurs.* Both of the latter, I believe, were amicably disposed, but a negociation could not be admitted, and to it we went. M'Nally presented so coolly, that I could plainly see I had but little chance of being missed, so I thought it best

* John and Henry Sheares were first hanged and then beheaded for high treason on July 14, 1798. McNally was, along with Curran, one of the defense counselors at the preceding trial. McNally's role in this affair was ambiguous—he may have supplied the prosecutors with the details of the defense strategy. See Fitzpatrick, *The Secret Service under Pitt,* chap. xxi. Bagenal Harvey was to become commander-in-chief of the rebel forces at the Battle of Ross, June, 1798. See below, pp. 285 ff.

to lose no time on my part. The poor fellow staggered, and cried out, "I am hit!" and I found some twitch myself at the moment which I could not at the time account for. Never did I experience so miserable a feeling. He had received my ball directly in the curtain of his side. My doctor rushed at him with the zeal and activity of a dissecting surgeon, and in one moment, with a long knife, which he thrust into his waistband, ripped up his clothes, and exposed his naked carcase to the bright sun.

The ball appeared to have hit the buckle of his gallows (yclept suspenders), by which it had been partially impeded, and had turned round, instead of entering his body. Whilst I was still in dread as to the result, my second, after seeing that he had been so far protected by the suspenders, inhumanly exclaimed, "By J——s, Mac! you are the only rogue I ever knew that was *saved* by the *gallows*."

On returning home, I found I had not got off quite so well as I had thought; the skirt of my coat was perforated on both sides, and a scratch just enough to break the skin had taken place on both my thighs. I did not know this whilst on the ground, but it accounts for the *twitch* I spoke of.

My opponent soon recovered, and after the *precedent* of being wounded by a King's Counsel, no barrister could afterwards decently refuse to give him satisfaction. He was, therefore, no longer insulted, and the poor fellow has often told me since, that my shot was his salvation. He subsequently got Curran to bring us together at his house, and a more zealous friendly partisan I never had, than M'Nally proved himself, on my contest for the city of Dublin.

THEATRICAL RECOLLECTIONS

FROM MY youth I was attached to theatrical representa-
tions, and have still a clear recollection of many of
the eminent performers of my early days. My grandmother, with whom I resided for many years, had silver
tickets of admission to Crow-street Theatre, whither I
was very frequently sent.

The play-houses in Dublin were then lighted with tal-
low candles, stuck into tin circles hanging from the middle
of the stage, which were every now and then snuffed by
some performer; and two soldiers, with fixed bayonets,
always stood like statues on each side the stage, close to
the boxes, to keep the audience in order. The galleries
were very noisy and very *droll*. The ladies and gentlemen
in the boxes always went dressed out nearly as for court;
the strictest etiquette and decorum were preserved in
that circle; whilst the pit, as being full of critics and wise
men, was particularly respected, except when the young
gentlemen of the University occasionally forced themselves in, to revenge some insult, real or imagined, to a
member of their body; on which occasions, all the ladies,
well-dressed men, and peaceable people generally, de-
camped forthwith, and the young gentlemen as generally
proceeded to beat or turn out the residue of the audience,
and to break every thing that came within their reach.
These exploits were by no means uncommon; and the
number and rank of the young culprits were so great, that
(coupled with the impossibility of selecting the guilty,)
the college would have been nearly depopulated, and
many of the great families in Ireland enraged beyond

measure, had the students been expelled or even rusti-
cated.

I had the honour of being frequently present, and (as
far as in *mêlée,*) giving a helping hand to our encounters
both in the play-houses and streets. We were in the habit
of going about the latter, on dark nights, in coaches, and,
by flinging out halfpence, breaking the windows of all
the houses we rapidly drove by, to the astonishment and
terror of the proprietors. At other times, we used to
convey gunpowder squibs into all the lamps in several
streets at once, and by longer or shorter fusees contrive
to have them all burst about the same time, breaking every
lamp to shivers and leaving whole streets in utter dark-
ness. Occasionally we threw large crackers into the china
and glass-shops, and delighted to see the terrified shop-
keepers trampling on their own porcelain and cut-glass,
for fear of any explosion. By way of a treat, we used
sometimes to pay the watchmen to lend us their cloaks
and rattles: by virtue whereof, we broke into the low
prohibited gambling-houses, knocked out the lights, drove
the gamblers down stairs, and then gave all their stakes
to the watchmen. The whole body of watchmen belonging
to one parish (that of the round church) * were our sworn
friends, and would take our part against any other watchmen in Dublin. We made a permanent subscription, and
paid each of these regularly seven shillings a week for
his *patronage.* I mention these trifles, out of a thousand
odd pranks, as a part of my plan, to show, from a comparison of the past with the present state of society in
the Irish metropolis, the extraordinary improvement

---

* St. Andrew's Church, built in 1793 on Hoggen Green, near
Trinity College. It was often called the "round church" because
it was built somewhat in the shape of an ellipse. It was destroyed
by fire in 1860. Evidently the parish was established before the
church itself, as Barrington had become an M.P. by the time the
"round church" was actually built.

which has taken place in point of decorum within the last half-century. The young gentlemen of the University then were in a state of great insubordination;—not as to their learning, but their wild habits: indeed, the singular feats of some of them would be scarcely credible now; and they were so linked together, that an offence to one was an offence to all. There were several noblemen's sons with their silver-laced gowns, who used to accompany us, with their gowns turned inside out: yet our freaks arose merely from the fire and natural vivacity of uncontrolled youth: no calm, deliberate vices,—no low meannesses,— were ever committed: that class of young men now termed dandies we then called macaronies; and we made it a standing rule to thrash them whenever we got a fair opportunity: such also as had been long tied to their "mothers' apron-strings" we made no small sport with when we got them clear inside the college: we called them *milksops,* and if they declined drinking as much wine as ordered, we always dosed them, as in duty bound, with tumblers of salt and water till they came to their *feeding,* as we called it. Thus generally commenced a young man of fashion's noviciate above fifty years ago. However, our wildness, instead of increasing as we advanced in our college courses, certainly diminished, and often left behind it the elements of much talent and virtue. Indeed, I believe there were to the full as good scholars, and certainly to the full as high gentlemen educated in the Dublin University then, as in this wiser and more cold-blooded era.

I remember, even before that period, seeing old Mr. Sheridan* perform the part of Cato at one of the Dublin theatres; I do not recollect which: but I well recollect his dress, which consisted of bright armour under a fine laced scarlet cloak, and surmounted by a huge, white, bushy,

* I.e., Thomas Sheridan (1719–88), father of Richard Brinsley Sheridan.

well-powdered wig (like Dr. Johnson's), over which was stuck his helmet. I wondered much how he could kill himself without stripping off the armour before he performed that operation! I also recollect him particularly (even as if before my eyes now) playing Alexander the Great, and throwing the javelin at Clytus, whom happening to miss, he hit the cupbearer, then played by one of the hack performers, a Mr. Jemmy Fotterel. Jemmy very naturally supposed that he was hit *designedly,* and that it was some *new light* of the great Mr. Sheridan to slay the cup-bearer in preference to his friend *Clytus* (which certainly would have been a less unjustifiable manslaughter), and that therefore he ought to tumble down and make a painful end, according to dramatic custom time immemorial. Immediately, therefore, on being struck, he reeled, staggered, and fell very naturally, considering it was his *first death;* but being determined on this unexpected opportunity to make an impression upon the audience, when he found himself stretched out on the boards at full length, he began to roll about, kick, and flap the stage with his hands most immoderately; falling next into strong convulsions, exhibiting every symptom of exquisite torture, and at length expiring with a groan so loud and so long that it paralyzed even the people in the galleries, whilst the ladies believed that he was really killed, and cried aloud.

Though then very young, I was myself so terrified in the pit that I never shall forget it. However, Jemmy Fotterel was, in the end, more clapped than any Clytus had ever been, and even the murderer himself could not help laughing most heartily at the incident.

The actresses both of tragedy and genteel comedy formerly wore large hoops, and whenever they made a speech walked across the stage and changed sides with the performer who was to speak next, thus veering backwards and forwards, like a shuttlecock, during the entire

[199]

performance. This custom partially prevailed in the continental theatres till *very* lately.

I recollect Mr. Barry,* who was really a remarkably handsome man, and his lady (formerly Mrs. Dancer); also Mr. Digges,† who used to play the *Ghost* in *"Hamlet."* One night in doubling that part with Polonius, Digges forgot, on appearing as the *Ghost,* previously to rub off the bright red paint with which his face had been daubed for the other character. A spirit with a large red nose and vermilioned cheeks was extremely novel and much applauded. There was also a famous actor who used to play the *Cock* that crew to call off the *Ghost* when Hamlet had done with him: this performer did his part so well that every body used to say he was the best *Cock* that ever had been heard at Smock-alley, and six or eight other gentry of the dunghill species were generally brought behind the scenes, who, on hearing him, mistook him for a brother cock, and set up their pipes all together: and thus, by the infinity of crowing at the same moment, the hour was the better marked, and the *Ghost* glided back to the other world in the midst of a perfect chorus of cocks,—to the no small admiration of the audience.

Of the distinguishing merits of the old actors, or indeed of many of the more modern ones, I profess myself but a very moderate judge. One thing, however, I am sure of;—that, man or boy, I never admired tragedy, however well personated. Lofty feelings and strong passions may be admirably mimicked therein; but the ranting, whining, obviously premeditated starting, disciplined gesticulation, &c.—the committing of suicide in melliflu-

---

* Spranger Barry (1719–77) built the Crow Street Theatre in 1758.

† West Digges (1720–86), popular eighteenth-century actor. For an interesting anecdote about Sheridan and Digges see Constantia Maxwell's *Dublin under the Georges* (London, 1936), pp. 229–30.

ous blank verse, and rhyming when in the agonies of death,—stretch away so *very* far from nature, as to destroy all that illusion whereon the effect of dramatic exhibition in my mind entirely depends. Unless occasionally to witness some very celebrated new actor, I have not attended a tragedy these forty years; nor have I ever yet seen any tragedian on the British stage who made so decided an impression on my feelings as Mr. Kean,* in some of his characters, has done. When I have seen other celebrated men enact the same parts, I have remained quite tranquil, however my judgment may have been satisfied: but he has made me *shudder,* and that, in my estimation, is the grand triumph of the actor's art. I have seldom sat out the last murder scene of any play except *Tom Thumb,* or *Chrononhotonthologos,†* which certainly are no burlesques on some of our standard tragedies.

Kean's Shylock, and Sir Giles Overreach, seemed to me neither more nor less than actual *identification* of those portraitures: so much so, in fact, that I told him myself, after seeing him perform the first-mentioned part, that I could have found in my heart to knock his brains out the moment he had finished his performance.

Two errors, however, that great actor has in a remarkable degree: some of his *pauses* are so long, that he appears to have forgotten himself; and he *pats his breast* so often, that it really reminds one of a nurse patting her infant to keep it from squalling: it is a pity he is not aware of these imperfections!

The effect produced by even one actor, or one trivial incident, is sometimes surprising. The dramatic trifle called "Paul Pry" has had a greater run, I believe, than any piece of the kind ever exhibited in London. I went to see it, and was greatly amused—not altogether by the

* Edmund Kean (1787–1833), one of the greatest actors of his day.
† Burlesques by Henry Fielding and Henry Carey, respectively.

piece, but by the ultra oddity of one performer. Put any handsome, or even human-looking person, in Liston's place, and take away his umbrella, and Paul Pry would scarcely bring another audience. His countenance certainly presents the drollest set of stationary features I ever saw, and has the uncommon merit of being exquisitely comic *per se,* without the slightest distortion: no *artificial* grimace, indeed, could improve his *natural.* I remember O'Keeffe,* justly the delight of Dublin; and Ryder,† the best Sir John Brute, Ranger, Marplot, &c in the world: the prologue of "Bucks have at ye All!" was repeated by him four hundred and twenty-four times. O'Keeffe's Tony Lumpkin, Vandermere's Skirmish, Wilder's Colonel Oldboy, &c. &c. came as near nature as acting and mimicry could possibly approach. There was also a first edition of Liston as to drollery, on the Dublin stage, usually called "Old Sparkes." ‡ He was very tall, and of a very large size; with heavy-hanging jaws, gouty ancles, big paunch, and sluggish motion; but his comic face and natural drollery were irresistible. He was a most excellent actor in every thing he could personate: his grotesque figure, however, rendered these parts but few. Peachum, in the *Beggar's Opera,* Caliban, (with *his own* additions) in *The Tempest,* and all bulky, droll, low characters, he did to the greatest perfection. At one time, when the audiences of Smock-alley were beginning to flag, Old Sparkes told Ryder, if he would bring out the after-piece of *The Padlock,* and permit him to manage it, he would ensure him a succession of good nights. Ryder gave him his way, and the bills announced a first appearance in the part of Leonora: the *débutante* was reported to be a Spanish lady. The public curiosity was

* John O'Keefe (1747–1833), dramatist and actor.
† Thomas Ryder, at various times manager of both the Crow Street and Smock Alley theatres.
‡ Isaac Sparks (1719–76).

excited, and youth, beauty, and tremulous modesty were all anticipated; the house overflowed; impatience was unbounded; the play ended in confusion, and the overture of *The Padlock* was received with rapture. Leonora at length appeared; the clapping was like thunder, to give courage to the *débutante,* who had a handsome face, and was very beautifully dressed as a Spanish Donna, which it was supposed she really was. Her gigantic size, it is true, rather astonished the audience. However, they willingly took for granted that the Spaniards were an immense people, and it was observed that England must have had a great escape of the Spanish Armada, if the men were proportionably gigantic to the ladies. Her voice too was rather of the hoarsest, but that was accounted for by the sudden change of climate: at last, Leonora began her song of "Sweet Robin"—

> Say, little foolish fluttering thing,
> Whither, ah! whither would you wing?

and at the same moment Leonora's mask falling off, Old Sparkes stood confessed, with an immense gander which he brought from under his cloak, and which he had trained to stand on his hand and screech to his voice, and in chorus with himself. The whim took: the roar of laughter was quite inconceivable: he had also got Mungo played by a *real* black: and the whole was so extravagantly ludicrous, and so entirely to the taste of the Irish galleries at that time, that his "Sweet Robin" was encored, and the frequent repetition of the piece replenished poor Ryder's treasury for the residue of the season.

No modern comedy, in my mind, equals those of the old writers. The former are altogether devoid of that high-bred, witty playfulness of dialogue so conspicuous in the works of the latter. Gaudy spectacle, commonplace clap-traps, and bad puns, together with forced or mongrel sentiment, have been substituted to "make the unskilful laugh," and to the manifest sorrow of the "judicious." Perhaps so much the better :—as, although there are now most excellent scene-painters and fire-workers, the London stage appears to be almost destitute of competent performers in the parts of genuine comedy, and the present London audiences seem to prefer gunpowder, resin, brimstone, musquetry, burning castles and dancing ponies, to any human or Christian entertainments, evidently despising all those high-finished comic characters, which satisfy the understanding and owe nothing to the scenery.

There is another species of theatrical representation extant in France—namely, scriptural pieces; half burlesque, half melodrame. These are undoubtedly among the drollest things imaginable; mixing up in one unconnected mass, tragedy, comedy, and farce, painting, music, scenery, dress and undress, decency and indecency! *

I have seen many admirable comedians on the continent. Nothing can possible exceed Mademoiselle Mars, for instance, in many characters: but the French are all actors and actresses from their cradles; and a great number of performers, even at the minor theatres, seem to me to *forget* that they are playing, and at times nearly make the audience forget it too! Their spectacle is admirably good; their dancing excellent, and their dresses

* "Samson pulling down the hall of the Philistines" is the very finest piece of *spectacle* that can be conceived!—"Susannah and the Elders" is rather too naked a concern for the English ladies to look at, unless through their fans: transparent ones have lately been invented, to save the expense of blushes at the theatres, &c. But the most whimsical of their scriptural dramas is the exhibition of Noah as a *ship-builder,* preparatory to the deluge. He is assisted by large gangs of angels working as his journeymen, whose great solicitude is to keep their wings clear out of the way of their hatchets, &c. At length the whole of them *strike* and turn out for wages, till the arrival of a body of *gens d'armes* immediately brings them to order, by whom they are threatened to be sent back to heaven if they do not *behave themselves!* [Barrington's footnote].

beautiful. Their orchestras are *well filled,* in every sense of the word, and the level of musical composition not so low as *some* of Mr. Bishop's effusions. Their singing however is execrable; their tragedy rant; but their *prose* comedy very nature itself!

In short, the French beyond doubt exceed all other people in the world with regard to theatrical matters: and as every man, woman, and child in Paris is equally attached to *spectacle,* every house is full, every company encouraged, all tastes find some gratification. An Englishman can scarcely quit a Parisian theatre, without having seen himself or some of his family characteristically and *capitally* represented: the *Anglais* supply certainly an inexhaustible source of French mimicry; and as we cannot help it, do what we will, our countrymen now begin to practise the good sense of laughing at it themselves! John Bull thinks that roast beef is the finest dish in the whole world, and that the finest fellow in Europe is the man that eats it: on both points, the Frenchman begs leave, *tout à fait,* to differ with John; and nothing can be sillier than to oppose opinions with a positive people, in their own country, and who never yet, right or wrong, gave up an argument.

PROCESSION OF THE TRADES

NOTHING can better show the high opinion entertained by the Irish of their own importance, and particularly by that celebrated body called the Corporation of Dublin, than the following incident. Mr. Willis, a leather-breeches-maker in Dame-street, and a famous orator at the Corporation meetings, holding forth one day about the parochial watch (a subject which he considered as of the utmost general importance,) discoursed as follows: —"This, my friends, is a subject neither trifling nor obscure; the character of our Corporation is at stake on your decision!—recollect," continued he, "recollect, brother freemen, that the *eyes of all Europe are upon us !*"

One of the customs of Dublin which prevailed in my early days made such a strong impression upon my mind, that it never could be obliterated. The most magnificent and showy procession, I really believe, except those of Rome, then took place in the Irish metropolis every third year, and attracted a number of English quite surprising, if we take into account the great difficulty existing at that time with regard to travelling from London to Dublin.

The Corporation of the latter city were by the terms of their charter bound, once in three years, to perambulate the limits of the Lord Mayor's jurisdiction, to make stands or stations at various points, and to skirt the Earl of Meath's Liberties—a part of the city at that era in great prosperity, but forming a local jurisdiction of its own, (in the nature of a manor,) totally distinct from that of Dublin.

This procession being in fact partly intended to mark

and to designate the extreme boundaries of his Lordship's jurisdiction, at those points where they touch the Earl of Meath's Liberty, the Lord Mayor thrust his sword through the wall of a certain house;—and then concluded the ceremony by approaching the sea at low water, and hurling a javelin as far upon the sands as his strength admitted, which was understood to form the boundary between him and Neptune.

The trade of Dublin is comprised of twenty-five corporations, or guilds, each independent of the other, and represented, as in London, by a common council. Every one of these comprised its masters, journeymen, and apprentices;—and each guild had a patron saint, or protector, whose image or emblem was on all great occasions dressed up in appropriate habiliments.

For this procession, every member of the twenty-five corporations prepared as for a jubilee. Small funds only were collected, and each individual gladly bore his extra charges—the masters and journeymen being desirous of outvying one another, and conceiving that the gayer they appeared on that great day, the more consideration would they be entitled to throughout the ensuing three years! Of course, therefore, such as could afford it spared no expense: they borrowed the finest horses and trappings which could be procured; the masters rode—the journeymen walked, and were succeeded by the apprentices.

Every corporation had an immense carriage, with a great platform and high canopy,—the whole radiant with gilding, ribbons, and draperies, and drawn by six or eight horses equally decked and caparisoned;—their colours and flags flying in all directions. On these platforms, which were fitted up as work-shops, were the implements of the respective trades, and expert hands were actually at work during the entire perambulation, which generally lasted eight or nine hours.—The procession indeed took two hours to pass. The narrow-weavers wove ribbons which they threw to the spectators:—the others tossed into the air small patterns of the fabric they worked upon: the printers were employed in striking off innumerable hand-bills, with songs and odes to the Lord Mayor.

But the smiths' part of the spectacle was the most gaudy: they had their forge in full work, and were attended by a very high phaeton adorned in every way they could think of—the horses covered with flowers and coloured streamers. In this phaeton sat the most beautiful girl they could possibly procure, in the character of wife to their patron, Vulcan. It is unnecessary to describe her dress: suffice it to say, it approached that of a Venus as nearly as decency would permit: a blue scarf, covered with silver doves, was used at her discretion, and four or five little Cupids, attired like pages, (aiming with bows and arrows at the ladies in the windows,) played at her feet. On one side rode, on the largest horse which could be provided, a huge fellow, representing Vulcan, dressed *cap-a-pie* in coal-black armour, and flourishing an immense smith's sledge-hammer! On the other side pranced his rival, Mars, on a tawdry-caparisoned charger, in shining armour, (with an immensity of feathers and horse-hair) and brandishing a two-edged glittering sword six or eight feet long—Venus meantime seeming to pay much more attention to her gallant than to her husband. Behind the phaeton, rode Argus, with an immense peacock's tail; whilst numerous other gods and goddesses, saints, devils, satyrs, &c. were distributed in the procession.

The skinners and tanners seemed to undergo no slight penance; a considerable number of these artisans being dressed up close in sheep and goat skins of different colours. The representatives of the butchers were enveloped in hides, with long towering horns, and rode along brandishing knives and cleavers!—a most formidable-looking corporation! The apothecaries made up and distributed pills and boluses on their platform, which was furnished

[208]

with numerous pestles and mortars so contrived as to sound, in the grinding, like bells, and pounding out some popular air. Each corporation had its appropriate band and colours; perfect order was maintained; and so proud was the Dublin mob of what they called their *fringes,* that on these peculiar occasions, they managed to behave with great decorum and propriety.

I never could guess the reason why—but the crowd seemed ever in the most anxious expectation to see *the tailors,* who were certainly the favourites. The master-tailors usually borrowed the best horses from their customers; and as they were not accustomed to horseback, the scene was highly ludicrous. A tailor on a spirited horse has always been esteemed a curiosity: but a troop of a hundred and fifty tailors, all decked with ribbons and lace and every species of finery, on horses equally smart, presented a spectacle outvying description! The journeymen and apprentices walked—except that number of workmen on the platform. St. Crispin with his last, St. Andrew with his cross, and St. Luke with his gridiron, were all included in the show; as were the city officers in their full robes and paraphernalia. The guild of merchants, being under the especial patronage of the Holy Trinity, could not, with all their ingenuity, find out any unprofane emblem, except a shamrock, of huge dimensions! the three distinct leaves whereof are on one stalk. This, by the way, offered St. Patrick means of explaining the Trinity, and thereby of converting the Irish to Christianity; and, hence, the shamrock became the national emblem of Ireland. The merchants had also a large ship on wheels, drawn and manned by *real* sailors.

This singular procession I twice witnessed: it has since been abolished, after having worked well, and done no harm, from the days of the very first Lord Mayor of Dublin. The city authorities, however, began at length to think venison and claret would be better things for the same expense; and so it was decided that the money should remain in the purse of the Corporation, and a wretched substitute for the old ceremony was arranged. The Lord Mayor and sheriffs, with some dozen of dirty constables, now perambulate these bounds in privacy and silence;—thus defeating, in my mind, the very *intention* of their charter, and taking away a triennial prospective object of great attraction and pride to the inhabitants of the metropolis of Ireland, for the sole purpose of gratifying the sensual appetites of a city aristocracy, who court satiety and indigestion at the expense of their humbler brethren.

ALDERMEN OF SKINNERS' ALLEY

ORANGE societies, as they are termed, were first formed by the Protestants to oppose and counteract the turbulent demonstrations of the Catholics, who formed the population of the south of Ireland. But at their commencement, the Orangemen certainly adopted a principle of interference which was not confined to religious points alone, but went to put down *all* popular insurrections which might arise on any point. The term, *Protestant ascendancy,* was coined by Mr. John Gifford,* (of whom more hereafter) and became an epithet very fatal to the peace of Ireland. Many associations indeed were, from time to time, originated: some for *reform;* others to oppose it; some for *toleration,* others for intolerance! There were good men and loyal subjects among the members of each; including many who never entertained the most distant idea of those disastrous results to be apprehended, at the feverish period preceding the revolution of 1798, from any encouragement to innovation.

I followed up the principles my family had invariably pursued from their first settlement in Ireland; namely, an attachment divided between the Crown and the people. In the year 1795, I saw that the people were likely to grow too strong for the Crown; and therefore became at once, not indeed an *ultra*—but one in whom loyalty absorbed almost every other consideration. I willingly united in every effort to check the rising spirit of popular

* John Giffard became editor of the *Dublin Journal,* which favored the government and violently opposed the United Irishmen.

[211]

disaffection—the dreadful results of which were manifested in the atrocities acting throughout France, and in the tottering state of the crowns of Europe.

I had been previously initiated by my friend, Doctor Duigenan,* judge of the Prerogative Court, into a very curious but most loyal society, whereof he was grandmaster at the time of my election; and as this club differed essentially from any other in the empire, it may be amusing to describe it—a labour which nobody has hitherto, I believe, undertaken.

This curious assemblage was called "The Alderman of Skinners' Alley:" it was the first Orange association ever formed; and having, at the period I allude to, existed a full century in pristine vigour, it had acquired considerable local influence and importance. Its origin was as follows:—After William the Third had mounted the English throne, and King James had assumed the reins of government in Ireland, the latter monarch annulled the then existing charter of the Dublin Corporation, dismissed all the aldermen who had espoused the revolutionary cause, and replaced them by others attached to himself. In doing this he was certainly justifiable;—the deposed aldermen, however, had secreted some little articles of their paraphernalia, and privately assembled in an alehouse in Skinners' Alley, a very obscure part of the capital: here they continued to hold Anti-Jacobite meetings; elected their own lord mayor and officers; and got a marble bust of King William, which they regarded as a sort of deity! These meetings were carried on till the battle of the Boyne put William in possession of Dublin, when King James's aldermen were immediately cash-

* Patrick Duigenan (1735–1826) was a Fellow of Trinity College and was also active in the Irish Parliament. By all accounts he was the most rabid anti-Catholic of his day. (I have often wondered whether Joyce rather ironically derived from this gentleman the name of Paddy Dignam in *Ulysses*.)

iered, and *the Aldermen of Skinners' Alley* reinvested with their mace and aldermanic glories.

To honour the memory of their restorer, therefore, a permanent association was formed, and invested with all the memorials of their former disgrace and latter reinstatement. This organization, constituted near a century before, remained, I fancy, quite unaltered at the time I became a member. To make the general influence of this association the greater, the number of members was unlimited, and the mode of admission solely by the proposal and seconding of tried *aldermen*. For the same reason, no class, however humble, was excluded—equality reigning in its most perfect state at the assemblies. Generals and wig-makers—King's Counsel and hackney clerks, &c. all mingled without distinction as brother-aldermen:—a lord mayor was annually appointed; and regularity and decorum always prevailed—until, at least, towards the *conclusion* of the meetings, when the aldermen became more than usually noisy and exhilarated,—King William's bust being placed in the centre of the supper-table, to over-look their extreme loyalty. The times of meeting were monthly; and every member paid sixpence per month, which sum (allowing for the absentees) afforded plenty of eatables, porter and punch, for the supping aldermen.

Their charter-dish was *sheeps' trotters* (in allusion to King James's running away from Dublin):—rum-punch in blue jugs, whiskey-punch in white ones, and *porter* in its *pewter,* were scattered plentifully over the table; and all regular formalities being gone through, and the eating part of the ceremony ended, the real *business* began by a general chorus of "God save the King!" whereupon the grand engine, which, as a loyal and facetious shoemaker observed, would *bind* every *sole* of them together, and commemorate them *all* till the end of time,

[213]

was set at work by order of the *lord mayor*. This engine was the charter-toast, always given with nine times nine! and duly succeeded by vociferous acclamations.

The 1st of July, (anniversary of the battle of the Boyne) [old style] was the favourite night of assembly: then every man unbuttoned the knees of his breeches, and drank the toast on his bare joints—it being pronounced by *his lordship* in the following words, composed expressly for the purpose in the year 1689; afterwards adopted by the Orange Societies generally; and still, I believe, considered as the charter-toast of them all.

This most ancient and unparalleled *sentiment* runs thus:—

ORANGE TOAST

"The glorious,—pious,—and immortal memory of the great and good King William:—not forgetting Oliver Cromwell, who assisted in redeeming us from popery, slavery, arbitrary power, brass-money, and wooden shoes. May we never want a Williamite to kick the * * * * of a Jacobite!—and a * * * * for the *Bishop of Cork!* And he that won't drink this, whether he be priest, bishop, deacon, bellows-blower, grave-digger, or any other of the fraternity of *the clergy;*—may a north wind blow him to the south, and a west wind blow him to the east! May he have a dark night—a lee shore—a rank storm—and a leaky vessel, to carry him over the river Styx! May the dog Cerberus make a meal of his r——p, and Pluto a snuff-box of his scull; and may the devil jump down his throat with a red-hot harrow, with every pin tear out a gut, and blow him with a *clean* carcase to hell! *Amen!*"

The extraordinary zeal wherewith this toast was drunk, could only be equalled by the enthusiasm with which the blue and white jugs and pewter pots were

* According to Constantia Maxwell, "Peter Browne, (d. 1735), Bishop of Cork and Ross, wrote a 'Discourse upon drinking Healths' in 1716, in which he denounced the practice as leading to drunkenness and ill-feeling" (*Dublin under the Georges*, p. 102n.).

resorted to, to ascertain the quality of the potation within: both processes serving to indicate the quantity of loyalty entertained by every alderman towards the King, Doctor Duigenan, and the Protestant Religion!—they then rebuttoned the knees of their breeches (trousers had not come into fashion), and sat down *to work* again in downright earnest. Mr. Powell, a jolly apothecary, (till he was killed, by *singing* I suppose,) led, in my time, the vocal band; and after a dozen speeches, accompanied by numerous replenishments of the jugs, &c. every body who had *any thing to do in the morning* generally withdrew, leaving the rest of the loyalists to finish the last drop.

The idea of "Orange Societies" arose, in my opinion, from this association. I believe it exists still; but has, I understand, degenerated into a sort of *half-mounted* club;—not exclusive enough for gentlemen, and too fine for wig-makers: it has sunk into a paltry and unimportant corporate utensil.

I recollect an amusing circumstance which many years back occurred in this lodge. Until politics grew too hot, Napper Tandy and several other of the *patriots* were *aldermen:* but finding that ultra-loyalty was making way too fast for their notions, they sought some fair opportunity of seceding from the club, stealing the mace, and regenerating the whole board and establishment of Skinners'-alley! and the opportunity was not long wanting.

An apothecary, of the name of M'Mahon, had become an alderman solely to avoid being considered a friend of the Pope: this, in point of reality, he was; but since, at that period, his creed was not the popular one, he conceived that he might thrive better in his business by appearing a staunch Protestant; or at least might learn, by association, some valuable secrets, and then betray them to his own sect.

But M'Mahon, although a clever person, was, like many an honest fellow, vastly more candid when he got "the sup in" than he had ever intended to be, indeed, in these circumstances, whatever a man thinks often comes out in spite of him, as if it disagreed with his liquor! Thus one unfortunate night, "Doctor M'Mahon, the apothecary," (as he was termed in Armiger-street,) having made too free amongst his brother-aldermen and been completely overmastered by the blue jug, forgot his company, and began to speak rather unkindly of King William. His worthy associates, who had made similar applications to the *blue* and *white,* took fire at this *sacrilege* offered to their patron saint: one word brought on another;—the Doctor grew outrageous; and, in his paroxysm, (not having the fear of flogging before his eyes,) actually *damned* King William! proceeding, in the enthusiasm of his popery, most thoughtlessly for himself and for the unhappy king's bust then staring before him, to strike it with his huge fat fist plump in the face!

The bust immediately showed most evident and marvellous symptoms of maltreatment by the apothecary; its beautiful virgin white marble appearing to be actually stained with blood! This miracle caused one of the aldermen to roar out in a fright—"That villain, M'Mahon, has broken the king's nose!"—"The king's nose?" ran throughout the room: some, who had been dozing, hearing this cry of high treason from every quarter, rose and rushed with the rest upon the Doctor: his clothes were soon turned into ribbons, and the cry of "throw him out of the window!" was unanimously and resolutely adopted: the window was opened; the Doctor, after exerting all his muscular powers, (and he was a strong, active man) was compelled to yield to numbers, and out he went into the street, very much to the ease and satisfaction of the loyal aldermen. The window was now closed again, the "Glorious Memory" drunk, the king's nose washed clean from the blood formerly belonging to the Doctor's knuckles, (which His Majesty's feature had unmercifully scarified) and all restored to peace and tranquillity.

As for the poor Doctor, out he went, as we have said, clean and cleverly, one good story. But (whether through chance or Providence we will not pretend to determine,) fortunately for him, a lamp and lamp-iron stood immediately under the window whereby he had made so sudden an exit! Hence, the Doctor's route downwards was impeded by a crash against the lamp; the glass and other materials all yielded to the precious weight, and very probably prevented the pavement from having the honour of braining him: he held a moment by the iron, and then dropped quite gently into the arms of a couple of guardians of the night, who, attracted by the uproar in the room above, and seeing the window open, and the Doctor getting out feet foremost, conceived that it was only a drunken frolic, and so placed themselves underneath "to keep the gentleman out of the gutter."

The Doctor scarcely waited to thank his preservers, set out pretty well sobered to his home, and the next day, summoning all the humane and *patriotic* aldermen, to whom he told his own story, they determined to secede and set up a new corps at the King's Arms in Fowns's- [*sic*] street. The old aldermen defended their conduct as loyal subjects; the others stigmatized it as the act of a set of man-slaughterers: these old and young guards of the British Constitution from that day set about *advertising* each other, and making proselytes on either side; and the *Orange* and *United Irishmen* parties gained as many recruiting serjeants by the fracas, as there were permanents or seceders amongst those illustrious aldermen.

As nothing is so much calculated to gratify the aldermen of Skinners'-alley as anecdotes respecting his Holiness the Pope, or their eminences the cardinals, I am happy in being enabled to afford them one, of which I

[217]

was an eye-witness. I had the honour of touching his Holiness's bull to the late Sir Francis Gould, (of gallant memory) and of seeing the beautiful candles therewith —six feet and an inch in their sockets: and if the *saving clause* in the bull should disappoint the aldermen, they must blame the caution of Cardinal Gonsalvi for having it inserted (though, I believe, a lay Cardinal). I regret that at present I can furnish them with no other anecdotes of the kind, (at least that came within my own knowledge;) but the following will serve excellently well to elucidate the Pope's bulls of absolution.

A few years since, the present Sir John Bourke, of Glinsk, Bart. travelled with his new married lady and establishment to Rome—not solely for his pleasure, but, as an Irish Catholic, to pay his respects to the Pope, kiss his Holiness' toe, and purchase antiquities.

The late Sir Francis Gould, then at Paris, requested Sir John (before me) that, as he fancied he felt himself in a declining state of health, and unable to travel so far as Rome, he (Sir John) would take the proper steps, through Cardinal Gonsalvi, to procure him from his Holiness a bull of plenary absolution, and, if possible, an indulgence also; adding that Sir John might *hint* to the Cardinal that he intended to bequeath a good deal of his property amongst the clergy.

Sir John undertook the matter,—proceeded to Rome, —saw the Cardinal, and, as far the absolution went, succeeded. He was himself at the same time created "Marchese de Bourke of the Holy Roman Empire;" and a bull was duly made out for Sir Francis Gould, at very considerable expense. Sir John received also a couple of blessed candles, six feet long, to burn whilst the bull was being read. Its express terms and conditions, however, were:—"Provided the penitent, Sir Francis Gould, should not again voluntarily commit the same sins now forgiven;" (which list included nearly all the sins the

Cardinal could think of!) in the other case, the forgiveness would be void, and the two sets of sins come slap upon the soul of Sir Francis at once, no doubt with compound interest;—and which nothing but severe penance, some hundred full masses, and a great deal of massmoney, would ever be able to bring him through.

Sir John having brought home the bull, magnificently enclosed, and sewed up in a silk bag sealed officially by the Cardinal, informed Sir Francis (as we were all dining together at Bourke's Hotel) that he had that day unpacked his luggage, had the Pope's bull perfectly safe, and would hand it to him instantly.

Sir Francis asked him its exact purport. "I have had two others," said he; "but they are null, for I sinned again, and so can't depend upon them."

Sir John informed him of the purport, so far as his Latin went: when Sir Francis calmly said, "My dear Bourke, don't give me the bull *yet awhile:* its operation I find, is only retrospective, and does not affect sins committed after its delivery: why did you not bring me one that would answer always?"

"Such a one would cost a damned deal more," replied Sir John.

"Well then," said Sir Francis, "send it to me in about ten days or a fortnight—*not sooner:* it will answer pretty well, as I am about taking away a beautiful young creature, my landlady's daughter, next week, and I should have that sin to answer for, if you gave me the bull before I had her clean out of Paris!"

He kept his word, took off the girl, then got the *absolution;* and in a very short time, poor fellow! was afforded, by death, an opportunity of trying its efficacy.

III

SOME IRISHMEN
OF THE DAY

GEORGE ROBERT FITZGERALD

A VERY illustrative anecdote of the habits of former times is afforded by the celebrated rencontre between George Robert Fitzgerald of Turlow, member for Mayo, and Mr. Richard Martin of Connemara, member for Galway county, which occurred nearly half a century ago. Both were gentlemen of great public notoriety: both men of family and of fortune. But of all the con-, trasts that ever existed in human nature, theirs was in the superlative degree; for modern biography does not present a character more eminently vindictive and sanguinary than the one, or an individual more signalised by active humanity and benevolence than the other.

With the chief of Connemara* I have now been nearly forty years in a state of uninterrupted friendship:—failings he has—"let him who is faultless throw the first stone!" The character I should give of him may be summed up in a single sentence. "Urbanity toward women; benevolence toward men; and humanity toward the brute creation." I must observe, however, that he is one of those good fellows who would rather do any body's business than his own; and durst look any thing in the face rather than his own situation. As to his *charity,* I cannot say too much; as to his *politics,* I cannot say too little.

His unfortunate antagonist, Mr. Fitzgerald, has long since met his miserable fate. Mr. Martin still lives; and

* Martin inherited a vast amount of land in Connemara (Constantia Maxwell says "more than half a million acres" [*Country and Town in Ireland under the Georges* (London, 1940), p. 54]). Like Barrington, he ended his days in France, where he had gone to escape his creditors.

seems to defy, from the strength of his constitution, both time and the destroyer. If *ever* he should become defunct, there is not a bullock, calf, goose, or hack, but ought to *go into deep mourning* for him.*

The virulent animosity and unfinished conflicts between these celebrated personages once formed a subject of very general conversation. When the bullets of holster pistols flatten against the ribs of a gentleman, there can be no great use in fighting any more with *him:* it is better to break fresh ground with some more vulnerable amateur; and as "fire eating" was at the period I allude to in full taste and fashion, no person who felt a *penchant* for chivalry need wait a single hour for a thrust. Every gentleman then wore his sword or *couteau de chasse,* which there could be no trouble in drawing.

I was quite unacquainted with the true state of the quarrel between these parties, or the facts of their rencontres; and have begged my friend Martin to give me a circumstantial detail, lest I might mistake and be called a "bouncer:" he was so obliging as to comply; and I conceive that his MS. statement is so perspicuous and fair, almost amounting to perfect impartiality—in that conversational style, too, best calculated for narrative,— that I determine to give it in nearly the same words; and when it is combined with a few facts which I learned from another friend, I venture to think that a better outline of Mayo and Galway lords, commoners, judges, country gentlemen, and *fire eaters,* cannot be found. As, however, there is nothing in it chivalrous in the *ladies'* way—the whole being about *hate* with not one particle respecting *love,* I fear it will not be a favourite sketch with the gentler part of the creation. To make them amends, I'll search my old trunks, and find if possible some pretty sketch that has *nothing but love* or *marriage*

* Martin in 1822 introduced in the British Parliament the first bill for the prevention of cruelty to animals.

in it, which they shall have as well dressed and garnished as they can reasonably expect from so old a *cuisinier;* and now, with their kind permission, we will proceed to County Mayo.

"George Robert Fitzgerald, having a deadly hate to all the Brown family, but hating most Lord Altamont, rode up one morning from Turlow to Westport House, and asked to see the big wolf-dog called the 'Prime Sergeant.' When the animal appeared, he instantly shot it, and desired the servants to tell their master that 'until the noble peer became charitable to the wandering poor whose broken meat was devoured by hungry wolf-dogs, *he* would not allow any such to be kept.' He, however, left a note to say that he *permitted* Lady Anne, Lady Elizabeth, and Lady Charlotte Brown, each to keep one *lap-dog.*

"Proud of this exploit, he rode into Lord Sligo's town of Westport, and proclaimed in the marketplace that he had just shot the *Prime Sergeant* dead. The whole town was alarmed; an uproar arose: but after some debate among the wisest or rather the *stoutest* people in the town, whether George Robert Fitzgerald ought not to be arrested if possible for this deliberate murder of Counsellor Brown; he quieted all by saying, 'I have shot a much worthier *animal,* the big watch-dog.' *

"I was at this time much attached to the family; and debating in my own mind how best to conduct myself toward my friends, I determined not to tell George Robert my opinion, as it would be in effect to declare that Lord Altamont wanted courage to defend his own honour. I therefore resolved on seeking some more plausible

---

* The Prime Sergeant of the Irish bar was then Lord Sligo's brother—a huge, fat, dull fellow; but the greater *lawyer* of the family. Prime Sergeant Brown was considered as an oracle by the whole county of Mayo: yet there could scarcely be found a man less calculated to *tell fortunes.* The watch-dog was named after him [Barrington's footnote].

ground of quarrel, which soon presented itself; for at the summer assizes of Mayo, holden at Castlebar, Charles Lionel Fitzgerald prosecuted his elder brother George Robert for false imprisonment and savage conduct toward their father, upon whom George Robert had fastened a chain and dray!

"The affair came on before Lord Carleton, and I volunteered in the only cause I ever pleaded.*

"An affidavit was produced, stating that the father was *not* confined. I observed, 'that Robert Fitzgerald had long notice of this cause coming on; and that the best answer would be the *attendance* of the father when he was called as one of the magistrates in the commission for the county of Mayo.'

"Remesius Lennon, a battered old counsellor, on the other side, observed that the father was one of the worst men living, and that it would be unjust to censure any son for confining such a public nuisance.

"I opposed putting off the trial of George Robert, and concluded to this effect:—'Though believing that, in course of a long life, this wretched father had committed many crimes, yet the greatest crime against society and the greatest sin against Heaven that he ever perpetrated, was having *begotten the traverser.*'

"On this, George Robert said, smiling, 'Martin, you look very healthy—you take good care of your *constitution;* but I tell you, that you have this day taken very bad care of your *life.*'

"The trial went on; and it was *proved,* among a great number of other barbarities, that the father *was* chained

* Mr. Richard Martin had been called to the Irish bar, as the eldest sons of the respectable families of Ireland then were, not, as might be supposed, to practise for others, but with a supposition that they would thereby be better enabled to defend their own *territories* from judgments, mortgagees, custodiums, &c. &c., and to "stave off" vulgar demands, which if too speedily conceded, might beget very serious inconveniences [Barrington's footnote].

by his son George Robert to a dray, and at times to a muzzled bear: a respectable jury found the traverser guilty; and Lord Carleton sentenced him to three years' imprisonment, and to pay a fine to the King of five hundred pounds.

" 'Kissing' at this time went 'by favour;' and Mr. Conally, the brother-in-law of George Robert, obtained from the late Duke of Buckingham, then Lord Lieutenant, the pardon and release of Fitzgerald.

"Some months after, I happened to pass through Castlebar, and learned that Mr. Fitzgerald was in the town. I had heard of his denunciations, but my determination was, neither to *avoid* nor *seek* my antagonist. Desirous of ascertaining what I had to expect, I requested a friend to call on him, and, after conversation on some ordinary subject, to say that *I* had been in the town.

"This was done, and George Robert answered, 'that he hoped, whenever we met, it would not be as *enemies.*'

"My friend reported this: but, on the whole, I thought it as well not to seek any occasion of meeting a person who, I apprehended, might, so soon after our dispute, be induced to depart from his pacific resolution; I therefore proceeded on my journey to Dublin.

"Mrs. Crawford, I found, had been engaged to play for a few nights at Crow Street theatre, and I determined to see her *Belvidera.* I had not long taken my seat in the front row of the stage-box, when I heard a noisy, precipitate step, and an order given in a commanding tone for the box to be opened. I turned, and saw Mr. Fitzgerald, who took his place on the next row. His look indicated rage, and I therefore left my place in front, and took my seat on the same row with him. He stared for a moment or two directly into my face, then turned away and laughed, on which I asked, 'Have you any thing particular to say to *me,* Mr. Fitzgerald?'

[227]

"He answered, with a stern look of defiance—'Only to tell you that I followed you from Castlebar, to proclaim you the *bully* of the Altamonts.'

" 'You have said enough, Mr. Fitzgerald; you no doubt expect to hear from me, and it shall be early in the morning.'

" 'I shall hear from you to-morrow!' he repeated, contemptuously, making, as he spoke, a blow at me, and adding, 'this will refresh your memory.' He then pulled back his body from behind the curtain of the box, and instantly retreated toward the lobby.

"My feet got entangled in the curtain when I rushed out to follow my antagonist, and I fell upon the floor. The present Lord Howden, then Major Craddock, kindly lifted me up. When on my feet, I sprang into the lobby, which was crowded almost to an overflow. I uttered all that rage could dictate, accused Fitzgerald of cowardice, and told him he had created the present *scene* in order that we should be both bound over to the peace.

" 'You have got a blow,' replied he: 'I desire to disgrace you, and when you are punished to my liking *that* way (and not before) you shall have the *satisfaction* of being shot, or run through the body.'

"Next day, I met the late Lord Donoughmore, and he most kindly said, if I required it, he would deliver a message to Fitzgerald. I said, 'No, I could not think of embroiling any friend of mine with such a fellow; that I would wear my sword, and trust to my opportunities of meeting Fitzgerald.'

"I watched his house closely for several days, but he did not appear. At this critical moment, a Mr. George Lyster called upon me, and said he would take my message to Fitzgerald.

"I answered, 'that of all things I most desired to meet him; that I found I could not unkennel the fox; and that I would thank whomsoever should succeed in putting us face to face.' I was, however, cautious of employing Lyster, knowing him to be Fitzgerald's cousin, and supposing it possible he might have been employed by Fitzgerald himself: this induced me to try him and to say, 'As you have *offered* to go to this gentleman, I will thank you to appoint the *earliest moment* for a meeting.'

"Mr. Lyster drew not back, but went to his cousin's house, and was ushered by one of the servants into the drawing-room. Mr. Fitzgerald shortly entered, and as soon as Mr. Lyster hinted his business, our hero desired the footman to send one of the valets: when the latter entered, Fitzgerald said, 'Francis, bring my cudgel with the green riband.' When Fitzgerald got this weapon, he addressed his relative thus—'How dare you bring a *message* to me? Hold out your finger with the diamond-ring upon it!' Poor Lyster obeyed, ignorant of his design, and with one blow Fitzgerald broke the finger, and the band of the ring, which fell on the floor, 'Now,' proceeded he, 'I order you to take up the ring, and present it to me.' As if thunderstruck, Lyster obeyed. When Fitzgerald got possession of the ring, he put it into paper, and returned it to Lyster, saying, 'Young fellow, take care of the ring! put it up very safe, and don't swear I robbed you of a present from some fair one.'

"This dialogue (recounted to me by Lyster himself) was followed by several blows, which cut and battered the young man severely. At last, he rushed to the window, drove his head through a pane of glass, and cried out for assistance. The police, hearing the cry, soon assembled; and not finding any of the city magistrates, they having seized both parties, conducted them into the presence of Mr. Justice Robinson.

"The judge first heard Lyster, and seeing him severely bruised, and supposing his skull might be fractured, declared that the prisoner could not be bailed.

"Fitzgerald now, on the other hand, asked to have his

examination entered against Lyster. He stated, 'that Lyster was his relative, and protected by him, and that I had *influenced* the young man to deliver a message from from me. He said, 'that Mr. Lyster *had* delivered such a *message:* that *he had* answered mildly, that he would not fight Mr. Martin; whereon, (says Fitzgerald,) this young gentleman said, 'Then you must fight *me*.' My answer was, that I would not fight *any man;* on which, continued George Robert, he made several blows of the cudgel I hold in my hand (his own) at me. I happened to be more dexterous than my assailant, and was fortunate enough to take the weapon out of his hands, and in my own defence was obliged to strike in turn, or I should have been murdered.'

"The old judge, believing every word of so plausible a statement, said, 'I have heard enough; I commit Lyster for trial, and bind over Mr. Fitzgerald to prosecute; and I do so, expressing my approbation of Mr. Fitzgerald's manly conduct, in refusing to fight Mr. Martin, and thus appealing for redress to the laws of his country.'

"Shortly after this curious scene, I heard that Fitzgerald was at Castlebar, and had it intimated to him that I should be there. I travelled with Mr. H. Flood * in his carriage, and he kindly offered to be my friend, which I declined—fearing to have exposed him to some insult.

"I had sent my duelling pistols by a fellow who got drunk on the road, and forgot his errand;—so that I remained some hours at Lord Lucan's house, expecting in vain their arrival, during which period I heard that Mr. Fitzgerald was parading the town with a number of persons from Turlow, his own estate, famous for its mobs trained to every kind of outrage. I heard, too, that he said, I waited for Lord Altamont's carriage, which, ob-

* This was the celebrated Henry Flood, the antagonist of Grattan—certainly the ablest statesman of his day. He had himself fought more than once; and had killed Mr. Eager, the father of Lord Clifden, of Gowran [Barrington's footnote].

served he significantly, *would not arrive*. Here I have to remark that I had written a note to Lord Altamont, to say that I would gladly compound for a slight wound in the expected affair, and that I requested his carriage might be in waiting for me at Castlebar, which is only eight miles from Westport. George Robert had heard this, and said to the mob, 'Mr. Martin expects Altamont's carriage, but he may wait long enough; for though the horse is a brave animal, I fancy Altamont's are like the owner, and will not stand the smell of powder.'

"These taunts reached me; and procuring a case of the common holster pistols my servant rode with, I determined to use them: but they were so stiff in the trigger that I could hardly let them off.* I fastened on my sword, and putting my hand under Doctor Merlin's arm, walked into the town, and soon saw Fitzgerald, followed by his mob. He too wore his sword, and I instantly told him to draw. He answered that he was lame, the pavement bad, and that he could not keep his footing; that I had Lord Lucan's mob on my side; and that, in short, he would not fight me.

"I then said, 'You will find me in the barrack-yard, where I shall remain.'

" 'I shall be in no hurry, after having struck you for your pertness,' said he.

"On this I flung a switch into his face, walked to the barrack, and got sentries posted, with orders to keep out all persons but Mr. Fitzgerald and his friend, whilst we should be fighting. He and Mr. Fenton soon appeared: he had a good case of pistols in his hand, while I had the wretched tools I named.

"I stood against a projecting part of the barrack wall, and desired Mr. Fitzgerald to come as close as he

* Martin engaged in so many duels that he won the nickname of "Hair-trigger Dick."

pleased. He said a cannon would not carry *so far*. I answered, 'I will soon cure that, for I will now march up until I lay my pistol to your face.' I accordingly advanced, until our pistols touched. We both fired: he missed me, but I hit him full in the breast, and he fell back, supporting himself by a projection of rock, and exclaiming, 'Honour, Martin, honour!'

"I said,—'If you are not disabled, I will wait as long as you choose!'

"At this moment, he couched treacherously like a cat, presented, fired, and hit me. I returned the fire, and hit him; he again recovered, came up, begged my pardon, asked to shake hands, and said, 'Altamont has caused all this, and now would not send you his carriage;—let us both kick him!'

"Flood met me at the gate, and I leaned on him. I was taken to Doctor Lendser's, to have the wound dressed, but on the way desired my servant to go with my compliments and inquire how Mr. Fitzgerald felt. Mr. Flood said, 'On no account make any inquiry, or, if he lives, you will have a second fight.' I was foolish, as will appear, and sent.

"I had not been many moments in bed when my hero entered the room with a careful, timid step. He said, 'Doctor, how do you find Mr. Martin?' I was quite surprised, but said, 'I am very well, and hope you are not badly hurt.'

"He then addressed me, and observed, 'Doctor Merlin insulted me, and I consider him a bully, and instrument of yours, and as such I will make *you* accountable.'

"I answered, 'If I account with you, on a mutual understanding that Doctor Merlin is beneath your notice, I shall have to fight him also for such an imputation:— so put your renewed quarrel on some other ground. If you say you did not ask my pardon, I will fight you again;

or if you say you are fond of such *amusement,* I will fight 'until my eyelids can no longer wag.'

" 'Shall you be at Sligo?' was Mr. Fitzgerald's *reply.*

"I said, 'It was not my present purpose; but if he *wished* it, I would be there, and that immediately.'

"He named the day, to which I assented. It was *reported,* but I cannot vouch for the fact, that a party was sent to intercept and murder me. Shortly after I reached Sligo, my opponent sent Sir M. Crafton to say, that 'Mr. Fitzgerald did not require any further renewal of the quarrel;' and thus the affair ended. My surprise at Fitzgerald's being alive and well, after having received two shots from *horse-pistols* full upon him, was soon cleared up; he had *plated his body* so as to make it completely bullet proof. On receiving my fire, he fell from the force of the balls striking him direct, and touching his concealed armour.—My wound was in the body.

"The elegant and gentlemanly appearance of this man, as contrasted with the savage treachery of his actions, was extremely curious and without any parallel of which I am aware."

WOLF TONE

THEOBALD WOLF TONE was one of the most remarkable of the persons who lost their lives in consequence of that wild democratic mania, which at the period treated of in the former sketch, had seized upon the reason of so many otherwise sensible individuals. His catastrophe cannot fail to be interesting.

This gentleman's enthusiastic mind was eternally surrounded by the mist of visionary speculation: it was a fine sailer, but wanted ballast. He had distinguished himself somewhat in the University as a desultory declaimer; but, in my judgment, that was the full extent of his powers. He was neither high-born, nor wealthy:—in fact, I fear even a steady competency was not at his command; and hence his spirit, naturally restless, was additionally goaded and inflamed.

It is a curious circumstance that Mr. Tone, a decided revolutionist and rebel, married, improvidently enough, one sister, whilst Mr. Thomas Reynolds, who betrayed the friends of Tone and of himself, espoused another.

Tone was called to the Irish bar; but had been previously over-rated, and did not succeed. I though it a pity (as he was really a good-hearted person,) that he should not be fairly tried, and, if possible, pushed forward; and being myself high on the circuit, I took him round in my carriage three times, and then thought well of him; but he was too light and visionary; and as for law, was quite incapable of imbibing that species of science. His person was unfavourable—his countenance thin and sallow; and he had in his speech a harsh guttural pronunciation of the letter R—a defect shared by him in common with Mr. Croker, of the Admiralty, who indeed resembled him in personal appearance greatly, but was somewhat Tone's inferior in elocution.

It is my belief, that Tone could not have succeeded in any steady civil profession. He was not worldly enough, nor had he sufficient common sense for his guidance. His biography has been repeatedly published, and I only intend here to allude to the extraordinary circumstances of his death;—an event upon which I confess I had many painful feelings, and not the less so from its being connected with my own judicial functions.

He had been taken in arms by Sir John Borlase Warren, at sea, in a French frigate, proceeding to land troops in Ireland. He wore the uniform of a French officer; but being recognized, brought prisoner to Dublin, and delivered over for trial to the provost-marshal and military authorities, he was of course condemned to be hanged. I did not see him under these distressing circumstances, nor in truth was it my wish to do so; for although there existed between us no actual friendship, still I had a strong feeling for a gentleman with whom I had been so well acquainted.

It occurred to his counsel that the jurisdiction of martial-law could not extend to him, as it only operated on land, and he had been taken at sea. An application was therefore made to the Common Pleas, to have him brought up by Habeas Corpus, in order (the point being ascertained) to be regularly tried before the competent tribunal—the court of Admiralty. The Habeas Corpus being granted, was served on General Craig, who then commanded in Dublin, but who refused to obey it, and was attached for his disobedience; an order being consequently made for the general and some of his staff to be taken into custody by the officers of the court.

To me (as judge of the Admiralty,) this appeal was most distressing. Had Tone the least chance of escape in any court, or upon any trial, it might have been otherwise; but he could not be defended; and to have him brought before me only to witness his conviction, and to pronounce his sentence, shocked me extremely. His friends thought this course might prolong his fate a considerable time, and it was supposed that something might intermediately occur calculated to effect a commutation of the capital punishment. I knew better! I was convinced that his execution was determined on: it was unavoidable, and I felt *great* uneasiness.

The court having ordered General Craig, and Major Sandys, (provost-marshal) to be arrested for disobedience, both these gentlemen submitted, and the *pursuivant* was then directed to bring up the body of Theobald Wolf Tone, on the writ of Habeas Corpus. The judges sat patiently awaiting the officer's return: and the decision being of great importance, the court was crowded to suffocation.

A considerable time elapsed, and still the *pursuivant* returned not. At length he appeared, with horror in his looks, and scarcely able to speak. He informed the court that Mr. Tone, feeling certain of execution by order of the military, and being ignorant of the motion which his friends thought might give him some chance for his life, had cut his throat from ear to ear, and, he believed, was dying! A surgeon now attended, who reported that the prisoner had certainly cut his throat, but that recovery was possible: the incision was long and deep, but had missed the artery, and he still lived. Of course, the trial was postponed; every friend he had, (and I think he had many amongst the bar,) rejoicing that poor Tone had escaped a public execution. He lingered awhile:—and will it be believed, that when the wound had been connected, and whilst life still seemed to be precarious, owing to the extreme inflammation,—I say, will it be believed that there existed cruelty sufficient in the breast of any human

[236]

creature to advise his execution—though it would have been impossible to put the sentence in force without inserting the rope within the wound, and nearly tearing away the unfortunate gentleman's head from his body? Yet such advice was given, for "the sake of example;"— and rejected, I am happy to say, with horror! I will spare the man who gave it the ignominy which would thence attach to his name were it mentioned.

HAMILTON ROWAN AND THE BAR

THERE were few persons whose history was connected with that of Ireland during my time, who excited my interest in a greater degree than Mr. Hamilton Rowan. The dark points of this gentleman's character have been assiduously exhibited by persons who knew little or nothing of his life, and that too, long after he had ceased to be an obnoxious character. I will endeavour to show the obverse of the medal; and I claim the meed of perfect disinterestedness, which will, I think, be awarded, when I state that I never had the least social intercourse with Mr. Rowan, whose line of politics was always decidedly opposed to my own.

Archibald Hamilton Rowan (I believe he still lives) is a gentleman of most respectable family and of ample fortune: considered merely as a private character, I fancy there are few who will not give him full credit for every quality which does honour to that station in society. As a philanthropist, he certainly carried his ideas even beyond reason, and to a degree of excess which I really think laid in his mind the foundation of all his enthusiastic proceedings, both in common life and in politics.

The first interview I had with this gentleman did not occupy more than a few minutes: but it was of a most impressive nature, and though now eight-and-thirty years back, appears as fresh to my eye as if it took place yesterday: in truth, I believe it must be equally present to every individual of the company who survives, and is not too old to remember any thing.

There is generally in every metropolis some temporary

incident which serves as a common subject of conversation; something which *nominally* excites interest, but which in fact nobody cares a *sou* about, though for the day it sells all the newspapers, and gives employment to every tongue, till some new occurrence happens to work up curiosity and change the topic.

In 1788, a very young girl, of the name of Mary Neil, had been ill-treated by a person unknown, aided by a woman. The late Lord Carhampton was supposed to be the transgressor, but without any proof whatsoever of his Lordship's culpability. The humour of Hamilton Rowan, which had a sort of Quixotic tendency to resist all oppression and to redress every species of wrong, led him to take up the cause of Mary Neil with a zeal and enthusiastic perseverance which nobody but the knight of La Mancha could have exceeded. Day and night the ill-treatment of this girl was the subject of his thoughts, his actions, his dreams: he even went about preaching a kind of crusade in her favour, and succeeded in gaining a great many partisans among the citizens; and in short, he eventually obtained a conviction of the woman as accessory to a crime, the perpetrator whereof remained undiscovered, and she accordingly received sentence of death. Still Mary Neil was not bettered by this conviction: she was utterly unprovided for, had suffered much, and seemed quite wretched. Yet there were not wanting persons who doubted her truth, decried her former character, and represented her story as that of an impostor: this not only hurt the feelings and philanthropy, but the pride of Hamilton Rowan; and he vowed personal vengeance against all her calumniators, high and low.

At this time about twenty young barristers, including myself, had formed a dinner club in Dublin: we had taken large apartments for the purpose; and, as we were not yet troubled with *too much* business, were in the habit of faring luxuriously every day, and taking a bottle of the best claret which could be obtained.*

There never existed a more cheerful, nor half so cheap a dinner club. One day, whilst dining with our usual hilarity, the servant informed us that a gentleman below stairs desired to be admitted *for a moment.* We considered it to be some brother-barrister who requested permission to join our party, and desired him to be shown up. What was our surprise, however, on perceiving the figure that presented itself!—a man, who might have served as model for a Hercules, his gigantic limbs conveying the idea of almost supernatural strength: his shoulders, arms, and broad chest, were the very emblems of muscular energy; and his flat, rough countenance, overshadowed by enormous dark eyebrows, and deeply furrowed by strong lines of vigour and fortitude, completed one of the finest, yet most formidable figures I had ever beheld. He was very well dressed: close by his side stalked in a shaggy Newfoundland dog of corresponding magnitude, with hair a foot long, and who, if he should be voraciously inclined, seemed well able to devour a barrister or two without overcharging his stomach:— as he entered, indeed, he alternately looked at us and then up at this master, as if only awaiting the orders of the latter to commence the onslaught. His master held in his hand a large, yellow, knotted club, slung by a leathern thong round his great wrist: he had also a long smallsword by his side.

This apparition walked deliberately up to the table; and having made his obeisance with seeming courtesy, a short pause ensued, during which he looked round on all

* One of us, Counsellor Townley Fitgate, (afterwards chairman of Wicklow County,) having a pleasure-cutter of his own in the harbour of Dublin, used to send her to smuggle claret for us from the Isle of Man: he made a friend of one of the tidewaiters, and we consequently had the very best wines on the cheapest possible terms [Barrington's footnote].

the company with an aspect, if not stern, yet ill-calculated
to set our minds at ease either as to his or his dog's
ulterior intentions.

"Gentlemen!" at length he said, in a tone and with an
air at once so mild and courteous, nay so polished, as
fairly to give the lie, as it were, to his gigantic and
threatening figure: "Gentlemen! I have heard with very
great regret that some members of this club have been
so indiscreet as to calumniate the character of Mary Neil,
which, from the part I have taken, I feel identified with
my own: if any present hath done so, I doubt not he will
now have the candour and courage to avow it.—*Who
avows it?*" The dog looked up at him again; he returned
the glance; but contented himself, for the present, with
patting the animal's head,* and was silent: so were we.

The extreme surprise indeed with which our party was
seized, bordering almost on consternation, rendered all
consultation as to a reply out of the question; and never
did I see the old axiom that "what is everybody's business
is nobody's business" more thoroughly exemplified. A
few of the company whispered each his neighbour, and I
perceived one or two steal a fruit-knife under the table-
cloth, in case of extremities; but no one made any reply.
We were eighteen in number; and as neither would or
could answer for the others, it would require eighteen
replies to satisfy the giant's single query; and I fancy
some of us *could not* have replied to his satisfaction, and
stuck to the truth into the bargain.

He repeated his demand (elevating his tone each time)
thrice: "Does any gentleman avow it?" A faint buzz now

* Rowan's fondness for animals apparently went beyond the
ordinary kinds of pets: according to Alfred Webb, Rowan noted
that, upon his return from America (earlier in his career), "after
a very rough passage, I landed at Portsmouth—my raccoon dead,
my bear washed overboard, and my opossum lost in the cable tier
—and I returned to Cambridge" (*A Compendium of Irish Biography,* pp. 457–58).

[241]

circulated round the room, but there was no *answer* whatsoever. Communication was cut off, and there was a dead silence: at length our visitor said, with a loud voice, that he must suppose, if any gentleman had made any observations or assertions against Mary Neil's character, he would have had the *courage* and spirit to avow it: "therefore," continued he, "I shall take it for granted that my information was erroneous; and, in that point of view, I regret having *alarmed* your society." And, without another word, he bowed three times very low, and retired backwards toward the door, (his dog also backing out with equal politeness,) where, with a salaam doubly ceremonious, Mr. Rowan ended this extraordinary interview. On the first of his departing bows, by a simultaneous impulse, we all rose and returned his salute, almost touching the table with our noses, but still in profound silence; which *bowing* on both sides was repeated, as I have said, till he was fairly out of the room. Three or four of the company then ran hastily to the window to be *sure* that he and the dog were clear off into the street; and no sooner had this satisfactory *denouement* been ascertained, then a general roar of laughter ensued, and we talked it over in a hundred different ways: the whole of our arguments, however, turned upon the question "which had behaved the *politest* upon the occasion?" but not one word was uttered as to which had behaved the *stoutest*.

This spirit of false chivalry, which took each entire possession of Hamilton Rowan's understanding, was soon diverted into the channels of political theory; and from the discussion of general politics, he advanced to the contemplation of sedition.* His career in this respect was short:—he was tried and convicted of circulating

* Rowan was one of the earliest members of the United Irishmen.

a factious paper,* and sentenced to a heavy fine and a long imprisonment, during which, political charges of a much more serious nature were arrayed against him. He fortunately escaped from prison to the house of Mr. Evans, of Portrenne, near Dublin, and got off in a fishing-boat to France, where, after numerous dangers, he at length arrived safely. Rowan subsequently resided some years in America, in which country he had leisure for reflection, and saw plainly the folly and mischief of his former conduct. The government found that his contrition was sincere; he eventually received His Majesty's free pardon; and I have since seen him and his family at the Castle drawing-rooms in dresses singularly splendid, where they were well received by the Viceroy and by many of the nobility and gentry: and people should consider that His Majesty's free pardon for political offences is always meant to *wipe away* every injurious feeling from his subjects' recollection.

The mention of Mr. Rowan reminds me of an anecdote of a singular nature, extremely affecting, and which at the time was the subject of much conversation: and as a connexion was alleged to exist between him and the unfortunate gentleman to whom it relates, (which connexion had nearly proved fatal to Mr. Rowan,) I consider this not an inappropriate place to allude to the circumstance.

Mr. Jackson, an English clergyman, who had come over to assist in organizing a revolution in Ireland, had been arrested in that country, tried, and found guilty of high treason in corresponding with the enemy in France.†

* The pamphlet was entitled, "Citizen soldier, to arms!" and was issued in 1792. At Rowan's trial in 1794, Curran was counsel for the defense.

† Unfortunately for the Reverend Mr. William Jackson, his close friend John Cockayne revealed all the details of the plot to the government. For this, Cockayne received a pension of £250.

I was in court when Mr. Jackson was brought up to receive sentence of death; and I believe whoever was present must recollect it as one of the most touching and uncommon scenes which appeared during that eventful period.*

He was conducted into the usual place where prisoners stand to receive sentence. He was obviously much affected as he entered; his limbs seemed to totter, and large drops of perspiration rolled down his face. He was supposed to *fear death,* and to be in great terror. The judge began the usual admonition before he pronounced sentence: the prisoner seemed to regard it but little, appearing abstracted by internal agony. This was still attributed to apprehension: he covered his face, and seemed sinking: the judge paused—the crowd evinced surprise—and the sheriff, on examination, declared the prisoner was *too ill* to *hear* his sentence. Meanwhile, the wretched culprit continued to droop: and at length, his limbs giving way, he fell! A visitation so unexampled created a great sensation in the court: a physician was immediately summoned, but too late; Jackson had eluded his denouncers, and was no more.

It was discovered that, previous to his coming into Court, he had taken a large quantity of arsenic and aquafortis mixed in tea. No judgment of course was pronounced against him. He had a splendid funeral:† and, to the astonishment of Dublin, it was attended by several members of Parliament and barristers! a Mr. Tigh, and Counsellor Richard Guinness, were amongst them.

* This occurred on April 30, 1795.
† And—Barrington might have added—was buried in St. Michan's Church, in spite of being guilty of both suicide and high treason.

THE SEVEN BARONETS

AMONGST those parliamentary gentlemen frequently to be found in the coffee-room of the House, were certain baronets, of very singular character, who, until some division called them to vote, passed the intermediate time in high conviviality. Sir John Stuart Hamilton, a man of small fortune and large stature, possessing a most liberal appetite both for solids and fluids—much wit, more humour, and indefatigable cheerfulness,—might be regarded as their leader.

Sir Richard Musgrave, who (except on the abstract topics of politics, religion, martial law, his wife, the Pope, the Pretender, the Jesuits, Napper Tandy, and the whipping-post,) was generally in his senses, formed, during those intervals, a very entertaining addition to the company.

Sir Edward Newnham, member for Dublin County, afforded a whimsical variety by the affectation of early and exclusive transatlantic intelligence. By repeatedly writing letters of congratulation, he had at length extorted a reply from General Washington, which he exhibited upon every occasion, giving it to be understood by significant nods, that he knew vastly more than he thought proper to communicate.

Sir Vesey Colclough, member for County Wexford, who understood books and wine better than any of the party, had all his days treated money so extremely ill, that it would continue no longer in his service! and the dross (as he termed it) having entirely forsaken him, he *bequeathed* an immense landed property, during his life, to the uses of custodiums, elegits, and judgments, which never fail to place a gentleman's acres under the especial guardianship of the attorneys. He was father to that excellent man, John Colclough, who was killed at Wexford,* and to the present Cesar Colclough, whose fall might probably have afforded rather less cause of regret.

Sir Vesey added much to the pleasantry of the party by occasionally forcing on them deep subjects of literature, of which few of his companions could make either head or tail: but to avoid the *imputation* of ignorance, they often gave the most ludicrous *proofs* of it on literary subjects, geography and astronomy, with which he eternally bored them.

Sir Frederick Flood, also member for County Wexford, whose exhibitions in the Imperial Parliament have made him tolerably well known in England, was very different in his habits from the last-mentioned baronet; —his love of money and spirit of ostentation never losing their hold throughout every action of his life. He was but a second-rate blunderer in Ireland. The bulls of Sir Boyle Roche (of whom we shall speak hereafter) generally involved aphorisms of sound sense, whilst Sir Frederick's (on the other hand) possessed the qualification of being pure nonsense.

He was a *pretty*, dapper man, very good-tempered; and had a droll habit, of which he could never effectually break himself (at least in Ireland) :—whenever a person at his back whispered or suggested any thing whilst he was speaking in public, without a moment's reflection he almost always involuntarily repeated the suggestion *literatim*.

Sir Frederick was once making a long speech in the Irish parliament, lauding the transcendent merits of the Wexford magistracy, on a motion for extending the criminal jurisdiction in that county, to keep down the

* I.e., during the uprising of 1798.

disaffected. As he was closing a most turgid oration, by declaring "that the said magistracy ought to receive some signal mark of the Lord Lieutenant's favour,"—John Egan, who was rather mellow, and sitting behind him, jocularly whispered, "and be whipped at the cart's tail:" —"And be whipped at the cart's tail!" repeated Sir Frederick unconsciously, amidst peals of the most uncontrollable laughter.

Sir John Blacquiere flew at higher game than the other baronets, though he occasionally fell into the trammels of Sir John Hamilton. Sir John Blacquiere was a little deaf of one ear, for which circumstance he gave a very singular reason:—his seat, when secretary, was the outside one on the treasury bench, next to a gangway; and he said that so many members used to come perpetually to whisper him—and the buzz of importunity was so heavy and continuous, that before one claimant's words had got out of his ear, the demand of another forced its way in, till the ear-drum, being overcharged, absolutely burst! which, he said, turned out conveniently enough, as he was then obliged to stuff the organ tight, and tell every gentleman that his physician had directed him not to use *that* ear at all, and *the other* as little as possible!

I will now advert to Sir Boyle Roche, who certainly was, without exception, the most celebrated and entertaining anti-grammarian in the Irish Parliament. I knew him intimately. He was of a very respectable Irish family, and, in point of appearance, a fine, bluff, soldier-like old gentleman. He had numerous good qualities; and having been long in the army, his ideas were full of honour and etiquette—of discipline, and bravery. He had a claim to the title of Fermoy, which however he never pursued; and was brother to the famous Tiger Roche, who fought some desperate duel abroad, and was near being hanged for it. Sir Boyle was perfectly well bred in all his habits; had been appointed gentleman-usher at the Irish Court, and executed the duties of that office to the day of his death with the utmost satisfaction to himself as well as to every one in connexion with him. He was married to the eldest daughter of Sir John Cave, Bart.; and his lady, who was a "bas bleu," prematurely injured Sir Boyle's capacity (it was said) by forcing him to read—Gibbon's *Rise and Fall of the Roman Empire*—[*sic*] whereat he was so cruelly puzzled without being in the least amused, that, in his cups, he often stigmatized the great historian as a low fellow, who ought to have been kicked out of company wherever he was, for turning people's thoughts away from their prayers and their politics to what the devil himself could make neither head nor tail of!

His perpetually bragging that Sir John Cave had given him his *eldest* daughter, afforded Curran an opportunity of replying,—"Aye, Sir Boyle," and depend on it, if he had had an *older* one still, he would have given her to you." Sir Boyle thought it best to receive the repartee as a compliment, lest it should come to her ladyship's ears, who, for several years back, had prohibited Sir Boyle from all allusions to chronology.

This baronet had certainly one great advantage over all other bull and blunder makers: he seldom launched a blunder from which some fine aphorism or maxim might not be easily extracted. When a debate arose in the Irish House of Commons on the vote of a grant which was recommended by Sir John Parnel, Chancellor of the Exchequer, as one not likely to be felt burthensome for many years to come,—it was observed in reply, that the house had no just right to load posterity with a weighty debt for what could in no degree operate to their advantage. Sir Boyle, eager to defend the measures of government, immediately rose, and, in a few words, put forward the most unanswerable argument which human ingenuity could possibly devise. "What, Mr. Speaker!" said he, "and so we are to beggar ourselves for fear of

[248]

vexing posterity! Now, I would ask the honourable gentleman, and this *still more* honourable House, why we
should put ourselves out of our way to do anything for
posterity:—for what has *posterity* done for *us?*"

Sir Boyle, hearing the roar of laughter which of course
followed this sensible blunder, but not being conscious
that he had said anything out of the way, was rather
puzzled, and conceived that the House had misunder-
stood him. He therefore begged leave to explain, as he
apprehended that gentlemen had entirely mistaken his
words: he assured the House "that by *posterity* he did not
at all mean our *ancestors,* but those who were to come
immediately after *them.*" Upon hearing this *explanation,*
it was impossible to do any serious business for half an
hour.

Sir Boyle Roche was induced by Government to fight
as hard as possible for the Union:—so he did, and I
really believe fancied, by degrees, that he was right. On
one occasion, a general titter arose at his florid picture
of the happiness which must proceed from this event.
"Gentlemen (said Sir Boyle) may titther, and titther,
and titther, and may think it a bad measure; but their
heads at present are hot, and will so remain till they grow
cool again; and so they can't decide right now; but when
the *day of judgment* comes, *then* honourable gentlemen
will be satisfied at this most excellent Union. Sir, there is
no Levitical degrees between nations, and on this occasion I can see neither sin nor shame in *marrying our own
sister.*"

He was a determined enemy to the French Revolution,
and seldom rose in the House for several years without
volunteering some abuse of it. "Mr. Speaker," said he,
in a mood of this kind, "if we once permitted the villainous
French masons to meddle with the buttresses and walls of
our ancient constitution, they would never stop nor stay,
sir, till they brought the foundation-stones tumbling down

about the ears of the nation! There," continued Sir Boyle, placing his hand earnestly on his heart, his powdered head shaking in unison with his loyal zeal, whilst he described the probable consequences of an invasion of Ireland by the French republicans; "There, Mr. Speaker! if those Gallican villains should invade us, Sir, 'tis on *that very table,* may-be, these honourable members might see their own destinies lying in heaps a-top of one another! Here perhaps, Sir, the murderous *marshall-law-men* (Marseillois) would break in, cut us to mince-meat, and throw our bleeding heads upon that table, to stare us in the face!"

Sir Boyle, on another occasion, was arguing for the Habeas Corpus Suspension Bill in Ireland:—"It would surely be better, Mr. Speaker," said he, "to give up not only a *part,* but, if necessary, even the *whole,* of our constitution, to preserve *the remainder!*"

This Baronet having been one of the Irish Parliamentary curiosities before the Union, I have only exemplified his mode of blundering, as many ridiculous sayings have been attributed to him. He blundered certainly more than any public speaker in Ireland; but his bulls were rather logical perversions, and had some strong point in most of them.

JOHN PHILPOT CURRAN

THERE have been few public men whose characters have afforded a more ample field for comment than that of Mr. Curran, and there are *very* few who have been more miserably handled by their biographers. Young men, who fancied they knew him because they were latterly in his society, in fact knew him not at all. None but the intimates of his earlier and brighter days, and, even among such, those only who had mixed with him in general as well as professional society, could possibly estimate the inconsistent qualities of that celebrated orator. There was such a mingling of greatness and littleness, of sublimity and meanness, in his thoughts and language, that cursory observers (confused amidst his versatility and brilliance,) quitted Curran's society without understanding any thing relating to him beyond his buoyant spirits and playful wit. But towards the close of his day, this splendour dissipated, and dark and gloomy tints appeared too conspicuously, poor fellow! for his posthumous reputation. He felt his decline pressing quick upon him, and gradually sank into listless apathy.

Even so early as 1798, his talents and popularity seemed to me to have commenced a slow but obvious declension. By seceding from parliament in the preceding year, he had evacuated the field of battle and that commanding eminence from whence he had so proudly repulsed all his enemies. His talents, it is true, for a while survived; but his habits of life became contracted, his energies were paralyzed, his mind rambled, he began to prose,—and, after his appointment to the Rolls, the world seemed to be closing fast upon him.

My intimacy with Curran was long and close. I knew every turn of his mind and every point of his capacity. He was not fitted to pursue the niceties of detail;—but his imagination was infinite, his fancy boundless, his wit indefatigable. There was scarce any species of talent to which he did not possess some pretension. He was gifted by Nature with the faculties of an advocate and a dramatist; and the lesser but ingenious accomplishment of personification (without mimicry,) was equally familiar to him. In the circles of society, where he appeared every body's superior, nobody ever seemed jealous of the superiority.

Curran's person was mean and decrepit: very slight, very shapeless—with nothing of the gentleman about it; on the contrary, displaying spindle limbs, a shambling gait, one hand imperfect, and a face yellow, furrowed, rather flat and thoroughly ordinary. Yet his features were the very reverse of disagreeable: there was something so indescribably dramatic in his eye and the play of his eyebrow, that his visage seemed the index of his mind, and his humour the slave of his will. I never was so happy in the company of any man as in Curran's for many years. His very foibles were amusing.—He had no vein for poetry; yet fancying himself a bard, he contrived to throw off pretty verses: he certainly was no musician; but conceiving himself to be one, played very pleasingly: Nature had denied him a voice; but he thought he could sing; and in the rich mould of his capabilities, the desire here also bred, in some degree, the capacity.

It is a curious, but a just remark, that every slow, *crawling* reptile is in the highest degree disgusting; whilst an insect, ten times uglier, if it be sprightly and seems bent upon enjoyment, excites no shuddering. It is so with the human race: had Curran been a dull, slothful, inanimate being, his talents would not have redeemed his personal defects. But his rapid movements,—his fire,—his spar-

[252]

kling eye,—the fine and varied intonations of his voice,—
these conspired to give life and energy to every company
he mixed with; and I have known ladies who, after an
hour's conversation, actually considered Curran a *beauty,*
and preferred his society to that of the finest fellows
present. There is, however, it must be admitted, a good
deal in the circumstance of a man being *celebrated,* as regards the patronage of women.

Curran had a perfect *horror* of fleas: nor was this
very extraordinary, since those vermin seemed to show
him peculiar hostility. If they infested a house, my friend
said, that "they always flocked to his bed-chamber, when
they heard he was to sleep there!" I recollect his being
dreadfully annoyed in this way at Carlow; and, on making his complaint in the morning to the woman of the
house, "By heavens! Madam," cried he, "they were in
such numbers, and seized upon my carcass with so much
ferocity, that if they had been *unanimous,* and all pulled
one way, they must have dragged me out of bed entirely!"

I never saw Curran's opinion of himself so much dis-
concerted as by Mr. Godwin, whom he had brought, at
the Carlow assizes, to dine with Mr. Byrne, a friend of
ours, in whose cause he and I had been specially employed as counsel. Curran, undoubtedly, was not happy in
his speech on this occasion—but he thought he was.
Nevertheless, we succeeded; and Curran, in great spirits,
was very anxious to receive a public compliment from Mr.
Godwin, as an eminent literary man, teasing him (half-
jokingly) for his opinion of his speech. Godwin fought
shy for a considerable time; at length, Curran put the
question home to him, and it could no longer be shifted.

"Since you *will* have my opinion," said Godwin, fold-
ing his arms, and leaning back in his chair with much
sang froid, "I really never did hear any thing so bad as
your *prose*—except your *poetry,* my dear Curran!"

An anecdote of a very different nature terminated one

of our trips to London:—I had long known that there existed what Curran called "a refined friendship" between him and a Miss H., at Spa and elsewhere. She was afterwards a friend of Holman, the player, and finally married Major * * * an associate of Mr. Hastings. Curran asked me one day, if I was too squeamish to go and sup with a former *chère-amie* of his who had pressed him to come that night, and permitted him to bring a companion. He told me who it was, and I was quite pleased at the idea of knowing a person of whom I had heard so much in Ireland.

We were received with the greatest cordiality and politeness by Miss H.: another young lady and two children were in the room. Curran was most humorous and enlivening, and every thing foreboded a cheerful *petit soupé* when the lady told Curran she wished to speak a word to him in the next room. They accordingly withdrew. I was in conversation with the governess and children, when I heard a noise like the report of a small pistol, and Curran immediately rushed into the apartment—Miss H. marching majestically after him. He took no notice of me, but snatching up his hat, darted down stairs and into the street with the utmost expedition. I really conceived that she had fired at him; and feeling dubious as to my own probable fate, (without a word passing) pounced upon my *chapeau,* and made after my friend in no small haste. I could not, however, open the street-door, and therefore gave myself up for a murdered man, particularly on the bell ringing violently: but the revulsion of my feelings was quite heavenly when I heard Miss H.'s voice over the banisters calling to her maid to "open the street-door for the gentleman." I lost no time in making good my retreat, but did not see Curran again till next morning.

I had the greatest curiosity to know the cause of his sudden flight; upon which he told me, but without any symptom of wit or humour, that she was the most violent-tempered woman existing; that on their going into the *boudoir* together, she informed him that she was then considerably distressed for a sum of money for two or three months; and that as she had never been under any pecuniary obligation to him, she would now ask one—namely, the loan of the sum she wanted, on her own note. Curran, who was particularly close, dreading the amount, anticipated her demand by hoping she did not suppose he could be so mean as to require her note for any little advance he might have it in his power to make; and was happy in handing her *half* the sum at his command in London—taking as he spoke a £10 note out of his pocketbook. "By Heavens! Barrington," said Curran, "her look petrified me: she gazed for a moment at the note—tore it to atoms, muttering the word 'rascal!' and when I was preparing to make an apology, hit me plump on the side of the head, with a fist at least as strong as any porter's! I thought my brains were knocked out!—did you not hear the crack?" inquired he. "To be sure I did," said I. "Did she say any thing," continued he, "after I was gone away?"—"She *only* said," replied I, "that you were the greatest rascal existing," (hereat Curran trembled hugely) "and that she would next day find you out wherever you were, and expose you all over London as a villain and a seducer!"

Curran turned pale as ashes,—made some excuses for leaving the room,—and about dinner-time I found I had carried my joke too far;—for I received a note stating that he was necessitated to start for Ireland directly on particular business, and would be off in the mail.

I never told him the truth, particularly since the lady was soon after married, as I have related, and had a noble establishment in London, and as I learned that Curran had found means to make his peace with the offended fair, at whose table he became a frequent guest.

Mrs. * * * afterwards broke her neck by a fall down stairs: and some people averred that a flask or two of champagne had been playing tricks upon her. She was most agreeable in her address and manner (her Amazonian paroxysms always excepted). The extraordinary length of her feet, (which were like a pair of brackets) should have saved her from tumbling any where; whilst, if I could judge my report, it was miraculous how Curran's pegs preserved him on the perpendicular.

IV

THE NATIONAL SCENE

SINGULAR CUSTOMS IN THE
IRISH PARLIAMENT

A VERY singular custom prevailed in the Irish House of Commons which never was adopted in England, nor have I ever seen it mentioned in print. The description of it may be amusing.

On the day whereon the routine business of the budget was to be opened, for the purpose of voting supplies, the Speaker invited the whole of the members to dinner in the House, in his own and the adjoining chambers. Several peers were accustomed to mix in the company; and I believe an equally happy, joyous, and convivial assemblage of legislators never were seen together. All distinctions as to government or opposition parties were totally laid aside; harmony, wit, wine, and good-humour reigning triumphant. The Speaker, Clerk, Chancellor of the Exchequer, and a very few veteran financiers, remained in the House till the necessary routine was gone through, and then joined their happy comrades—the party seldom breaking up till midnight.

On the ensuing day the same festivities were repeated; but on the third day, when the report was to be brought in, and the business discussed in detail, the scene totally changed;—the convivialists were now metamorphosed into downright public declamatory enemies, and, ranged on opposite sides of the House, assailed each other without mercy. Every questionable item was debated—every proposition deliberately discussed—and more zealous or assiduous senators could no where be found than in the very members who, during two days, had appeared to commit the whole funds of the nation to the management of half a dozen arithmeticians.

But all this was consonant to the national character of the individuals. Set them at table, and no men enjoyed themselves half so much; set them to business, no men ever worked with more earnestness and effect. A steady Irishman will do more in an hour, when fairly engaged upon a matter which he understands, than any other countryman (so far, at least, as my observation has gone) in two. The persons of whom I am more immediately speaking: they certainly were extraordinarily quick and sharp! I am, however, at the same time, ready to admit that the lower orders of officials—such, for instance, as mere clerks in the public offices, exhibited no claim to a participation in the praise I have given their superiors: they were, on the other hand, frequently confused and incorrect; and amongst that description of persons I believe there were then fewer competent men than in most countries.

Another custom in the House gave rise to a very curious anecdote, which I shall here mention. The members of Parliament formerly attended the House of Commons in full dress:—an arrangement first broken through by the following circumstance:—

A very important constitutional question was debating between government and the opposition; a question, by the by, at which my English reader will probably feel surprised; namely, "as to the application of a sum of £60,000, then lying *unappropriated* in the Irish Treasury, being a balance after paying all debts and demands upon the country or its establishments." The numbers seemed to be nearly poised,—although it had been supposed that the majority would incline to give it to the king, whilst the opposition would recommend laying it out upon the country; when the serjeant-at-arms reported that a member wanted to force into the House *undressed,* in dirty boots, and splashed up to his shoulders.

The speaker could not oppose custom to privilege, and

[260]

was necessitated to admit him. It proved to be Mr. Tottenham, of Ballycarny, County Wexford, covered with mud, and wearing a pair of huge jack-boots! Having heard that the question was likely to come on sooner than he expected, he had (lest he should not be in time) mounted his horse at Ballycarny, set off in the night, ridden nearly sixty miles up to the Parliament-House direct, and rushed in, without washing or cleaning himself, to vote for *the country*. He arrived just at the critical moment! and critical it was, for the numbers were in truth *equal,* and his casting vote gave a majority of one to "the country" party.

This anecdote could not die while the Irish Parliament lived; and I recollect, "Tottenham in his boots" remaining, down to a very late period, a standing toast at certain patriotic Irish tables.*

One interesting scene at which I was present merits especial description, on many accounts. No other instance of the kind has occurred in the British Empire in my time; and as it forms a very important record with relation to the independent political state of Ireland at the period, and has not yet been made the subject of any historical detail or observation, it cannot fail to be interesting in every point of view:—I allude to the trial of a peer of the realm of Ireland for murder, by the House of Lords in Dublin, after the acknowledgment of Irish independence.

The grand and awful solemnity of that trial made a deep impression on my memory: and, coupled with the recollection that it proclaimed indisputably the sovereignty of the Irish nation, its effect on a contemplative mind was of a penetrating nature.

Robert, Earl of Kingston, stood charged with the murder of Colonel Fitzgerald, by shooting him in his bed-

* The phrase is also preserved in *Finnegans Wake*: "That is tottinghim in his boots" (p. 284, n. 2).

[261]

chamber. The relation of the circumstances of that event would be, in every point of view, improper, and would only serve to recall painful recollections long since sunk into oblivion. I therefore abstain from any further allusion to them. Justice required the trial of the accused party at the bar of his peers:—but as no similar case had occurred in Ireland within the memory of man, it was requisite to consult precedents upon the subject, in order to render his Lordship's trial conformable to the *Lex Parliamentaria* common to both countries. These precedents were accordingly sought by the proper officers; and as his Lordship was very popular, and his provocation maddening,—and as all were ignorant of the evidence which was to be brought forward, the whole affair was of a most exciting nature to every man, more especially to those individuals who possessed the noble Lord's acquaintance.

Owing to the great numbers of attendants, the full muster of Peers, and the extensive preparations of every kind necessary, in order to adhere to precedent, the House of Lords was supposed to be insufficiently large for the occasion.

The Irish House of Peers was considered one of the most beautiful and commodious chambers possible. It combined every appearance of dignity and comfort: the walls were covered with tapestry, representing the battle of the Boyne, and the entire *coup-d'oeil* was grand and interesting; but being, as I have said, considered too small for all the purposes of the trial in question, the House of Commons was made ready in preference.

Whoever had seen the interior of the Irish House of Commons, must have admired it as one of the most chaste and classic models of architecture. A perfect rotunda, with Ionic pilasters, enclosed a corridor which ran round the interior. The cupola, of immense height, bestowed a magnificence which could rarely be surpassed; whilst a gallery, supported by columns divided into compartments, and accommodating 700 spectators, commanded an uninterrupted view of the chamber.

This gallery, on every important debate, was filled, not by reporters, but by the superior orders of society— the first rows being generally occupied by ladies of fashion and rank, who diffused a brilliance over, and excited a gallant decorum in that assembly which the British house certainly does not appear very sedulously to cultivate.

This fine chamber was now fitted up in such a way as to give it the most solemn aspect. One compartment of seats in the body of the House was covered with scarlet cloth, and appropriated to the Peeresses and their daughters, who ranged themselves according to the table of precedence. The Commons, their families and friends, lined the galleries: the whole house was superbly carpeted, and the Speaker's chair newly adorned for the Lord Chancellor.—On the whole, it was by far the most impressive and majestic spectacle ever exhibited within those walls.

At length the Peers entered, according to their rank, in full dress, and richly robed. Each man took his seat in profound silence: and even the ladies (which was rather extraordinary) were likewise still. The Chancellor, bearing a white wand, having taken his chair, the most interesting moment of all was at hand, and its approach really made me shudder.

Sir Chichester Fortescue, king-at-arms, in his party-coloured robe, entered first, carrying the armorial bearings of the accused nobleman emblazoned on his shield: he placed himself on the left of the bar. Next entered Lord Kingston himself, in deep mourning, moving with a slow and melancholy step. His eyes were fixed on the

[263]

ground; and walking up to the bar, he was placed next to the king-at-arms, who then held his armorial shield on a level with his shoulder.

The supposed executioner then approached, bearing a large hatchet with an immense broad blade. It was painted black except within about two inches of the edge, which was of bright polished steel. Placing himself at the bar on the right of the prisoner, he raised the hatchet about as high as his Lordship's neck but with the shining edge averted; and thus he remained during the whole of the trial. The forms, I understood, prescribed that the shining edge should be averted, until the pronouncing of judgment, when, if it were unfavourable, the blade was instantly to be turned by the executioner *towards* the prisoner, indicating at once his sentence and his fate.

I could not reconcile my mind to the thought of such a consummation. I knew the late Lord Kingston, and had a high regard for him; and hence I felt a very uneasy sensation, inasmuch as I was profoundly ignorant of what would be the termination of the awful scene.

The usual legal ceremonies were now entered on:—the charge was read—the prisoner pleaded not guilty—and the trial proceeded. A proclamation was made, (first generally, then name by name,) for the witnesses for the prosecution to come forward. It is not easy to describe the anxiety and suspense excited as each name was called over. The eyes of every body were directed to the bar where the witness must enter, and every little movement of the persons who thronged it was held to be intended to make room for some accuser. None, however, appeared —thrice they were called, but in vain: and it was then announced that "no witnesses appearing, to substantiate the charge of murder against Robert, Earl of Kingston, the trial should terminate in the accustomed manner." The Chancellor proceeded to put the question; and every Peer, according to his rank, arose and deliberately walking by the chair in which the Chancellor was seated, placed his hand as he passed solemnly on his heart, and repeated, "Not guilty, upon my honour!" (The bishops were, very properly, precluded from voting in these criminal cases.) After all had passed, which ceremony occupied an hour, the Chancellor rose and declared the opinion of the Peers of Ireland,—"That Robert, Earl of Kingston was not guilty of the charge against him." His lordship then broke his wand, descended from his chair, and thus ended the trial—most interesting because it had at once a strong political and constitutional bearing, and affected a nobleman universally beloved. The result was highly satisfactory to every one who had learned the circumstances which led to the fatal event for which the Earl of Kingston was arraigned, whose conduct, though strictly justifiable neither in law nor morality, might have been adopted by the best of men under similar provocation.

POLITICAL CONDUCT OF
THE AUTHOR

THE INTRODUCTION of the following letter and extracts (though somewhat digressive from my original intention in compiling this work,) is important to me, notwithstanding they relate to times so long past by; inasmuch as certain recent calumnies* assiduously propagated against me demanded at my hands a justification of my conduct towards government, at the period of the Union. With this view, the letter in question was written to my friend Mr. Burne, whom I requested to communicate its contents to my connexions in Dublin, or indeed to any person who might have been prejudiced against me by those aspersions. Having, however, reason to fear that only a very partial circulation of my letter took place, I have adopted this opportunity of giving it full publicity by mixing it up with these sketches:—

PARIS, RUE DE RICHELIEU, 2nd May, 1825.
"MY DEAR FRIEND,

"I am well aware that the reports you mention as to my 'having broken trust with the government in the years 1799 and 1800,' had been at one period most freely circulated: but I could scarcely suppose the same would be again and lately revived, to do me injury on a very important concern. This has not been altogether without its operation, and I feel it a duty to myself unequivocally to

* Most likely rumors to the effect that Barrington had received favors from the government at the same time that he was strenuously opposing the Act of Union. These "calumnies" are probably true.

refute such imputation. The fact is proved in few words:
—I *could* not break my trust with the government, for I
never accepted any trust from them. I never entered into
any stipulation or political engagement with *any* government; and every public act which I did—every instance
of support which I gave,—resulted from my own free
agency and unbiassed judgment.

"My first return to Parliament, in the year 1790, for
the city of Tuam, was altogether *at my own expense*. I
had once before stood a contested election for Ballynakill,
formerly my father's borough: I was under no tie nor
obligation to the government: I had not then, nor have I
ever had, any patron; I never, in fact, solicited patronage:
I never submitted to the dictation of any man in my life:
my connexion with government therefore was my own
choice, and the consequent support I gave to Lord Westmoreland's administration, of my own free will. I liked
Lord Buckinghamshire (Major Hobart) individually,
and lived much in his society: I respected Lord Westmoreland highly, and he has always been very obliging
to me during a period of seven-and-thirty years, whenever he had an opportunity. During his administration I
accepted office; and on his recall, he recommended Lord
Camden to return me to Parliament. Mr. Pelham did so
for the city of Clogher; but made no sort of *terms* with
me, *directly or indirectly*. In the autumn of 1798, Mr.
Cooke wrote to me that a Union would probably be submitted to Parliament; and to this communication I
promptly replied, that I must decline all further support
to any government which should propose so destructive
a measure, at the same time tendering my seat. He replied, 'That I should think better of it.'

"Lord Cornwallis came over to carry this great measure; and I opposed him, Lord Castlereagh, and the Union in every stage of the business, and by every means in

my power, both in and out of Parliament. Lord Cornwallis was defeated: he tried again;—Lord Castlereagh had purchased or packed a small majority in the interval, and the bill was carried. In January, 1800, I received a letter from Lord Westmoreland, stating that as Clogher had been a government seat, he doubted if I could in honour retain it. I had already made up my mind to resign it when required. I mentioned the subject to Mr. Forster, the Speaker, who thought I was not bound to resign; however, I acceded to the suggestion of Lord Westmoreland, and accepted an Escheatorship.* But no office in his Majesty's gift—no power, no *deprivation*, would have induced me to support the Union.

"I stood, at my own expense, a very smartly contested election for Maryborough, Queen's County, in which I was supported by Sir Robert Staples, Mr. Cosby of Stradbally Hall, Dean Walsh, Colonel Pigot, Mr. Warburton, (member for the county) the Honourable Robert Moore, (against his brother, the Marquess of Drogheda) &c., and by the tenantry of the present Lord Maryborough. I was outvoted by a majority of three—the scale being turned against me by Lord Castlereagh, who sent down Lord Norbury, the Crown Solicitor, and several such-like gentry for the purpose. With that election my political career concluded: but I am happy and proud to state that, at its termination, I retained the confidence and esteem of every body whose friendship I considered it desirable to retain. Lord Westmoreland bears the most unexceptional testimony to my straight-forward conduct: I have been honoured by his friendship, without intermission, down to the present day; and the following

---

* Members of the Irish Parliament had to go through the ritual of accepting some such meaningless post as the Escheatorship of Munster in order to resign. Cf. the English institution of the Chiltern Hundreds.

extracts from his Lordship's letters to me, wherein he states his desire to bear witness to my strict conduct in my transactions with government, form the best refutal of all the calumnies against me.

"Since the period of my retirement from public life, two of my then most intimate friends (namely, the present Chief Justice Bush and the present Attorney-general Plunkett) have succeeded beyond their most sanguine expectations, yet certainly not beyond their just merits. No government could pass such men by, at the bar, if they chose to claim offices. They took the same, and nearly as strong an anti-Union part as I did; but, after the Union, my public pursuits were nearly at an end.* Ireland lost all charms for me; the Parliament (the source of all my pride, ambition, and gratification as a public man) had been bought and sold; I felt myself as if nobody,— became languid, careless, and indifferent to every thing. I was no longer in fact in my proper sphere: my health rapidly declined; and I neither sought for nor would have accepted any other government office in Ireland.

"Most of these facts, my dear Burne, you have been long acquainted with; and this is solely a recapitulation of some circumstances which I have no other means of making generally known. You will use it as you think may best serve me; and it only remains for me to repeat, what you already know, that I am most sincerely

"Yours ever,

"JONAH BARRINGTON."

JOHN BURNE, ESQ. K.C.
MERRION-SQUARE.

Extracts of letters from the Earl of Westmoreland to Sir Jonah Barrington, enclosed to Mr. Burne:—

* Note, however, that Barrington remained a Judge of the Admiralty until he was deposed from the Bench by both Houses of Parliament in 1830.

LONDON, March 28th, 1795,

"MY DEAR SIR,

* * * * * "I shall always be obliged to you whenever you will have the goodness to let me know what is
going on on your side of the water, wherein I am convinced you will always bear a very considerable part. I
must at the same time assure you that no man's name is
more in public repute than your own.

"Lord Camden left town this morning, and I have not
failed to assure him of your talents and spirit, which
were so useful to my government on many occasions; and
which, as I am satisfied he also will find useful, so is he
equally disposed, I believe, to give them that countenance
they deserve.

* * * * * * *

"The state of Ireland since I left you is most wonderful, but the reign of faction seems drawing to a close.

"I beg to be remembered to all friends, and am,

"Dear Sir, yours very faithfully,
"WESTMORELAND." *

To JONAH BARRINGTON, ESQ. one of His
Majesty's Counsel at Law, &c. &c.
MERRION-SQUARE, DUBLIN.

Much correspondence took place between his Lordship and me after that period, in which he was always
equally kind. Indeed, in that kindness he never varied:
and after knowing me seven-and-thirty years, (the most
important of all revolutions having during that interval
taken place in Ireland,) and after I had directly and
diametrically opposed, in Parliament and out of it, his
Lordship's opinion and acts upon that great question;—
the following extract of another letter from the same
nobleman (dated 1817) proves that he never has changed

* The Earl of Westmoreland became Viceroy of Ireland in
1790, and was succeeded in this post by Lord Camden in 1795.

[270]

his opinion of my honourable conduct toward the King's government, (and permits me to state his approbation of that conduct,) every part of which he must have well known; since he had been, with very little intermission, a member of the British Cabinet during the entire period.

(Abstract.)
PARIS, 19th August, 1817.

"DEAR SIR,

* * * * * * *

* * * * "I have enclosed you a letter of introduction to Sir C. Stuart, and will certainly speak to him as you wish, and shall have great pleasure if it should prove of any convenience to you or your family: and I assure you I have always much satisfaction in giving my testimony to the honourable manner in which you have *always* conducted yourself in the political relations wherein you have stood with me.

"I am your very faithful servant,
"WESTMORELAND."

I also added the following, by way of postscript, to my explanatory letter to Mr. Burne :—

"I think, my dear Burne, that after these testimonials, he must be a daring enemy who will re-assert the calumnies against me. I apprehend that few public men can show more decided proofs of honour and consistency,— or more fair and disinterested conduct than I displayed when I found it necessary to oppose the government. I must also observe, on a principle of gratitude, that throughout the whole course of my public life, I have uniformly experienced from the government and ministers of *England,* (let me here particularize Lord Stowell,) at all times and on all occasions, (whether supporting or opposing them) the greatest kindness, justice, and considerate attention; together with a much greater interest,

[271]

in any concerns of mine submitted to them, than I could possibly have conceived—much less have expected.

"But His Majesty's public functionaries in Ireland were men of a different bearing: after the *surveillance* of a national parliament was extinguished, the country was, as it were, given over to them, bound hand and foot, and they at once assumed new powers, which before they durst not have aimed at. I possess knowledge respecting some of them, of the communication of which they are not aware; and I am not inclined to permit certain individuals to go to their graves without hearing my observations. When the proper time arrives, I shall not be silent.

"Again, dear Burne, yours,
"J. BARRINGTON."

On reading over the foregoing postscript of the letter to my poor friend Burne (who has lately paid his debt on demand to Nature) some observations occur to me respecting Ireland herself, her parties, and species of government, not uncongenial to the subject of my letter. The justice of these observations, each day's experience tends to prove; and I firmly believe, every member of the British government at this moment (except one) views the matter precisely as I do. They find it difficult, however, to disentangle themselves from the opinions which have been so frequently expressed by them heretofore, and which, had they been equally informed then as now, I apprehend would never have been entertained. The people of England, and also of some continental kingdoms, are fully aware of the distracted state of Ireland, but are at a loss to account for it. It is, however, now in *proof,* that twenty-seven years of Union have been twenty-seven years of beggary and of disturbance; and this result, I may fairly say, I always foresaw. The only question now asked is, "What is to be done?" and the

[272]

only comment on this question that it is in my power to make is, "a council of peace is better than a council of war." Much of the unfortunate state of that country may be attributed to the kindred agency of two causes— namely, fanaticism in Ireland, and ignorance (I mean, want of true information) in Great Britain. The Irish are deluded by contesting factions, and by the predominance of a couple of watch-words; whilst the great body of the English people know as little of Ireland (except of its disturbances) as they do of Kamschatka: and the King's ministers, being unluckily somewhat of different opinions, go on debating and considering what is best to be done, and meanwhile doing nothing: if they do not take care, in a little time there will be nothing left *them* to do.

I firmly believe England now means well and honourably to the Irish nation on all points, but think she is totally mistaken as to measures. Neither honourable intentions, nor the establishment of Sunday-schools, nor teaching the four rules of arithmetic, nor *Bible Societies,* can preserve people from starving: education is a very sorry substitute for food; and I know the Irish well enough to say, they never will be taught any thing upon an empty stomach. Work creates industry, and industry produces the means of averting hunger: and when they have work enough and food enough, they may be turned to *any thing*. I speak now, of course, of the lowest orders: the class immediately above those is very unmanageable, because supported by its starving inferiors, who now depend upon it alone for subsistence. The nature and materials of the present Irish constitution, indeed, appear to me totally unadapted to the necessities of that country.

It is but too obvious that the natural attachment which ought to subsist between Great Britain and Ireland is *not increasing,* though on the due cultivation of that attachment so entirely depends the strength, the peace, and the prosperity of the United Empire; yet I fearlessly repeat that the English members of the Imperial Parliament mean well by Ireland, and only require to ascertain her true circumstances to act for her tranquillization. Politically they may be sure that the *imperium in imperio,* as at present operating in that country, is not calculated to reform it. The protecting body of the country gentlemen have evacuated Ireland, and in their stead we now find official clerks, griping agents, haughty functionaries, proud clergy, and agitating demagogues. The resident aristocracy of Ireland, if not quite extinguished, is hourly diminishing:—and it is a political truism, that the co-existence of an oligarchy without a cabinet; of a resident executive and an absent legislature; of tenants without landlords, and magistracy without legal knowledge:—must be, from its nature, as a form of constitution, at once incongruous, inefficient, and dangerous. Nobody can appreciate the native loyalty of the Irish people better than his present Majesty,* whose reception in Ireland was enthusiastic: they adored him when he left it; and amidst millions of reputed rebels, he wanted no protection: every man would have been his life-guard! I speak not however of corporations or guilds—of gourmands, or city feasters: these have spoken for themselves, and loudly too. His Majesty's wise and paternal orders were ridiculed and disobeyed by them the very moment his back was turned! With such folks the defunct King William seems more popular than the living King George.

Good government, and the sufferance of active local factions are, in my view of things, utterly incompatible.

* I.e., George IV, whose visit to Ireland in 1821 was the first by a reigning monarch since the Battle of the Boyne. Barrington's defense of this reprobate stems from the fact that His Majesty's brother, the Duke of Clarence, later William IV, had taken Barrington's only son into his family and had been responsible for his education.

Faction and fanaticism (no matter on which side ranged) ought to be put down to the ground—*gently,* if possible; but if a *strong hand* be necessary, it should not be withheld. The spectator often sees the game better than the player, and in Ireland it has now proceeded too far to be blinked at. The British cabinet may be somewhat divided; but they will soon see the imperative necessity of firmness and unanimity. It is scandalous that the whole empire should thus be kept in a state of agitation by the pretended theological animosities of two contending sects—a great proportion of whose respective partisans are in no way influenced by religion—the true object of their controversy being *"who shall get the uppermost?"*

DUKE OF WELLINGTON, AND
MARQUESS OF LONDONDERRY

M Y PERSONAL acquaintance with the Duke of Wellington originated accidentally, soon after I commenced public life; and so clearly shows the versatility of men, the fallibility of judgment, and the total uncertainty of all human prediction, that I cannot avoid mentioning it.

In 1793, when I was in high repute, most prosperous at the bar, living in the first ranks of society, a distinguished favourite at the vice-regal court, and designated as a candidate for the first offices of my profession,— I occasionally gave large splendid dinners, according to the habit invariably adopted in those times, by persons circumstanced like myself. At one of those entertainments, Major Hobart (Lord Buckinghamshire) ; Sir John Parnel; Isaac Corry; I think, Lord Limerick; Sir John (afterwards Lord) de Blacquiere; and Lords Llandaff, Dillon, Yelverton; the Speaker;—in all, upwards of twenty noblemen and commoners, did me the honour of partaking my fare. Lord Clonmell sent me his two grand cooks, and a most cheerful party was predicted. The House had sat late that day, and etiquette never permitted us to go to dinner, where the speaker was a guest, until his arrival, unless he had especially desired us to do so.

The speaker did not join us till nine o'clock, when Sir John Parnel brought with him, and introduced to me, Captain Wellesley and Mr. Stewart, two young members, who having remained in the House, he had insisted on their coming with him to my dinner, where he told them good cheer and a hearty welcome would be found —and in this he was not mistaken.

Captain Arthur Wellesley had, in 1790, been returned to parliament for Trim, county Meath, a borough under the patronage of his brother, the Earl of Mornington. He was then ruddy-faced and juvenile in appearance, and popular enough among the young men of his age and station. His address was unpolished; he occasionally spoke in Parliament, but not successfully, and never on important subjects; and evinced no promise of that unparalleled celebrity and splendour which he has since reached, and whereto intrepidity and decision, good luck and great military science, have justly combined to elevate him.

Lord Castlereagh was the son of Mr. Stewart, a country gentleman, generally accounted to be a very clever man, in the North of Ireland. He was a professed and not very moderate *patriot,* and at one time carried his ideas of opposition exceedingly far,—becoming a leading member of the Reform and Liberal societies.

Lord Castlereagh began his career in the Irish Parliament, by a motion for a committee to inquire into the representation of the people, with the ulterior object of a reform in Parliament. He made a good speech and had a majority in the House, which he certainly did not expect, and I am sure did not *wish for.* He was unequal and unwilling to push that point to further trial; the matter cooled in a few days; and after the next division, was deserted entirely. Mr. Stewart, however, after that speech, was considered as a very clever young man, and in all points well taught and tutored by his father, whose marriage with the Marquess of Camden's sister was the remote cause of all his future successes—how sadly terminated! *

At the period, to which I allude, I feel confident, nobody could have predicted that one of those young gentlemen would become the most celebrated English general of his era, and the other, one of the most mischievous

* Castlereagh committed suicide in 1822.

[277]

statesmen and unfortunate ministers that has ever appeared in modern Europe. However, it is observable, that to the personal intimacy and reciprocal friendship of those two individuals, they mutually owed the extent of their respective elevation and celebrity:—Sir Arthur Wellesley never would have had the chief command in Spain but for the ministerial manoeuvring and aid of Lord Castlereagh; and Lord Castlereagh never could have stood his ground as a minister, but for Lord Wellington's successes.

At my house, the evening passed amidst that glow of well-bred, witty, and cordial vinous conviviality, which was, I believe, peculiar to high society in Ireland.

From that night, I became rather intimate with Captain Wellesley and Mr. Stewart; and perceived certain amiable qualities in both, which a change of times, or the intoxication of prosperity, certainly in some degree tended to diminish. Indeed, if Lord Wellington had continued until now the same frank, open-hearted man, he certainly must have been better proof against those causes which usually excite a metamorphosis of human character than any one who had ever preceded him. Still, if possible, he would have been a greater man; at least, he would have better drawn the distinction between a warrior and a hero —terms not altogether synonymous. Many years subsequently to the dinner-party I have mentioned, I one day met Lord Castlereagh in the Strand, and a gentleman with him. His Lordship stopped me, whereat I was rather suprised, as we had not met for some time; he spoke very kindly, smiled, and asked if I had forgotten my old friend, Sir Arthur Wellesley?—whom I discovered in his companion; but looking so sallow and wan, and with every mark of what is called a worn-out man, that I was truly concerned at his appearance. But he soon recovered his health and looks, and went as the Duke of Richmond's secretary to Ireland; where he was in all material traits still Sir Arthur Wellesley—but it was Sir Arthur Wellesley judiciously improved. He had not forgotten his friends, nor did he forget himself. He said that he had accepted the office of secretary only on the terms that it should not impede or interfere with his military pursuits; and what he said proved true, for he was soon sent, as second in command, with Lord Cathcart to Copenhagen, to break through the law of nations, and execute the most distinguished piece of treachery that history records.*

On Sir Arthur's return he recommenced his duty of secretary; and during his residence in Ireland, in that capacity, I did not hear one complaint against any part of his conduct either as a public or private man. He was afterwards appointed to command in Spain; an appointment solicited, and I believe expected, by Sir John Doyle. It might be entertaining to speculate on the probable state of Europe at present, if Sir John had been then appointed generalissimo. I do not mean to infer any disparagement to the talents of Sir John, but he might have pursued a different course, not calculated, as in Sir Arthur's instance, to have decided (for the time being) the fate of Europe.

A few days before Sir Arthur's departure for Spain, I requested him to spend a day with me, which he did. The company was not very large, but some of Sir Arthur's military friends were among the party:—the late Sir Charles Asgill, the present General Meyrick, &c. &c. I never saw him more cheerful or happy. The bombardment of Copenhagen being by chance stated as a topic of remark, I did not join in its praise; but, on the other hand, muttered that I never did nor should approve of it.

"Damn it, Barrington," said Sir Arthur, "why? what do you mean to say?" "I say, Sir Arthur," replied I,

* A reference to the bombardment of Copenhagen by the British in 1807.

"that it was the very best devised, the very best executed, and the most just and necessary 'robbery and murder' now on record!" He laughed, and adjourned to the drawing-room, where Lady B. had a ball and supper as a *finish* for the departing hero.

In 1815, having been shut up in Paris during the siege, I went out to Nivelly, to pay a visit to the Duke before our troops got into the city. I had not seen him since the last day he dined at my own house; but he had intermediately much changed.

I knew his Grace when Captain Wellesley—Sir Arthur Wellesley—Secretary Wellesley—Ambassador Wellesley—and Duke of Wellington. In the first stage of this career, I was his equal; in the last, nobody is. However, it is a fine reflection for the contemporaries of great people, that it will be "all the same a hundred years hence!" and Heroes, Diplomatists, &c. must either become very good-tempered fellows when they meet in the Elysian fields, or—there must be a very strong police to keep them in order.

I was present in one of the French chambers when the question of capitulation was discussed; and most undoubtedly Marshal Ney supported that measure upon the basis of a *general amnesty*. On any other, it never would have been listened to; the battle would have taken place early next morning; and the Duke of Wellington would have had to contest the most sanguinary and desperate engagement of his day with a numerous and well-appointed army, frantic with zeal to revenge their disgrace at Waterloo. This I know:—for I was (truly against the grain) kept more than twelve hours in the midst of it at Vilette, two days before the capitulation. I cannot but remark, that if Ney had been pardoned, and the horses not sent to Venice, the spirit of the capitulation would have been more strictly adhered to.

I must be rightly understood respecting Lord Londonderry, to whom, individually, I never had the slightest objection. As a private gentleman, I always found him friendly, though cold; and fair, though ambiguous. I never knew him break his word, and believe him to have been perfectly honourable upon every subject of private interest. But here my eulogy must close; for, with regard to public character, his Lordship must, I fear, be pronounced corrupt. When determined on a point, nothing could stop him. In Ireland, his career was distinguished by public bribery and palpable misrepresentations:—of which assertion, had I not indisputable and ample proof, I would not hazard it.

Mr. Pelham (now Earl of Chichester) was secretary to Lord Camden, when Lord Lieutenant. I had the good fortune and pleasure (for it was a great pleasure to me,) to be on very friendly terms with this amiable and engaging gentleman, and have seldom met any public personage I liked so well—moderate, honourable, sufficiently firm and sufficiently spirited: I had a real gratification in attaching myself not only to his measures, but to his society. In all our intercourse (which ceased with his departure) I found him candid and just, and experienced at his hands several public acts of kindness.

Mr. Pelham's parliamentary talents were not of a splendid order. The people of Ireland never required *stars* for ministers; but a fair and candid secretary was a great treat to them, and Mr. Pelham was making full way in public estimation. The last day I ever saw him in Ireland, he and his brother-in-law Lord Sheffield did me the favour of dining with me in Merrion Square. I perceived he was uncommonly dull, and regretted the circumstance much: he obviously grew worse,—at length laid his head upon the table, and when he departed was extremely ill: next day he was in a violent fever, his life was long despaired of, he recovered with difficulty, and, on his recovery, returned to England. Mr. Stewart (by

[281]

marriage the Lord Lieutenant's nephew,) was named as *locum tenens* during Mr. Pelham's absence, or (should he not return) until the appointment of another secretary. But he was soon discovered by his employers to be fit for *any* business; and as it had been long in the secret contemplation of the British ministry to extinguish the Irish Parliament, either by fraud or force,—and Lord Camden being considered too inactive (perhaps too conscientious and honourable) to resort to either of those weapons, it was determined to send over an old servant-of-all-work, who had fought till he was beaten, and negociated till he was outwitted. This person, (Lord Cornwallis) with the assistance of his young secretary, would stop at nothing necessary to effect the purpose, and they could, between them, carry a measure which few other persons, at that period, durst have attempted.

These fragments are not intended as political episodes. The result of that coalition every body knows: I shall only state so much of the transaction as relates to my own individual concerns. I had an interview with Lord Castlereagh, some time after he came into office, at Mr. Cooke's chambers. He told me he understood I expected to be the next solicitor-general, and had applied for the office. I answered, that I not only expected as much, but considered myself, under all circumstances, *entitled* to that preferment. He and Mr. Cooke both said, "yes;" and recommended me to make "my *party good* with Lord Clare," who had expressed "no indisposition" to the appointment. Had I not been supposed of some use to the government, I do not doubt but Lord Clare would have preferred many other more subservient gentry of my profession. But he knew that although Lord Westmoreland, on leaving Ireland, had made no express stipulation, he had subsequently gone as far as he could with Lord Camden, for my promotion. Lord Clare played me off cleverly until, in the month of August 1799, I was sent for in private by the secretary, Edward Cooke, who had been a particular confidential friend of mine for several years. Having first enjoined secrecy as to our conference, he told me that a measure of great import had been under consideration, in the English Cabinet, and might possibly be acted on: and then proceeding to acquaint me that Lord Clare had made no objection to my promotion, he asked in so many words if I would support the "question of 'a union,' if it should be brought forward?" I was struck as if by a shot! I had no idea of such a thing being now seriously contemplated, although I had often heard of it as a measure suggested in 1763. My mind had never any doubts upon the degrading subject, all thoughts whereof had been considered as banished for ever by the volunteers of 1782. I therefore replied at once, "No, never!"—"You'll think better of it, Barrington!" said he. "Never, by ———!" rejoined I: "never!" and the discussion was dropped, nor did I confide it to any save one individual, who differed with me very much, at least as to the mode of refusal.

I was determined, however, to know how the matter really stood; and, without touching on the late conversation, desired to be apprised whether they preserved the intention of appointing me solicitor-general. I received no other answer than the following letter from Lord Castlereagh, without any explanation;—but it was enveloped in a very long one from Mr. Cooke, headed "strictly private;" and, therefore, of course, still remaining so.

September 7, 1799

"My dear Sir,

"I am directed by his excellency, the Lord Lieutenant, to assure you, that he would be glad to avail himself of any proper opportunity of complying with your wishes: and that he regrets much, he is at present so particularly circumstanced with respect to the office of solicitor-general, that he feels it impossible to gratify your desire as to that appointment. I should, myself, have been very happy had I been able to communicate to you a more favourable result.

> "Dear Sir, yours very sincerely,
> "CASTLEREAGH."

I never had any thing more to do with the successive governments of Ireland,* and have used all forbearance in giving my opinion of Irish Lord Chancellors, except Mr. Ponsonby, whom nobody ever heard me praise as a very great lawyer, but whom every body has heard me term a just judge, and an honest friendly man.

Of Lord Camden, I believe, there was no second opinion in the circle wherein I moved:—a better man could not be; but instead of governing, he was governed: and intimately acquainted as I was with every procedure and measure during his administration in Ireland, I do most fully acquit him, individually, of the outrageous, impolitic, and ill-judged measures which distinguished his rule. As to Lord Clare, he was despotic, and the greatest enemy Ireland ever had. His father had been a Roman Catholic, and intended for a priest, but changed his tenets, became a barrister of great and just celebrity, and left many children.

Lord Clare was latterly my most inveterate enemy: the cause shall be no secret;—it arose from a vicious littleness of mind scarcely creditable, and proves to me that implacability of temper never exists without its attendant faults; and although it may be deprecated by cringing, is seldom influenced by feelings of generosity.

* Lord Castlereagh's letter to me put, in fact, a civil end to my dreams of promotion [Barrington's footnote].

IRISH REBELLION

I DINED at the house of Lady Colclough (a near relative of Lady Barrington,) in the town of Wexford,
in April, 1798. The company, so far as I recollect, consisted of about seventeen persons, amongst whom were
several other of Lady B.'s relatives, then members of the
grand jury: Mr. Cornelius Grogan, of Johnstown, a gentleman of very large fortune who had represented the
county; his two brothers, both wealthy men; Captain
Keogh, afterwards rebel governor of Wexford, the husband of Lady B.'s aunt; the unfortunate John Colclough,
of Tintern, and the still more unfortunate Mr. Colclough; Counsellor John Beauman; Counsellor Bagenal
Harvey, afterwards the rebel generalissimo; Mr. William Hatton, and some others. The conversation after
dinner turning on the distracted state of the country, became rather too free, and I begged some of the party to
be more moderate, as our ways of thinking were so different, and my public situation did not permit me, especially at that particular period, to hear such strong language: the loyalists amongst us did not exceed four or
five.

The tone of the conversation was soon lowered, but
not before I had made up my mind as to the probable fate
of several in company, though I certainly had no idea
that, in little more than a month, a sanguinary rebellion
would desolate my native land, and violent deaths, within
three months, befall a great proportion of that joyous
assemblage. I had seen enough, however, to convince me
that all was not right; and that, by plunging one step
further, most of my relatives and friends would be in

imminent danger. The party however broke up; and next morning, Mr. Beauman and myself, happening to meet on the bridge, talked over the occurrences of the previous day, uniting in opinion as to the inauspicious aspect of things, and actually proceeding to make out a list of those amongst the dinner-party whom we considered likely to fall victims!—and it so turned out that *every one* of our predictions was verified.* It was superficial observation alone that led me to think as I did at that moment, but a decided presentiment of what eventually happened soon after took possession of me; and indeed so full was I of forebodings, that I have more than once been roused out of my sleep by the horrid ideas floating through my mind!

Bagenal Harvey, who had been my school-fellow and constant circuit-companion for many years, laughed, at Lady Colclough's, at my political prudery; assured me I was totally wrong in suspecting him; and insisted on my going to Bargay Castle, his residence, to meet some old Temple friends of ours on the ensuing Monday;—my relative Captain Keogh was to be of the party.

I accordingly went there to dinner, but that evening proved to me one of great uneasiness, and made a very disagreeable impression both on my mind and spirits. The company I met included Captain Keogh; the two un-fortunate Counsellors Sheers, who were both hung shortly afterwards; Mr. Colclough, who was hung on the bridge;

* Although Barrington specifically denies informing on his friends by name (see below), there is some show of truth in R. R. Madden's acid comment on this passage: "Sir Jonah's black list, made out merely for amusement, on the bridge of Wexford, by some invisible agency—of some bird of passage, perhaps of prey—must have been picked up and fortunately let fall at the feet of Mr. Secretary Cooke" (*The United Irishmen: Their Lives and Times* [2nd ed.; Dublin, 1858–60], IV, 234–35). On the other hand, all of these were already marked men, as Madden himself shows (*ibid.,* pp. 463 ff.), and Harvey, after all, had been com-mander-in-chief of the rebel forces.

Mr. Hay, who was also executed; Mr. William Hatton, one of the rebel directory of Wexford, who unaccountably escaped; and a gentleman of the bar whose name I shall not mention, as he still lives.

The entertainment was good, and the party cheerful. Temple freaks were talked over; the bottle circulated: but, at length, Irish politics became the topic, and proceeded to an extent of disclosure which utterly surprised me. With the Messrs. Sheers (particularly Henry) I had always been on terms of the greatest intimacy: I had extricated both of them not long before from considerable difficulty, through the kindness of Lord Kilwarden; and I had no idea that matters wherein they were concerned had proceeded to the lengths developed on that night. The probability of a speedy revolt was freely discussed, though in the most artful manner, not a word of any of the party committing themselves: but they talked it over as a result which might be expected from the complexion of the times and the irritation excited in consequence of the severities exercised by the government. The chances of success, in the event of a rising, were openly debated, as were also the circumstances likely to spring from that success, and the examples which the insurgents would in such a case probably make. All this was at the same time talked over, without one word being uttered in favour of rebellion:—a system of caution which, I afterwards learned, was much practised for the purpose of gradually making proselytes without alarming them. I saw through it clearly, and here my presentiments came strong upon me. I found myself in the midst of absolute though unavowed conspirators. I perceived that the explosion was much nearer than the government expected; and I was startled at the decided manner in which my host and his friends spoke.

Under these circumstances, my alternative was evidently to quit the house or give a turn to the conversation. I therefore began to laugh at the subject, and ridicule it as quite visionary, observing jestingly to Keogh—"Now, my dear Keogh, it is quite clear that you and I, in this famous rebellion, shall be on different sides of the question; and of course one or the other of us must necessarily be hanged at or before its termination—I upon a lamp-iron in Dublin, or you on the bridge of Wexford. Now, we'll make a bargain!—if we beat you, upon my honour I'll do all I can to save your neck; and if your folks beat us, you'll save me from the honour of the lamp-iron!"

We shook hands on the bargain, which created much merriment, and gave the whole after-talk a cheerful character; and I returned to Wexford at twelve at night, with a most decided impression of the danger of the country, and a complete presentiment that either myself or Captain Keogh would never see the conclusion of that summer.

I immediately wrote to Mr. Secretary Cooke, without mentioning names, place, or any particular source of knowledge; but simply to assure him that there was not a doubt that an insurrection would break out at a much earlier period than the government expected. I desired him to ask me no questions, but said that he might depend upon the fact; adding that a commanding force ought instantly to be sent down to garrison the town of Wexford. "If the government," said I, in conclusion, "does not attend to my warning, it must take the consequences." My warning was not attended to; but His Majesty's government soon found I was right. They lost Wexford, and might have lost Ireland, by that culpable inattention.

The result need scarcely be mentioned; every member of that jovial dinner-party (with the exception of myself, the barrister before alluded to, and Mr. Hatton,) was executed within three months! and on my next visit to

Wexford, I saw the heads of Captain Keogh, Mr. Harvey, and Mr. Colclough on spikes over the court-house door.

Previously to the final catastrophe, however, when the insurgents had been beaten, Wexford retaken by our troops, and Keogh made prisoner, I did not forget my promise to him at Bargay Castle. Many certificates had reached Dublin of his humanity to the royalists whilst the town of Wexford was under his government, and of attempts made upon his life by Dixon, a chief of his own party, for his endeavouring to resist the rebel butcheries. I had intended to go with these directly to Lord Camden, the Lord Lieutenant; but I first saw Mr. Secretary Cooke, to whom I related the entire story and showed him several favourable documents. He told me I might save myself the trouble of going to Lord Camden; and at the same time handed me a dispatch received that morning from General Lake, who stated that he had thought it necessary, on recapturing Wexford, to lose no time in "making examples" of the rebel chiefs; and that accordingly, Mr. Grogan, of Johnstown, Mr. Bagenal Harvey, of Bargay Castle, Captain Keogh, Mr. Colclough, and some other gentlemen, had been hanged on the bridge and beheaded the previous morning.

I felt shocked beyond measure at this intelligence,—particularly as I knew Mr. Cornelius Grogan (an excellent gentleman, seventy years of age, of very large fortune and establishment,) to be no more a rebel than myself. Being unable, from infirmity, to walk without assistance, he was led to execution.

I was at all times ready and willing to risk my life to put down that spirit of mad democracy which sought to subvert all legal institutions, and to support every true principle of the constitution which protected us: but at the same time I must in truth and candour say, (and I say it with reluctance,) that, during those most sangui-

[289]

nary scenes, the brutal conduct of certain frantic royalists was at least on a parallel with that of the frantic rebels.

A short time after the recapture of Wexford, I traversed that county, to see the ruins which had been occasioned by warfare. Enniscorthy had been twice stormed, and was dilapidated and nearly burned. New Ross showed most melancholy relics of the obstinate and bloody battle of full ten hours' duration, which had been fought in every street of it. The numerous pits crammed with dead bodies, on Vinegar Hill, seemed on some spots actually elastic as we stood upon them; whilst the walls of an old windmill on its summit appeared stained and splashed with the blood and brains of the many victims who had been piked or shot against it by the rebels. The courthouse of Enniscorthy, wherein our troops had burned alive above eighty of the wounded rebels; and the barn of Scullabogue, where the rebels had retaliated by burning alive above 120 Protestants—were terrific ruins! The town of Gorey was utterly destroyed,—not a house being left perfect; and the bodies of the killed were lying half-covered in sundry ditches in its vicinity.

An unaccountable circumstance was witnessed by me on that tour immediately after the retaking of Wexford. General Lake, as I have before mentioned, had ordered the heads of Mr. Grogan, Captain Keogh, Mr. Bagenal Harvey, and Mr. Colclough, to be placed on very low spikes, over the court-house of Wexford. A faithful servant of Mr. Grogan had taken away his head; but the other three remained there when I visited the town. The mutilated countenances of friends and relatives, in such a situation, would, it may be imagined, give any man most horrifying sensations! The heads of Mr. Colclough and Harvey appeared black lumps, the features being utterly undistinguishable; that of Keogh was uppermost, but the air had made no impression on it whatever! His comely and respect-inspiring face (except the *pale* hue, scarcely to be called *livid,*) was the same as in life: his eyes were not closed—his hair not much ruffled: in fact, it appeared to me rather as a head of chiselled marble, with glass eyes, than as the lifeless remains of a human creature:— this circumstance I never could get any medical man to give me the least explanation of. I prevailed on General Hunter, who then commanded in Wexford, to suffer the three heads to be taken down and buried.

REBEL PORTRAITS

WHEN we read or hear of public and distinguished characters, whether good or bad, we are naturally disposed to draw in our mind a figure or face for each, correspondent to the actions which rendered the individual conspicuous. We are inclined, for instance, to paint in our imagination a rebel chieftain as an athletic powerful personage, with a commanding presence;—an authoritative voice to control; and impetuous bravery to lead on a tumultuous army of undisciplined insurgents. Were this always the case, insurrections would, perhaps, stand a better chance of being successful.

In the Irish Rebellion of 1798, the chief leaders had scarcely any of these attributes. *Numerically,* the rebels were sufficient, and more than sufficient, to effect all their objects; but they had no idea of discipline, and little of subordination. Their intrepidity was great, and their perseverance in the midst of fire and slaughter truly astonishing. Yet on every occasion it was obviously the *cause* and not the *leaders* that spurred them into action; when Irishmen *are* well officered they never yield.*

A spirit of uncompromising fortitude or enthusiastic

* The battle of Ross, in June, 1798, lasted ten hours. The rebel *officers* did nothing, the *men* every thing. While the commander-in-chief, Counsellor Bagenal Harvey, was standing on a hill nearly a mile distant, a boy twelve years old (Lett of Wexford town) called on the insurgents to follow him. He put himself at the head of ten thousand men—approached the town, and stormed it. The town took fire; the rebels got liquor; and they were killed in sleep and drunkenness. Nothing could have saved our troops had the rebels been well officered: General Johnston, who commanded the royalists, deserved great praise for his judgment on that critical occasion [Barrington's footnote].

gallantry generally spreads over the countenance some characteristic trait. Undisciplined followers are fascinated by ferocious bravery: they rush blindly any where, after an intrepid leader. But a languid eye, unbraced features, and unsteady movements, palpably betray the absence of that intellectual energy, and contempt of personal danger, which are indispensable qualities for a rebel chief.

To reflect on the great number of respectable and unfortunate gentlemen who lost their lives by the hands of the common executioner in consequence of that insurrection, is particularly sad;—indeed, as melancholy as any thing connected with the long misrule and consequent wretched state of brave and sensitive Ireland—which is *now,* at the termination of seven hundred years, in a state of more alarming and powerful disquietude than at any period since its first connexion with England.

I had been in long habits of friendship and intercourse with most of the leading chiefs of that rebellion. Their features and manners rise, as it were in a vision, before my face: indeed, after thirty long years of factious struggle and agitation, when nothing remains of Ireland's pride and independence but the memory, every circumstance occasioning and attending that period, and the subsequent *revolution* of 1800,* remains in freshest colours in the recollection of a man who *once* prided himself on being born an Irishman.

I made allusion, in a previous part of this work, to a dinner of which I partook in April, 1798, at Bargay Castle, County Wexford, the seat of Beauchamp Bagenal Harvey,—who, I may as well repeat here, was a month afterward general-in-chief over an army of more than thirty thousand men (mostly of his own county), brave and enthusiastic; and, in two months more, died by the hands of the hangman. He had been my school and class-

* I.e., The successful attempt by the government to get the Act of Union passed through the Irish Parliament.

[293]

fellow, and from nine years of age we held uninterrupted intercourse: he was a most singular example of mixed and opposite qualities; and of all human beings, I should least have predicted for him such a course, or such a catastrophe.

Harvey was son of one of the six Clerks of Chancery, who having amassed a very considerable fortune, purchased the estate and castle of Bargay. Beauchamp Bagenal, his eldest son, was called to the Irish bar, and succeeded to his father's estates. It was said that he was nearly related by blood to that most extraordinary of all the country gentlemen of Ireland, Beauchamp Bagenal, of Dunlickry, whose splendour and eccentricities were the admiration of the continent while he was making the grand tour (then reserved as part of the education of the very highest circles). This relationship was the subject of much merriment after a duel which Harvey's reputed kinsman provoked my friend to fight with him, in order to have the satisfaction of ascertaining, "whether or no the lad had metal."

Harvey's person was extremely unimposing. He was about five feet four inches in height; and that ancient enemy of all beauty, the small-pox, had shown him no mercy, every feature being sadly crimped thereby. His sharp peaked chin never approached toward a contact with his cravat, but left a thin scraggy throat to give an impoverished hungry cast to the whole contour, by no means adapted to the mien and port of a "commander of the forces." His scanty hair generally hung in straight flakes, and did not even pretend to be an ornament to his visage; his eye was quick but unmeaning; his figure thin and ill put together; his limbs short, slight, and wabbling; his address cheerful, but tremulous. On the whole, a more unprepossessing or unmartial-like person was never moulded by capricious nature.

Yet Harvey was a very good-tempered friendly man,

[294]

and a hearty companion. In common life he was extremely well conducted, and in the society of the bar often amusing, and never out of humour. He was the greatest punster of his profession, and piqued himself on that qualification, in which he often succeeded admirably. He had, in short, that sort of partial popularity with his bar contemporaries as rendered them always glad to have him in their society; but it was seldom any one inquired what had become of him when he was out of it. He had an ample store of individual courage; feared not single combat, and fought several duels intrepidly, though I do not think he ever *provoked* one. He shot Sir Harding Giffard, late Chief Justice of Ceylon, and obtained a very droll name through that achievement, which never forsook him during his lifetime.

Harvey was a person of the best fortune in his quarter of the county; of a Protestant family; and, being charitable and benevolent to his tenantry, was much beloved by them. Nobody in fact could dislike him: though he was flippant, he did not want sense; and presented an excellent example of those contradictory qualities so often discoverable in the same individual. He was considered by the heads of the United Irishmen to be well adapted —as a man of fortune and local influence in the most disaffected portion of their strongest county—to forward their objects: and he suffered his vanity so far to overcome his judgment, as, without the slightest experience to assume the command of a great army—for which purpose there were few men in Ireland so utterly unfit.

In his martial office, his head became totally bewildered; the sphere of action was too great—the object struggled for, too comprehensive. Nor did even his *personal* courage follow him to the field. His bravery, as against a single man, was neutralised in a tumult; and a mind naturally intrepid became bewildered, puzzled, and impotent. Amidst the roar of cannon, and the hurly-burly of the tumultuous and sanguinary battle of Ross, his presence of mind wholly forsook him, and he lost the day by want of tact and absence of spirit. His men fought hand to hand in the streets of Ross with the regular troops, of whom they slew a considerable number, including the Earl of Mountjoy; nor did they at last retire until they had not a single officer left to continue the engagement or lead them on to a renewed attack—which in all probability would have been effectual. Never did human beings show more decided bravery than the Irish peasantry in that bloody engagement. Thrice the town was theirs, and was finally lost by their inebriety and want of proper officers. Had Harvey captured New Ross, all Munster would have risen in his cause; and then indeed no royalist could have anticipated without dread the consequences. Officers and arms would have made the whole country inevitably theirs. When Wexford was retaken, Harvey concealed himself on an island, but was discovered, brought to that town, and without much ceremony hanged next day upon the bridge, toward the erection of which he had largely subscribed.

I could not but feel extreme regret at the sad fate which befell my old friend and school-fellow, who did not meet his destiny quite so firmly as his original manly bearing had inclined people to expect:—poor fellow! he idly strove by entreaty to avert, or at least retard it; and its infliction was aggravated by every species of indignity. In every thing except his politics, Harvey's character was unimpeachable.

I never knew two persons much more dissimilar than were the commander-in-chief of the insurgents and the rebel governor of Wexford, Captain Keogh. The latter was a retired captain of the British service, who had fought in America, and, like many others, had there received a lesson on *civil liberty* which never escaped his memory. He was married to an aunt of Lady Barrington;

and, for many years, when I went the circuit, I lived at his house, and had conceived the greatest friendship for him. He was a very clever man. His housekeeping was characterised by neatness, regularity, and cheerfulness. Every thing was good of its kind; and in that plentiful country, even luxuries were abundant. Calm, determined, moderate, and gentlemanly, Captain Keogh combined good sense with firmness and spirit. But, most unfortunately, ill-treatment sustained from Lord Chancellor Clare perverted half his good qualities, and metamorphosed him into a partizan, which was far from being his natural tendency.

He had a fine soldier-like person, above the middle size; his countenance was excellent; his features regular and engaging; his hair, rather scanty, receded from his forehead; his eyes were penetrating and expressive; and his complexion exhibited that partial ruddiness which we so frequently see in fine men approaching threescore. He was appointed rebel governor of Wexford, but among those savages soon lost his popularity; and had the insurgents continued much longer masters of the place, he would surely have been assassinated. He did what he durst on the side of humanity, and had supposed that his orders would be obeyed: but he was deceived; blood, and blood in torrents, was the object of *both* parties during that horrid summer. On the surrender of the town, Keogh was immediately convicted under martial law. He pleaded for himself; and I learn that on that occasion every body was affected. He knew his situation to be irretrievable, and his life forfeit; and he conducted himself at his execution with the utmost firmness, as became a gentleman and a soldier. He was hanged and beheaded on the bridge of which he also was a proprietor; and his head, was exhibited on a spike over the court-house door.

A singular circumstance occurred in Keogh's house while the rebels were in possession of Wexford. His

[297]

brother, a retired major in the British army, had also served in America, and lived with the captain in Wexford, but was a most enthusiastic royalist. Upon the rebels taking the place, he endeavoured to dissuade his brother from accepting the office of governor, but failing in the attempt, he retired to his own room and immediately blew his brains out!

The next of my friends and connexions who suffered by the hands of the executioner, was Mr. Cornelius Grogan of Johnstown Castle, a gentleman of large fortune, and great local interest and connexion. He had been twice high-sheriff and representative in Parliament for the county. He resided three miles from Wexford at his castle, where he had a deer-park on one thousand acres of good ground, besides a fine demesne. He lived as a quiet, though hospitable country gentleman. At this unfortunate period he had passed his seventieth year, and was such a martyr to the gout that his hands were wrapped up in flannel; and half carried, half hobbling upon crutches, he proceeded to the place of execution.

Mr. Grogan was in person short and dark-complexioned. His countenance, however, was not disagreeable, and he had in every respect the address and manners of a man of rank. His two brothers commanded yeomanry corps. One of them was killed at the head of his corps (the Castletown cavalry) at the battle of Arklow; the other was wounded at the head of *his* troop (the Healtford cavalry) during Major Maxwell's retreat from Wexford.

The form of a trial was thought necessary by General Lake for a gentleman of so much importance in his county. His case was afterward brought before Parliament, and argued for three successive days and nearly nights. His *crime* consisted in having been surrounded by a rebel army, which placed him under the surveillance of

[298]

numerous ruffians. They forced him one day into the town on horseback;—a rebel of the appropriate name of Savage always attending him with a blunderbuss, and orders to shoot him if he refused their commands. They one day nominated him a *commissary,* knowing that his numerous tenantry would be more willing in consequence to supply them. He used no weapon of any sort;—indeed, was too feeble even to *hold* one. A lady of the name of Seagriff gave evidence that her family were in want of food, and that she got Mr. Grogan to give her an *order* for some bread, which order was obeyed by the insurgents. She procured some loaves, and supplied her children; and for that bread (which saved a family from starvation) Mr. Grogan was, on the lady's evidence, sentenced to die as a felon—and actually hanged, when already almost lifeless from pain, imprisonment, age, and brutal treatment! The court-martial which tried him was not sworn, and only mustered seven in number. *His* witness was shot while on the way to give evidence of his innocence; and while General Lake was making merry with his staff, one of the first gentlemen in the county (in every point his superior) was done to death almost before his windows!

From my intimate knowledge of Mr. Grogan for several years, I can venture to assert most unequivocally (and it is but justice to his memory) that, though a person of independent mind and conduct as well as fortune, and an opposition member of parliament, he was no more *rebel* than his brothers, who signalised themselves in battle as *loyalists;* and the survivor of whom was *rewarded* by a posthumous bill of attainder against the unfortunate gentleman in question, by virtue of which estates of many thousands per annum were confiscated to the king. (The survivor's admitted *loyal* brother had been killed in battle only a few days before the other was

[299]

executed.) This attainder was one of the most flagitious acts ever promoted by any government:—but after ten thousand pounds costs to Crown officers, &c. had been extracted from the property, the estates were restored. I spent the summer of 1799 at Johnstown Castle, where I derived much private information as to the most interesting events of that unfortunate era.

It is, of course, most painful to me to recollect those persons whose lives were taken—some fairly—some, as I think, unfairly—at a time when military law had no restraint, and enormities were daily committed through it not much inferior to those practised by the rebels.

Sir Edward Crosby, a baronet with whom I was intimately acquainted, and who also lived tranquilly, as a country gentleman, upon a moderate fortune, near Carlow, was another person who always struck me to have been *murdered* by martial law. There was not even a rational *pretence* for *his* execution. His trial, with all its attending documents, has been published, and his innocence, in fact, made manifest. The president of the martial court was one Major Dennis, who some time after quitted the service—I shall not mention why. The sentence on Sir Edward was confirmed by Sir Charles Asgill, I must suppose through gross misrepresentation, as Sir Charles had himself known enough about *hanging* (though personally innocent) in America, to have rendered him more merciful, or at least more cautious in executing the first baronet of Ireland.

The entire innocence of Sir Edward Crosby has since, as I just now mentioned, been acknowledged by all parties. His manner was mild and well-bred: he was tall and genteel in appearance; and upward of fifty years of age. He had a wife who loved him; and was every way a happy man till he was borne to execution without the slightest cause. He was the elder brother of my old college friend, Balloon Crosby, whom I heretofore mentioned in relating my *rencontre* with Mr. Daly. He did not die with the courage of Keogh, but hoped for mercy to the last minute, relying on the interference of his old friend Judge Downes, who, however, proved but a broken reed.

THE WALKING GALLOWS

NEVER was there an era in the history of any country which, in so short a space of time, gave birth to such numerous and varied circumstances as did the memorable year 1798 in Ireland: nor was there ever yet an event so important as the Irish insurrection, but has afforded a veracious—or, at least, a tolerably impartial narrative. But the party rancour and virulent hatred of the religious sects in the south, the centre and west of Ireland (where the rebellion principally raged), operated to prevent any fair record of those scenes of bloodshed and atrocity which, on *both sides,* outraged every principle of morality and justice, and every feeling of consanguinity, honour, or humanity. The very worst qualities were fostered to full maturity, and the better ones turned adrift like discarded servants. Blood, fire, and famine were the only umpires resorted to by the contending parties.

Those barbarities were nearly, if not altogether, unexampled either in ancient or modern Europe: but is now thirty years since their termination; the surviving contemporaries are old enough to have their blood cooled and their prejudices moderated;—and they should have grown sufficiently dispassionate to speak of those scenes (if at all) with honesty and candour.

I was myself in the midst of the tumult: a zealous loyalist; an officer in the corps of barristers; an active partizan; in a word, a *strong* adherent of government— but not a *blind* one. I could not shut my eyes; I could not close my ears; I would not pervert my reason; and the full use of those faculties at that time, enables me now to state as an historic fact—which some will deny, and many may discredit—that the barbarities of that period (though not precisely) were pretty nearly balanced between the conflicting parties. Mercy was alike banished by both; and the instruments employed of death and torture, though dissimilar, were alike destructive: the bullet, sabre, bayonet, lash, and halter, being met by the pike, the scythe, the blunderbuss, the hatchet, and the firebrand.

Yet while human blood was pouring out in streams, and human beings consuming in fire, or writhing either upon rebel pikes or royal bayonets—will it be believed? —men had grown so familiarised to scenes of horror, that the eccentric humour of the Irish people was insusceptible of decrease. In the midst of tortures, either suffered or inflicted, it frequently broke out into the most ludicrous actions and expressions, proving to me that an Irishman's humour is so drilled into his nature, as to be inexhaustible even to the moment of his death (if that is not unusually too deliberate).

It is not in the nature, or within the comprehension, of the sober English people to form any judgment of what a true-born Irishman is capable of saying or doing in his deepest extremities: and I am sure they will give me little credit for veracity when I mention some instances which, I own, in any other country might be reasonably considered incredible. In no other place existing could the cruel and ludicrous be so mingled, as they were in the transactions of the sanguinary period in question; nor do I think there can be a better way to inform and amuse the reader, than by giving alternate anecdotes of the *royalists* and the *rebels,* leaving it to his own judgment to draw conclusions.—This one observation, however, it is necessary, in justice, to premise;—that the royalists were, generally speaking, of a higher class than the rebels —and had received the advantages of education, while the rebels were in a state of total ignorance and beggary.

[303]

The wanton barbarities, therefore, of the more enlightened classes have less ground of palliation than those of a demi-savage peasantry, urged by fanaticism, and blinded by ignorance. This observation was strongly impressed on my mind throughout the whole of that contest; and it would be acting unfairly toward the officer who so judiciously commanded the military corps I was then attached to, not to say, that, though an unqualified Protestant—an hereditary Huguenot, filled with that spirit of sectionary zeal which drove his eloquent ancestor from his native country; yet, during the whole of the rebellion, Captain Saurin never suffered the corps he led to indulge any religious distinctions;—scarcely, indeed, could his own sect be discovered by any particular of his acts, orders, or conduct; nor did that corps ever participate in, or even countenance, the violent proceedings so liberally practised by other military yeomen.

This line of conduct was most exemplary; and from a thorough knowledge of the constitutional attributes of the man, I am convinced that neither his philanthropy, toleration, humility, or other good qualities have been much increased by his *schooling,* for the last twenty years, in the Irish Four Courts.

Among the extraordinary characters that turned up in the fatal "ninety-eight," there were few more extraordinary than Lieutenant H——,* then denominated the "walking gallows;"—and such he certainly was, literally and practically.

Lieutenant H—— was about six feet two inches high; —strong, and broad in proportion. His strength was great, but of the dead kind, unaccompanied by activity. He could lift a ton, but could not leap a rivulet; he looked mild, and his address was civil—neither assuming nor at all ferocious. I knew him well, and from his countenance should never have suspected him of cruelty; but so cold-

* This man's name was Heppenstall.

[304]

blooded and so eccentric an executioner of the human race I believe never yet existed, save among the American Indians.

His inducement to the strange barbarity he practised I can scarcely conceive; unless it proceeded from that natural taint of cruelty which so often distinguishes man above all other animals when his power becomes uncontrolled. The propensity was probably strengthened in him from the indemnities of martial law, and by those visions of promotion whereby violent partizans are perpetually urged, and so frequently disappointed.

At the period alluded to, law being suspended, and the courts of justice closed, the "question" by torture was revived and largely practised. The commercial exchange of Dublin formed a place of execution; even *suspected* rebels were every day immolated as if *convicted* on the clearest evidence; and Lieutenant H——'s *pastime* of hanging *on his own back* persons whose physiognomies he thought characteristic of rebellion was, (I am ashamed to say) the subject of jocularity instead of punishment. What in other times he would himself have died for, as a murderer, was laughed at as the manifestation of loyalty: never yet was martial law so abused, or its enormities so hushed up as in Ireland. Being a military officer, the lieutenant conceived he had a right to do just what he thought proper, and to make the most of his time while martial law was flourishing.

Once, when high in blood, he happened to meet a *suspicious-looking* peasant from County Kildare, who could not satisfactorily account for himself according to the lieutenant's notion of evidence; and having nobody at hand to vouch for him, the lieutenant of course immediately took for granted that he *must* be a rebel strolling about, and imagining the death of His Most Gracious Majesty. He therefore, no other *court of justice* being at hand, considered that he had a right to try the man by his *own opinion;* accordingly, after a brief interrogation, he condemned him to die, and without further ceremony proceeded to put his own sentence into immediate execution.

However, to do the lieutenant justice, his *mode* was not near so tedious or painful as that practised by the grand signior, who sometimes causes the ceremony to be divided into three acts, giving the culprit a drink of spring water to *refresh* him between the two first; nor was it so severe as the burning old women formerly for witchcraft. In fact, the "walking gallows" was both on a new and simple plan; and after some kicking and plunging during the operation, never failed to be completely effectual. The lieutenant being, as before mentioned, of lofty stature, with broad and strong shoulders, saw no reason why they might not answer His Majesty's service upon a pinch as well as two posts and a cross-bar (the more legitimate instrument upon such occasions): and he also considered that, when a rope was not at hand, there was no good reason why his own silk cravat (being softer than an ordinary halter, and of course less calculated to *hurt* a man) should not be a more merciful choke-band than that employed by any *Jack Ketch* in the three kingdoms.

In pursuance of these benevolent intentions, the lieutenant, as a preliminary step, first knocked down the suspected rebel from County Kildare, which the weight of mettle [*sic*] in his fist rendered no difficult achievement. His garters then did duty as handcuffs: and with the aid of a brawny aide-de-camp (one such always attended him), he pinioned his victim hand and foot, and then most considerately advised him to pray for King George, observing that any prayers for his *own* d——d *Popish soul* would be only time lost, as his fate in every world (should there be even a thousand) was decided to all eternity for having imagined the death of so good a monarch.

During this exhortation, the lieutenant twisted up his long cravat so as to make a firm, handsome rope, and then expertly sliding it over the rebel's neck, secured it there by a double knot, drew the cravat over his own shoulders, and the aide-de-camp holding up the rebel's heels, till he felt him *pretty easy,* the lieutenant with a powerful chuck drew up the poor devil's head as high as his own (cheek by jowl), and began to trot about with his burden like a jolting cart-horse,—the rebel choking and gulping meanwhile, until he had no further solicitude about sublunary affairs—when the lieutenant, giving him a parting chuck, just to make sure that his neck was broken, threw down his load—the personal assets about which the aide-de-camp made a *present* of to *himself.*

The above *trotting* execution (which was humorously related to me by an eye-witness) took place in the barrack-yard at Kerry House, Stephen's Green. The *hangee* was, I believe, (*as it happened*) in reality a rebel.

Providence, however, which is said to do "every thing for the best," (though some persons who are half starving, and others who think themselves very unfortunate, will not allow it so much credit,) determined that Lieutenant H——'s loyalty and merits should meet their full reward in another sphere—where, being quite out of reach of all his enemies, he might enjoy his destiny without envy or interruption. It therefore, very soon after the rebellion had terminated, took the lieutenant into its own especial keeping; and despatched a raging fever to bring him off to the other world, which commission the said fever duly executed after twenty-one day's combustion;—and no doubt his ghost is treated according to its deserts; but nobody having since returned from those regions to inform us what has actually become of the lieutenant, it is still a *dead* secret, and I fancy very few persons in Ireland have any wish for the opportunity of satisfying their curiosity. People however give a shrewd guess, that it is *possible* he may be employed somewhere else in the very same way wherein he entertained himself in Ireland; and that after being duly furnished with a tail, horns, and cloven foot, no spirit could do infernal business better than the lieutenant.

THE ENNISCORTHY BOAR

A MOST ludicrous incident chanced to spring out of the most murderous conflict (for the numbers engaged) that had occurred during the merciless insurrection of 1798 in Ireland.

The murdered victims had not been effectually interred, the blood was scarcely dry upon the hill, and the embers of the burned streets not yet entirely extinguished in Enniscorthy, when, in company with a friend who had miraculously escaped the slaughter, and Mr. John Grogan, of Johnston, who was then seeking for evidence amongst the conquered rebels, to prove the injustice of his brother's execution, I explored and noted the principal occurrences of that most sanguinary engagement. I give them, in connexion with the preposterous incident which they gave rise to, to show in one view the *mélange* of fanaticism, ferocity, and whimsical credulity, which characterised the lower Irish at that disastrous epocha, as well as the absurd credulity and spirit of true intolerance which signalised their London brethren, in the matter of the silly incident which I shall mention.

The town of Enniscorthy, in the county of Wexford, in Ireland, (one of the first strong possessions that the English, under Strongbow, established themselves in,) is situate most beautifully on the river Slaney, at the base of Vinegar Hill; places which the conflicts and massacres of every nature, and by both parties, have marked out for posterity as the appropriate sites of legendary tales, and traditional records of heroism and of murder.

The town is not fortified; and the hill, like half a globe, rising from the plain, overlooks the town and

[309]

country, and has no neighbouring eminence to command it.

The first assault on this town by the rebels, and its defence by a gallant, but not numerous garrison, formed one of the most desperate, heroic, and obstinate actions of an infatuated people. It was stormed by the rebels, and defended with unflinching gallantry; but captured after a long and most bloody action, during which no quarter was given or accepted on either side. Those who submitted to be prisoners only preserved their lives a day, to experience some more cold-blooded and torturing extinction.

The orange and green flags were that day alternately successful. But the numbers, impetuosity, and perseverance of the rebels, becoming too powerful to be resisted, the troops were overthrown, the rout became general, and the royalists endeavoured to save themselves in all directions: but most of those who had the good fortune to escape the pike or blunderbuss were flung into burning masses, or thrown from the windows of houses, where they had tried to gain protection or conceal themselves.

The insurgents were that day constantly led to the charge, or, when checked, promptly rallied by a priest, who had figured in the French revolution in Paris—a Father Roche. His height and muscular powers were immense, his dress squalid and bloody, his countenance ruffianly and terrific; he had no sense either of personal danger, or of Christian mercy. That day courage appeared contagious, and even his aged followers seemed to have imbibed all the ferocity and blind desperation of their gigantic and fearless pastor.

The streets through which the relics of the royal troops must traverse to escape the carnage were fired on both sides by the order of Father Roche, and the unfortunate fugitives had no chance but to pass through volumes of flame and smoke, or yield themselves up to the ferocious pikemen, who chased them even into the very body of the conflagration.

My accompanying friend had most unwittingly got into the town, when in possession of the army, and could not get out of it on the sudden assault of the rebels. He had no arms. Many of them knew him, however, to be a person of liberal principles, civil and religious; but he with difficulty clambered to a seat high up in the dilapidated castle; where, unless as regarded the chance of a random shot, he was in a place of tolerable safety. There he could see much; but did not descend till the next morning; and would certainly have been shot at the windmill on Vinegar Hill had not the Catholic priests of his own parish vouched for his toleration and charity; and above all, that he had, early that year, given a large sum towards building a chapel and endowing a school for the cottagers' children.

Amongst the persons who lost their lives on that occasion was the Rev. Mr. Haydn, a very old and highly respected clergyman of the Established Church: he was much more lamented than the thirty priests who were hanged at the same period. He was piked or shot by the rebels in the street, and lay dead and naked upon the Castle Hill, till duly consumed by half-starving dogs, or swine of the neighbourhood, that marched without invitation into the town, to dine upon any of the combatants who were not interred too deep to be easily rooted up again.

After the rebellion had entirely ended, it was remarked in the neighbourhood, that what the peasants call a "slip of a pig," who had been busy with his neighbours carousing in Enniscorthy, as aforesaid, had, from that period, increased in stature and corresponding bulk to an enormous degree, and far outstripped all his contemporaries, not only in size, but (so far as the term could be applicable to a pig) in genuine beauty. At length his growth became almost miraculous; and his exact symmetry kept pace with his elevation.

This young pig was suffered to roam at large, and was universally admired as the most comely of his species. He at length rose to the elevation of nearly a heifer, and was too great a curiosity to remain in Ireland, where curiosities, animate and inanimate, human and beastly, are too common to be of any peculiar value, or even excite attention. It was therefore determined to send him over as a present to our Sovereign—as an olive-branch, so to speak, for the subdued and repentant rebels of Enniscorthy, and a specimen which, being placed in the Tower, might do great honour to the whole race of domestic swine, being the first tame gentleman of his family that ever had been in any royal menagerie.

This Enniscorthy miracle was accordingly shipped for Bristol, under the care of a priest, two rebels, and a showman, and in due season arrived in the metropolis of England. Regular notice of his arrival was given to the king's proper officers at the Tower, who were to prepare chambers for his reception, though it was maliciously whispered that the "olive branch," as the priest called the pig, was intended only second-hand for His Majesty; that is to say, after the party and showman should have pursed every loose shilling the folks of London might be tempted to pay for a sight of so amiable an animal. The pig took admirably; the showman (a Caledonian by birth) was economical in the expenditure, and discreet in his explanations. The pig became the most popular show at the east end; Exeter 'Change even felt it. However, fate ultimately restored the baboons and tigers to their old and appropriate rank in society.

This proceeding, this compliment of the *olive branch,* was neither more nor less than is generally used in the case of our most celebrated generals, admirals, and statesmen, (and occasionally our most gracious Sovereigns,) who, being duly disembowelled, spiced, swaddled, and screwed up in a box, with a white satin lining to it, (well stuffed, to make it easy,) are exhibited to their compatriots of all ranks, who can spare sixpence to see an oak trunk, covered with black, and plenty of lacquered tin nailed on the top of it. But here the pig was seen alive and merry, which every body (except testamentary successors) conceives has much the advantage over any thing that is inanimate.

I had myself, when at Temple, the honour of paying sixpence to see the fork which belonged to the knife with which Margaret Nicholson attempted to penetrate the person of His Majesty, King George the Third, at St. James's; and the Dean and Chapter of Westminster, through their actuaries, receive payment for showing the stone heads of patriots, poets, and ministers, whom they have secured in their tabernacle: Sir Cloudesley Shovel, who was drowned as an admiral; Major André, who was hanged as a spy; and Mr. Grattan, who should have been buried in Ireland.

The celebrity of the "olive branch" every day increased, and the number of his visitors so rapidly augmented, that the priest and showman considered that the day when he should be committed to the Tower would be to them no trifling misfortune. Even the ladies conceived there was something musical in his grunt, and some tried to touch it off upon their pianos. So gentle, so sleek and silvery were his well-scrubbed bristles, that every body patted his fat sides. Standing on his bare feet, his beautifully arched back, rising like a rainbow, overtopped half his visitors; and he became so great and general a favourite, that, though he came from Ireland, nobody even thought of inquiring whether he was a Papist or Protestant grunter!

One day, however, the most unforeseen and grievous misfortune that ever happened to so fine an animal, at

[313]

once put an end to all his glories, and to the abundant pickings of his chaplain.

It happened, unfortunately, that a Wexford yeoman, who had been at the taking and retaking of Enniscorthy, (a theme he never failed to expatiate on,) and had been acquainted with the pig from his infancy, as well as the lady sow who bore him, having himself sold her to the last proprietors, came at the time of a very crowded assembly into the room; and, as Irishmen never omit any opportunity of talking, (especially in a crowd, and, if at all convenient, *more* especially about themselves,) the yeoman began to brag of his acquaintance with the hog, the storming of the town, the fight, and slaughter; and, unfortunately, in order to amuse the company, by suggesting the cause of his enormous bulk and stature, mentioned, as a national curiosity, that the people in Ireland were so headstrong as to attribute his growth to his having eaten the Rev. Mr. Haydn, a Protestant clergyman of Enniscorthy, after the battle; but he declared to the gentlemen and ladies that could not be the fact, as he was assured by an eye-witness, a sergeant of pikemen amongst the rebels, that there were several dogs helping him, and some ducks out of the Castle court. Besides, the parson having been a slight old gentleman, there was scarcely as much flesh on his reverend bones as would have given one meal to a hungry bull-dog. This information, and the manner of telling it, caused an instantaneous silence, and set every English man and woman staring and shuddering around him, not one of whom did the pig attempt to put his snout on. The idea of a *Papist* pig eating a *Protestant* parson was of a nature quite unsupportable; both church and state were affected: their praises were now turned to execration; the women put their handkerchiefs to their noses to keep off the odour; every body stood aloof both from the pig and the showman, as if they were afraid of being devoured. The men

[314]

cursed the Papist brute, and the rebellious nation that sent him there; every one of them who had a stick or an umbrella gave a punch or a crack of it to the "olive branch;" and in a few minutes the room was cleared of visitors, to the astonishment of the yeoman, who lost no time in making his own exit. The keepers, now perceiving that their game was gone, determined to deliver him up, as *Master Haydn,* to the lieutenant of the Tower, to be placed at the will and pleasure of His Majesty.

The chaplain, showman, and two amateur rebels, now prepared to return to Wexford. Though somewhat disappointed at the short cut of their exhibition, they had no reason to find fault with the lining their pockets had got. The officers of the Tower, however, had heard the catastrophe and character of the "olive branch," and communicated to the lieutenant their doubts if he were a fit subject to mix with the noble wild beasts in a royal menagerie. Several consultations took place upon the subject; the lord chamberlain was requested to take His Majesty's commands upon the subject in council: the king, who had been signing some death-warrants and pardons for the Recorder of London, was thunderstruck and shocked at the audacity of an Irish pig eating a Protestant clergyman; and though no better Christian ever existed than George the Third, his hatred to pork from that moment was invincible, and became almost a Jewish aversion.

"The Tower! the Tower!" said His Majesty, with horror and indignation. "The Tower for an Irish hog that ate a pious Christian!—No, no—no, no, my lords. —Mr. Recorder, Mr. Recorder—here, see, see—I command you on your allegiance—shoot the pig, shoot him— shoot, Mr. Recorder—you can't hang.—Eh! you would if you could, Mr. Recorder, no doubt. But, no, no—let me never hear more of the monster. A sergeant's guard —shoot him—tell Sir Richard Ford to send his keepers

[315]

to Ireland to-night—to-night if he can find them—go, go—let me never hear more of him—go—go—go—go —shoot him, shoot him!"

The Recorder withdrew with the usual obeisances, and notice was given that at six next morning a sergeant's guard should attend to shoot the "olive branch," and bury his corpse in the Tower ditch, with a bulky barrel of hot lime to annihilate it. This was actually executed, notwithstanding the following droll circumstance that Sir Richard Ford himself informed us of.

Sir Richard was far better acquainted with the humour and management of the Irish in London, than any London magistrate that ever succeeded him: he knew nearly all of the principal ones by name, and individually, and represented them to us as the most tractable of beings, if duly come round and managed, and the most intractable and obstinate, if directly contradicted.

The Irish had been quite delighted with the honour intended for their compatriot, the Enniscorthy boar, and were equally affected and irritated at the sentence which was so unexpectedly and so unjustly passed on him; and, after an immediate consultation, they determined that the pig should be rescued at all risks, and without the least consideration how they were to save his life afterwards. Their procedure was all settled, and the rescue determined on, when one of Sir Richard's spies brought him information of an intended rising at St. Giles's to rescue the pig, which the frightened spy said must be followed by the Irish firing London, plundering the Bank, and massacring all the Protestant population—thirty thousand choice Irish being ready for any thing.

Sir Richard was highly diverted at the horrors of the spy, but judged it wise to prevent any such foolish attempt at riot, by anticipating His Majesty's orders; wherefore, early in the evening, a dozen policemen, one by one, got into the hog's residence, with a skilful butcher, who stuck him in the spinal marrow, and the "olive branch" scarcely brought life to the ground with him. The rescue was then out of the question, and in a very short time Doctor Haydn's Gourmand was not only defunct, but actually laid ten feet under ground, with as much quick-lime covered up over his beautiful body as soon left hardly a bone to discover the place of his interment.

Sir Richard told this anecdote, as to the execution, &c. with great humour. The Irish used to tell Sir Richard that a pig was dishonoured by any death but to make bacon of; that God had sent the breed to Ireland for that purpose only; and that, when killed for that purpose, they considered his death a natural one!

THE END.

APPENDIX

The Library at Cullenaghmore

Although Barrington assumes that all the titles listed in his grandfather's library are familiar to readers of taste, a few are perhaps less well known now than they were in the late eighteenth century. I offer the following identifications:

Killing No Murder. Supposed author, Edward Sexby (d. 1658). *A discourse proving it lawful to kill a tyrant according to the opinion of the most cele-brated ancient authors,* by Col. Titus alias William Allen. First published in Holland, 1657. This is a tract defending Cromwell.

The Patriot King. The Patriot King; or Irish Chief, by Francis Dobbs (1750–1811). A tragedy performed at the Smock Alley Theatre, Dublin, 1774.

Bailey's *Dictionary. Etymological English Dictionary,* by Nathan Bailey. First edition, 1721; thirty editions to 1802.

George Faulkner's Newspapers. George Faulkner (1699–1775) is remembered today principally as Swift's printer, but he amassed a large fortune from the publication of his own *Journal,* which was carried on for fifty years after his death.

Quintus Curtius in English. Evidently a reference to Quintus Curtius Rufus (fl. A.D. 41–54) whose biography of Alexander the Great, *De rebus gestris Alexandri magni,* was Englished by P. Pratt in 1821.

Nelson's *Fasts and Feasts. A Companion for the Festivals and Fasts of the Church of England: with collects*

[319]

and prayers for each solemnity, by Robert Nelson. London, 1704. Many editions—thirty-six by 1826.
The History of Peter Wilkins. The Life and Adventures of Peter Wilkins, by Robert Paltock. London, 1751. This is an interesting example of eighteenth-century travel-science fiction, in which the hero meets a race of winged folk. The males of this people are called "glumms" and the females "gawries," which explains Barrington's next "title," *Glums and Gouries.*

BIBLIOGRAPHY

Barrington, Jonah. *Historic Memoirs of Ireland.* 2 vols. London, 1835.
———. *Personal Sketches of His Own Times.* 3 vols. London, 1827–32.
Beckett, J. C. *The Making of Modern Ireland, 1603–1923.* London, 1966.
Chart, D. A. *The Story of Dublin.* London, 1907.
Craig, Maurice. *Dublin: 1660–1860.* London, 1952.
Curran, William Henry. *The Life of the Right Honourable John Philpot Curran.* Chicago, 1882.
D'Alton, E. A. *History of Ireland from the Earliest Times to the Present Day.* 6 vols. London, 1904–10.
Dickinson, P. L. *The Dublin of Yesterday.* London, 1929.
Falkiner, C. Litton. *Essays Relating to Ireland.* London, 1909.
Fisher, J. R. *The End of the Irish Parliament.* London, 1911.
Fitzpatrick, S. A. O. *Dublin: A Historical and Topographical Account of the City.* London, 1907.
Fitzpatrick, W. J. *Ireland before the Union.* Dublin, 1867.
———. *The Secret Service under Pitt.* London, 1892.
———. *"The Sham Squire," and the Informers of 1798.* London, 1866.
Gilbert, J. T. *A History of the City of Dublin.* 3 vols. Dublin, 1861.
Grattan, Henry. *Memoirs of the Life and Times of the Right Honourable Henry Grattan.* 5 vols. London, 1839–46.
Haliday, Charles. *The Scandinavian Kingdom of Dublin,*

edited with Some Notice of the Author's Life, by John P. Prendergast. Dublin, 1881.

Harvey, John. *Dublin, a Study in Environment*. London, 1949.

Inglis, Brian. *The Freedom of the Press in Ireland, 1784–1841*. London, 1954.

Kain, Richard M. "An American Looks at Barrington's 'Sketches,' " *nonplus*, No. 3 (Summer, 1960), pp. 69–75.

Lecky, W. E. H. *A History of Ireland in the Eighteenth Century*. 5 vols. London, 1892–96.

Le Fanu, W. R. *Seventy Years of Irish Life*. New York, 1894.

McDowell, R. B. *Irish Public Opinion, 1750–1800*. London, 1944.

Madden, R. R. *The Connexion between the Kingdom of Ireland and the Crown of England*. Dublin, 1845.

————. *The United Irishmen: Their Lives and Times*. 2nd ed. 4 vols. Dublin, 1858–60.

Maxwell, Constantia. *Country and Town in Ireland under the Georges*. London, 1940.

————. *Dublin under the Georges*. London, 1936.

Mercier, Vivian. *The Irish Comic Tradition*. Oxford, 1962.

Phillips, Charles. *Curran and His Contemporaries*. 4th ed. London, 1851.

Plowden, Francis. *History of Ireland, from Its Union with Great Britain in January, 1801, to October, 1810*. Dublin, 1811.

Torchiana, Donald T. "The World of Sir Jonah Barrington's Personal Sketches," *Philological Quarterly*, XLV, No. 1 (January, 1966), 321–45.

————. *W. B. Yeats and Georgian Ireland*. Evanston, Ill., 1966.

Webb, Alfred. *A Compendium of Irish Biography*. Dublin, 1878.

INDEX

Sparks, Isaac, 202 and n
The Spectator, 5
Stafford, Sir James, 17n
Sterne, Laurence, 57n
Stradbally, 8
Swift, Jonathan, 5, 79, 148, 154
and n
Swift, Theophilus, 152–58

Tandy, Napper, 175, 192n, 193,
215, 245
The Tempest, 202
Theatre: Smock Alley, 105 and
n; injurious to moral charac-
ter of young ladies, 133–36;
recollections of, 196–205
Theatre Royal, 182
Timogee, 8
Tipperary Resolutions, 191
Tom Thumb, 201
Tone, Wolfe, 192n, 234–37
Tottenham, Charles, 260–61
A Treatise on Tar-Water, 5, 75
Trim, 277
Trinity College ("University of
Dublin"), 75, 123–24, 131,
153–56, 196–98, 212n
Tuam, 139, 267
Turlow, 55, 60, 64–65, 223,
225

Ulysses, 190n, 212n
United Irishmen, 192n, 193n,
211n, 217, 242n, 286n, 295
University of Dublin. *See* Trinity College

Vinegar Hill, 290; Battle of,
309–11
The Virtues of Fasting Spittle,
75

Walsh, General Hunt, 128, 187
Washington, George, 89–90,
97, 245
Waterford, 54, 85, 151
Wedding customs, 99–116
Wellington, Duke of, 276–81
Westmoreland, Earl of, 145,
267–70, 282
Westport, 225, 231
Wexford, 245–46, 285–301
White Boys, 6 and n
The Wild Irish Girl, 74n
William III, 9–12, 32, 212–14,
216, 274
William IV, 182n, 274n

Yeats, William Butler, 39n
Yelverton, Barry, 190–92